REWRITING APOCALYPSE IN CANADIAN FICTION

Rewriting Apocalypse in Canadian Fiction

Marlene Goldman

McGill-Queen's University Press

Montreal & Kingston • London • Ithaca

© McGill-Queen's University Press 2005
ISBN 0-7735-2904-7

Legal deposit third quarter 2005
Bibliothèque nationale du Québec

Printed in Canada on acid-free paper that is 100% ancient forest free
(100% post-consumer recycled), processed chlorine free.

This book has been published with the help of a grant from the
Canadian Federation for the Humanities and Social Sciences,
through the Aid to Scholarly Publications Programme, using funds
provided by the Social Sciences and Humanities Research Council of
Canada.

McGill-Queen's University Press acknowledges the support of the
Canada Council for the Arts for its publishing program. It also
acknowledges the financial support of the Government of Canada
through the Book Publishing Industry Development Program (BPIDP)
for our publishing activities.

Library and Archives Canada Cataloguing in Publication

Goldman, Marlene., 1963–
    Rewriting Apocalypse in Canadian Fiction / Marlene Goldman.

Includes bibliographical references and index.
ISBN 0-7735-2904-7

    1. Canadian Literature (English) – 20th century – History and
criticism.   I. Title.

PS8191.A65G64 2005   c813'.5409   C2005-900896-2

Typeset in 10/13 Palatino by True to Type

This book is dedicated to Bob, Luke, and Emma

Contents

Acknowledgments

It is a great pleasure to thank the numerous and generous community of family, friends, and scholars – especially my graduate students in ENG 5043F, "Apocalyptic and Anti-apocalyptic Discourse in Canadian Literature" – who supported the writing and editing of this book. I would like to thank, in particular, those students who studied with me and who also worked closely with the Canadianist Group: Kristina Kyser, Viki Visvis, and Natalie Foy. While the book was being written, I had the good fortune to be inspired by my colleagues at the University of Toronto at Scarborough, Russell Brown, Donna Bennett, and Lora Carney; together we created the multimedia presentation "Closing Time: Apocalyptic Imagery in Canadian Culture." I would also like to thank Linda Hutcheon, Neil ten Kortenaar, and Garry Leonard, who read and commented on various aspects of the project.

A particular debt of gratitude is to Russell Brown and to Malcolm Woodland for commenting on drafts of particular chapters. While I began to think about my study, Russell Brown was developing his course on the Bible and Malcolm Woodland was working on his own book about apocalypse and Wallace Stevens; it was invaluable to be able to discuss my project with them. I also greatly benefited from discussions with Teresa Heffernan and Dominic Jenkins. As well, Rob Mancini was also a wonderful help in preparing the first draft of the manuscript for submission to McGill-Queen's Press.

I should also like to thank the editors of the following journals in which earlier drafts of parts of this book have previously appeared for their permission and support: *Essays on Canadian Writing*, *The University of Toronto Quarterly*, *Canadian Studies/Études Canadiennes*, and

Canadian Literature. I would also like to thank the anonymous readers for the ASPP who took the time to comment on the book.

Gratitude of the highest order is also due to Roger Martin of McGill-Queen's Press for his unwavering support and witty conversations as he shepherded the manuscript through the ASPP granting process. Thanks also to Claude Lalumière, the editor at McGill-Queens.

Finally, this book could not have been completed without the help, guidance, and inspiration of Elizabeth Jones, editor *par excellence* and my good friend, and I want to thank her most sincerely.

REWRITING APOCALYPSE IN CANADIAN FICTION

The Apocalyptic Paradigm

The apocalyptic paradigm pervaded Canadian literature from its beginnings. In documenting their experience, the explorers and settlers who left the Old World and arrived in the territory north of the forty-ninth parallel drew on the narrative of apocalypse – a story whose key vision portrays the "old world" being replaced by the new. This conceptual substitution, however, was never entirely successful, creating an ironic tension. For even though the explorers and settlers invoked apocalypse, the myth of a decadent earthly world abruptly and violently transformed into a perfect heavenly world never accurately defined the Canadian experience – an experience perhaps best described by Jacques Cartier, who likened the country to "the land God gave to Cain."[1] Indeed Canadian exploration more often invoked apocalyptic visions of hell than of paradise, as seen from Alexander Mackenzie's *River of Disappointment*, Simon Fraser's *Hell's Gate*, and the loss of life on John Franklin's first arctic land expedition.[2]

Early references to apocalypse by settlers also reflect a skeptical view of the traditional apocalyptic narrative. In *Roughing it in the Bush* (1852), for example, Susanna Moodie, the cultured, British foremother of Canadian letters, documented her departure from England and her first encounter with the New World. In an account dated 30 August 1832, she describes travelling up the mighty St Lawrence and records the breathtaking beauty of the countryside that looks to her "a perfect paradise at this distance" (19). Although the captain warns her that "'many things look well at a distance which are bad enough when near,'" so eager is she to put her "foot upon the soil of the new world for the first time" that she disregards his advice and steps ashore on Grosse Isle. When the veil is pulled aside – in this case, "the low range of bushes which formed a screen in front of the river" (20) – and the truth is revealed, Moodie discovers that, in contrast to the apocalyptic plot, this "second Eden" has not been purged and renovated; worse, it is a despoiled paradise that she must share with the non-elect – those deemed unworthy of ascending to paradise.

Although the word *apocalypse* conjures images of nuclear disasters and doomsday cults, this study is primarily concerned with how Canadian authors rewrite the narrative of apocalypse, which envisions the end of the world and the creation of a heavenly world reserved for God's chosen people. Rather than tell the story from the familiar perspective of the saved, the fictions under consideration adopt a characteristically Canadian approach and convey the experience of the disenfranchised, those denied entry into the new paradise and condemned to die. In *Survival* (1972), a popular critical guide to Canadian literature, Margaret Atwood remarks on Canadian writers' fascination with marginalized groups, finding "a superabundance of victims in Canadian literature" (39). And in *The Canadian Postmodern* (1988), Linda Hutcheon recalls Atwood's observation, arguing that postmodern writers typically adopt an "ex-centric" position: "the margin or the border is the postmodern space *par excellence*" (4). Hutcheon goes on to suggest that "[s]ince the periphery or the margin might also describe Canada's perceived position in international terms, perhaps the postmodern ex-centric is very much a part of the identity of the nation" (3). Owing to this "ex-centric" Canadian perspective, the writers examined in this study do not portray typical heroes – the warriors and the victors; instead, they give voice to the "story and the story-telling of the non-combatants or even the losers" (Hutcheon, "The Politics of Representation" 38).

The basic elements of the apocalyptic narrative include a transformative catastrophe and a subsequent revelation of ultimate truth. But apocalypse frequently blurs the boundary between art and life, a tendency that provokes a consideration of the broader social and historical context. While this study addresses such wider contexts (particularly when the works themselves draw attention to historical events such as the Second World War), it remains focused on the impact of apocalypse on contemporary Canadian fiction, and more precisely how this fiction articulates the perspective (borrowing Leonard Cohen's famous phrase) of apocalypse's "beautiful losers." To unveil Canadian writers' ongoing reliance on the apocalyptic paradigm, this study traces how the theological ideas derived from biblical exegesis – specifically, the narrative plot, characters, and imagery of the Revelation of Saint John the Divine – have been adapted and transposed into secular terms. Ultimately, the aim of this study is to demonstrate how contemporary Canadian authors translate the features of apocalypse into their fiction and, in accordance with the country's ongoing concern for the ex-centric and the victim, highlight the traumatic experience of those barred from paradise. In contrast to the traditional biblical apocalypse, contemporary Canadian fiction refuses to celebrate the destruction of evil and the creation of a new, heavenly world. Instead, these works highlight the devastation wrought by apocalyptic thinking on those accorded the role of the non-elect.

Prior to its particular impact on contemporary Canadian literature, the myth of apocalypse engendered a well-documented apocalyptic literary tradition: "Since its establishment as a literary genre in the century or so preceding the birth of Christ, apocalypse has held a special fascination for artists, in part because of its arresting imagery and powerful poetry, in part because of pride of place. It is, after all, ostensibly God's last word on his creation. The Revelation of St John, by many judgements the most complete and the finest of traditional apocalyptic texts, occupies the final place in the Christian canon, as if to reinforce by position the authority of its summarizing intent. Apocalyptic visions, particularly John's, began to inspire a significant body of imaginative literature and visual art in the later Middle Ages, and have continued to do so, variously and abundantly" (Zamora 1). Indeed, the principal writers of the English Renaissance – Spenser, Shakespeare, Donne, and later Herbert, Marvell, and Milton – relied on the myth of apocalypse; the apocalypse was "widely commended as utterly indispensable," both on the popular level and "by no less an authority than King James, who wrote that 'of all the scriptures, the buik of the Reuelatioun is maist meit for this our last age'" (Patrides 207).

Following the Renaissance, the myth of apocalypse continued to inspire England's most celebrated writers. In the poetry of Blake, Coleridge, Wordsworth, Shelley, and Keats, as critics such as M.H. Abrams and Morton D. Paley observe, a pervasive theme is the imminence of an apocalypse that will be succeeded by a millennium. The Romantic poets drew with great familiarity "upon the situations, figures, and language of the Book of Revelation" (Paley 5). But the apocalypticism of the English poets also had profound transatlantic dimensions: "Columbus himself suggested that the New World he had discovered was to be the locale of the new earth prophesied in Revelation. This belief was brought to America by the early Franciscan missionaries ... and entrenched by the fervent iteration of America's millennial destiny by the Puritan settlers of New England" (Abrams, "Apocalypse" 24). Apocalypse's biblical formulae and images are "woven into the fabric of the cultures and languages of the United States and Latin America" (Zamora 3). Not surprisingly, a tremendous amount of critical attention has been paid to the literary uses of apocalypse in US literature.[3] Here a divinely inspired apocalypse is frequently posited in contrast to its antithesis, entropy. The theory of entropy entails that the universe "is subordinated to a constant and irreversible process of 'dying' or, more precisely, of turning its energy into waste. The process can be neither stopped nor reversed – and there will be no regeneration" (Lewicki xv).

To date, critical discussion of the influence of apocalyptic narratives on Canadian literature has been limited.[4] In addition, owing to the USA's long-standing connection to the New Jerusalem (the heavenly city featured in Revelation), the theoretical models designed to study the apocalyptic paradigm have been formulated largely in conjunction with the USA's revolutionary historical tradition and national literature. While writers from diverse nations have adopted and adapted the biblical narrative, Canadian authors introduce particular twists to the familiar myth of the end by challenging rather than embracing apocalypse's key features, specifically, the purgation of the non-elect and the violent destruction of the earthly world in preparation for the creation of a divine one.

In Timothy Findley's retelling of the biblical Flood story in *Not Wanted on the Voyage* (1984), for instance, Noah's wife refuses to board the ark meekly. Instead, she returns to her beloved home and rails against the destruction of the world and all its inhabitants: "'If only you had seen all this when all this was living and divinely beautiful. The porch – the view – my cat [...] the view across these lawns ... the hill [...]. If only you had seen the world. [...] Half an hour – an hour, every day – you didn't have to sleep to dream. It was all out there – as real as you and me. *Wonderful!*'" (174). Findley's novel is characteristic of the fictions addressed in this study, which install the biblical narrative to interrogate it. The novel begins with a familiar quotation from Genesis: "And Noah went in, and his sons, and his wife, and his son's wives with him into the ark, because of the waters of the flood ..." (3). But the authority of the Bible is immediately under-cut by the sentence that follows: "Everyone knows it wasn't like that." The narrative proceeds to provide readers with an account of the Flood from the perspective of the traumatized victims of God's edict.

Of course, not every Canadian writer has challenged the apocalyptic paradigm. As Russell Brown observes, the mid-twentieth century saw the appearance of some relatively straightforward apocalyptic narratives, including Hugh MacLennan's *Barometer Rising* (1941), W.O. Mitchell's *Who Has Seen the Wind* (1947), and Sheila Watson's *The Double Hook* (1959). In each of these novels, a fortuitous disaster facilitates the emergence of a new, ideal order. MacLennan, whom many critics regard as the father of the Canadian novel,[5] frequently employed apocalyptic imagery in the service of Canadian national-ism: *Barometer Rising* dramatizes the Halifax Explosion of 1917 (the most devastating explosion before Hiroshima) as a momentous, apocalyptic event necessary if Canada was to leave behind its past as a British colony and move into the future as an autonomous nation. *Who Has Seen the Wind* provides a comic telling of an apocalyptic nar-rative when the mad prophet, Saint Sammy, crazed by the disasters of the Depression era, makes wild promises of God's vengeance that are seemingly fulfilled when a windstorm breaks down the sterile old order and initiates a new and better era. *The Double Hook*, with its bib-lical style and starkly symbolic narrative, adds a mythic dimension to the apocalyptic pattern in its tale of a community restored through the murder of Mrs Potter, the selfish, old matriarch; the burning of her home and seat of power; and the blinding of Kip, the commu-nity's seer.

These narratives, with their non-ironic and optimistic view of apocalypse, represent a short-lived phase in Canadian literature. The class and racial biases of *Barometer Rising* are especially troubling for contemporary readers, who notice that the fires unleashed by the explosion raze the slums where the recent immigrants and lower classes reside and that the new society poised to emerge at the end of *Barometer Rising* is composed of individuals of British and Scottish descent – elements that would have been welcome to Susanna Moodie. The historic traumas of mid-century and after – the revela-tions about the Holocaust, the use of nuclear weapons, followed by the Cold War with its continual threat of a more terrible disaster – have provided a historical context in which the apocalyptic model has come to seem too sinister to countenance. Thus, later works, including MacLennan's own *Voices in Time* (1980), call into question the enduring connection between apocalypse and the right to claim a place in the new world's New Jerusalem. They also challenge the idea that the emergence of a better world is necessarily predicated on a passage through an interval of violence and death. In *The Stone Angel* (1964), for example, Margaret Laurence tells the cautionary tale of Murray Lees, whose life was destroyed by his wife's embracing of an apocalyptic belief system. Later, in *The Diviners* (1974), Laurence suggests that a whole generation has come, terrifyingly, to feel itself the "children of the apocalypse." Robert Kroetsch explicitly examines and parodies the apocalyptic, evangelical politics that shaped his own formative years by creating, in *The Words of My Roaring* (1966), a historical novel about the 1935 Alberta general election in which Aberhart drew on the book of Revelation while portraying central Canada's "Big Shots" as agents of demonic evil. That book, like the two succeeding novels that completed Kroetsch's *Out West* triptych, wittily utilizes an explicitly apocalyptic pattern in order to suggest its dangers.

Works published in the latter half of the last century and in the early twenty-first century, however, reveal the radical shift in attitudes toward apocalypse that took place after the Second World War. Again, in this period, the array of apocalyptic fictions is vast: Jack Hodgin's *The Invention of the World* (1977); all of Timothy Findley's fictions; any number of Atwood's texts, particularly *Surfacing* (1972), *The Handmaid's Tale* (1985), *The Robber Bride* (1993), and *Oryx and Crake* (2003); William Gibson's *Burning Chrome* (1986); Barbara Gowdy's *Falling Angels* (1996) and *The White Bone* (1998); Anne Michaels's *Fugitive Pieces* (1996); Douglas Coupland's *Girlfriend in a Coma* (1998); and Rudy Wiebe's *A Discovery of Strangers* (1998) – to name only a few.[6]

Hodgin's comic novel traces the life of Donal Keneally, a charismatic Irishman who led his religious disciples from Ireland to Vancouver Island in search of Eden. Upon arriving, Keneally assumes tyrannical leadership of the Revelations Colony of Truth. Weaving past and present together, Hodgin's novel interrogates the seeds of fascism and the horrific impact of its quest to apply the myth of apocalypse to the real world. While the text repeatedly emphasizes that perfection and unity cannot be attained in this world, characters occasionally glimpse the truth in the guise of unviolated nature.

Atwood's novels also consider the decline of post-Second World

War civilization and the subsequent longing for perfection and revelation. *Surfacing*, like Hodgin's *Invention of the World*, concludes with an epiphany, a view of the Canadian wilderness that seemingly resurrects the dead and restores the divine to the earthly world. But the revelation is fleeting, as the protagonist admits: "No gods to help me now, they're questionable once more, theoretical as Jesus. They've receded, back to the past, inside the skull, it is the same place. They'll never appear to me again ... from now on I'll have to live in the usual way, defining them by their absence; and love by its failures, power by its loss. ... No total salvation, resurrection ... " (203–4). Atwood's later novels betray an increasingly pessimistic attitude toward the possibility of forestalling disaster. *The Handmaid's Tale*, a dystopian fantasy, like *Invention of the World* and Findley's *Not Wanted on the Voyage*, explores the dynamics of fascism and the repercussions of imposing biblical narratives on the world from the perspective of the non-elect. Atwood's futuristic tale depicts the experience of women in the Republic of Gilead, a theocracy founded by religious extremists in what was formerly the United States. In the new Republic, woman are used as reproductive slaves to bear children for the elect. In *The Robber Bride*, set at the end of the millennium, Atwood continues to meditate on the collapse of civil society, the nature of evil, and the possibility of redemption by drawing on biblical motifs. Here, however, evil is personified by Zenia, a woman explicitly identified with the figures of Jezebel and the Whore of Babylon from the biblical apocalypse. In *Oryx and Crake*, a brilliant scientist at a biotech firm initiates the apocalypse by creating a lethal virus and releasing it worldwide. In doing so, he eradicates all of humanity, save the race of perfect humans that he engineered and their sole human guardian.

The fictions by Gibson, Gowdy, Michaels, Coupland, and Wiebe offer equally despairing images of failed apocalypses, the absence of an earthly paradise, and the violence unleashed on the non-elect. Gibson's short-story collection *Burning Chrome*, like Atwood's futuristic narrative, provides readers with a post-apocalyptic vision. Gibson's narratives serve as elegies for Canada's once-bucolic West coast and its misguided inhabitants, who placed their faith in technology, shed their earthly bodies, and digitally encoded their minds in a bid to achieve immortality. Indeed, all of these fictions are elegies of one sort or another. Gowdy's novel *The White Bone*, an explicitly apocalyptic tale, recounts the slaughter of elephants by ivory poachers on the African plain and is narrated by the besieged

elephants themselves. Inspired by a myth of redemption, the traumatized survivors set out in search of a legendary white bone supposedly imbued with the power to lead them to paradise. Michaels's
Fugitive Pieces also tells the story of a traumatized survivor, the Jewish poet Jacob Beer, orphaned in childhood by the Nazis. Coupland's
Girlfriend in a Coma explicitly addresses the apocalypse, envisioning
a world in which everyone goes to sleep and dies three days after
Christmas in 1998, save a circle of friends who are chosen to witness
the catastrophe and to testify together to what they have seen and
felt. In its portrayal of humanity's corruption and the world's anti-
climactic, comatose end – not with a bang but a whimper – the novel
recalls US fiction's preoccupation with the tension between apocalypse and entropy. At one point, one of the chosen survivors literally
"whimpers" in the face of the entropic decay of the world: "There's
no point to the world now. It just erodes and becomes chaotic and
poisoned" (224). Wiebe's novel *A Discovery of Strangers* examines the
genocide of the Native peoples. Narrated in part by members of the
Tetsot'ine tribe, the narrative mourns the apocalyptic destruction of
the Natives and their harmonious way of life: "[A]t one time they
needed to think only of People, and of animals and coming weather,
and food, and the prevention and curing of possible illness; that was
the world of their land and they lived it. But suddenly a fireball
smashed through the sky: crash! – here are Whites! Now! And immediately the world is always on fire with something else, something
they have never thought about or had to do before; always, it seems,
burning out of its centre and rushing, destroying itself towards all
possible edges" (17). Indeed, Native North Americans have firsthand knowledge of apocalyptic disasters and the cultural and psychological devastation that attends being labelled the non-elect, as
Tom King's comic novel *Green Grass, Running Water* vividly demonstrates. In addition, works such as Joy Kogawa's *Obasan* and, more
recently, Kerri Sakamoto's *The Electrical Field* document the traumatic ordeal of Japanese Canadians who were labelled "enemy
aliens," interned, and stripped of their property during the Second
World War. As this study argues, in contrast to the writers at mid-
century, Canadian authors at century's end frequently portray the
repercussions of apocalyptic thinking from the perspective of
minorities who struggle with the traumatic aftermath of an apocalyptic catastrophe.

CANADIAN APOCALYPTIC TEXTS

The texts for this study were chosen primarily for the ways in which they highlight the key structural features of apocalypse: its reliance on intertexts and allegory, its dependence on the revelation of something hidden, its portrayal of the stark opposition between good and evil – an opposition that culminates in the sudden and violent destruction of the non-elect – and its status as "crisis literature." If these were the only criteria, however, an analysis of any number of works by earlier writers would have sufficed, most obviously those mentioned earlier by MacLennan, Mitchell, and Watson. There are, however, six works that best exemplify the paradigm and demonstrate the shift in attitudes toward apocalypse that occurred after the Second World War. These texts also explicitly address the troubling fact that apocalypse has never been restricted to the literary realm. All of the fictions in this study – Findley's *Headhunter* (1993), Michael Ondaatje's *The English Patient* (1992), Margaret Atwood's story "Hairball," from her collection *Wilderness Tips* (1991), Thomas King's *Green Grass, Running Water* (1993), and Joy Kogawa's *Obasan* (1981) – address the literary, psychological, political, and cultural repercussions of apocalypse; they also share a marked concern with the traumatic impact of apocalyptic violence and the loss experienced by the non-elect. Indeed, for Findley, Ondaatje, and Kogawa, the horrors of the Holocaust and the bombing of Japan provoked a radical re-evaluation of culture and human progress. Dealing explicitly with the Second World War, their fictions ask readers to consider what it means to come after Auschwitz by raising questions about humanity's relation to itself, to its culture, and to its texts. As inheritors of the skeptical postwar vision outlined earlier, the works under consideration simultaneously challenge the notion of apocalypse even as they install its discourse.

This study adopts an interdisciplinary approach that bridges literature, religion, history, and politics. The decision to take this approach springs from the growing critical awareness that the influence of apocalypse is pervasive and that it has never functioned solely as a discrete literary genre but has always shaped philosophical and political thinking, as well as historical events. Few critics have examined Canada's relationship to the apocalyptic narrative, owing, perhaps, to the United States' pre-eminent status as the apocalyptic nation – a view that dates back to the Puritan belief that the USA was to be "the City on the Hill," a sacred place that would demonstrate Christ's spirit on Earth and lead its adherents to Heaven. But a scholarly analysis of the broader cultural impact of apocalypse depicted in Canadian fiction is needed for the reasons outlined by critics such as Harold Bloom, M.H. Abrams, and Frank Kermode. According to Abrams, we have always been directly and indirectly influenced by "the imprint, in the narrative plot, characters and imagery, of the Revelation of Saint John the Divine." Whether we are believers or unbelievers, educated or uneducated, Abrams argues that "we, like our Western ancestors over the last two millennia, continue to live in a pervasively biblical culture, in which theological formulas are implicated in our ordinary language and we tend to mistake our inherited categories for the constitution of the world and the universal forms of thought" ("Apocalypse" 7–8). Perhaps Kermode puts it best when he reminds us that, while it may be easy to be satirical about conceptions of popular apocalypses and to ignore the dire warnings of theologians, it is potentially dangerous "to dismiss consideration of the degree to which the ideas and the literatures we value and some of the assumptions we ordinarily do not question are impregnated by an apocalypticism that is neither vulgar nor technical" ("Waiting for the End" 255). As the fictions in this study illustrate, Canada has not remained deaf to the siren song of apocalypse.

Yet, just as not all eschatological writings are apocalyptic, not all writings that contain apocalyptic ideas fall under the strict literary classification of "apocalypse." At the end of the millennium, the term "apocalypse" increasingly came into vogue; it is "often applied loosely to signify any sudden and visionary revelation, or any event of violent and large-scale destruction – or even anything which is very drastic" (Abrams, *Natural Supernaturalism* 41). Such a broad definition, however, does not typify the fictions discussed here. Instead, they rely on particular generic features characteristic of ancient apocalypses.

The first two chapters, on Findley's *Headhunter* and Ondaatje's *The English Patient*, introduce readers to the characteristic features of the apocalyptic paradigm, emphasizing and, in some instances, subverting its reliance on intertextuality, allegory, revelation, an overarching temporal perspective, and a stark opposition between good and evil, personified by the elect and the non-elect. Both Findley's

and Ondaatje's novels also underscore apocalypse's unsettling tendency to escape the bounds of the literary realm and shape our conception of events in the real world. These novels serve as a useful
starting point because, although they portray a range of apocalyptic
motifs, each draws attention to particular aspects of apocalypse.
Ondaatje's text, for instance, underscores the link between apocalypse and allegory and explores the implications of an allegorical
way of seeing. Both works also promote different strategies for
countering the apocalyptic plot. To destabilize apocalypse's stark
oppositions, Findley's novel relies on the salutary recognition of the
permeable boundary between good and evil, the elect and the non-
elect. By contrast, Ondaatje's novel treats apocalypse as an
inevitable part of human history and considers what can be salvaged
in the wake of the disaster.

The third chapter, on Atwood's short story "Hairball," contrasts
with the initial chapters on Findley's and Ondaatje's texts and with
the final chapters on King's and Kogawa's novels because Atwood's
story does not depict strategies for resisting apocalypse, particularly
those associated with prophetic eschatology. Instead, "Hairball"
demonstrates the horrific repercussions of unchecked apocalyptic
thinking, tracing, in particular, the gendered and racial aspects of
apocalypse and the cannibalistic violence at the heart of Revelation.
While Atwood's text depicts an apocalypse, it remains anti-apocalyptic because, rather than embrace the logic of apocalypse, it portrays apocalypse to warn against it. And although chapter 3 remains
distinct because it deals with the only truly apocalyptic text in the
study, nevertheless, in keeping with the first two chapters, it extends
the discussion of apocalypse beyond the bounds of literature by
implicitly linking the plot of Revelation to the conquest of Canada
and the Native peoples by the settler-invader society.

The final chapters on King's and Kogawa's novels examine the
impact of depicting apocalypse from the perspective of Canada's
non-elect. Whereas the conflict between Native and non-Native cultures is implicit in Atwood's stories, it is central to King's *Green Grass,
Running Water*, a novel that playfully interrogates non-Native society's reliance on the logic of apocalypse in its treatment of Native
peoples as the non-elect. And while Findley's, Ondaatje's, and
Atwood's fictions destabilize the apocalyptic paradigm by exposing
the repercussions of its brutality, King's novel takes the critique one
step further, illustrating that it is possible to resist apocalypse's

relentless linear teleology by drawing on the traditional Native figure of the circle.

Finally, in contrast to King's playful critique, Kogawa's *Obasan* offers a tragic account of the parallels between Canada's treatment of Native peoples and of Japanese Canadians during the Second World War: both groups were stripped of their rights and property and forcibly interned. In keeping with *Green Grass, Running Water, Obasan* prompts readers to acknowledge the impact of the myth of apocalypse on Canadian history.

A GRAMMAR OF APOCALYPSE

Given that this study deals explicitly with apocalyptic motifs, it is necessary, at this point, to summarize the genre's basic structural, thematic, and political elements – to review the "grammar" of apocalypse. And just as a summary of poetic tropes gives the reader a foundation for their application by diverse poets, the grammar provided below offers a foundation for the subsequent chapters' more detailed discussion of the use of apocalyptic motifs in Canadian fiction.

The idea of apocalypse falls under the general category of eschatology, the teachings of "the last things": "Eschatology gives an account of the final condition of man and the world as this is represented in scripture. The idea of a final condition of mankind and the world rests on the other idea that history is a moral process, with a goal towards which it is moving. In scripture this moral process is specifically a redemptive process of which the author and the finisher is God, He Himself being the end towards which mankind is being drawn" (Salmond 734). In his study of apocalypse, Douglas Robinson points out that, whereas the term eschatology is often believed to mean "the last things," the original meaning of *eschaton* is actually "the furthermost boundary," "the ultimate edge" in time or space (xii). The texts in this study, particularly Findley's *Headhunter* and Kogawa's *Obasan*, draw attention to spirituality's obsession with this "edge" – an obsession fuelled by the belief that lurking just beyond the edge is divine truth. As these texts indicate, however, tearing away the veil does not disclose God's truth. In these fictions, more often than not, the act of unveiling merely exposes that both the edge and what supposedly lies beyond it are human constructs.

Not all eschatological beliefs, however, are apocalyptic. For the purposes of this study, it is crucial to distinguish between two distinct approaches: prophetic and apocalyptic eschatology. As the subsequent chapters demonstrate, many texts base their protest against the traditional apocalyptic narrative – which calls for the eradication of this world in favour of the heavenly New Jerusalem – on the distinction between prophetic and apocalyptic eschatology. In Findley's *Headhunter*, for example, some individuals faced with a "world that had begun to fracture and fragment" refuse "to shed the past" and to conceive of themselves as pilgrims on a journey "into the future" (34–6). Prophetic eschatology (which, despite its name, should not be identified solely with the idea of prophecy) describes a religious perspective that focuses on "the prophetic announcement to the nation of the divine plans for Israel ... which he [the seer] translates into *the terms of plain history, real politics, and human instrumentality*" (Hanson 11; my emphasis). Simply put, prophetic eschatology envisioned God accomplishing divine plans within the *here and now*, within "the context of human history and by means of human agents" (Reddish 20).[7]

On the other hand, apocalyptic eschatology maintains that the prophet no longer retains the faith that redemption can occur in this world. In apocalyptic literature, hope does not lie in the anticipation of the restoration of an earthly community, but in the belief that God will bring an end to the profane world and create an entirely new one. Apocalypse thus produces "a doctrine of two aeons which follow one another and stand in antithetical relation: this world and the world to come, the reign of darkness and the reign of light" (Scholem 6). In apocalypse, hope and retribution occur outside the range of human history. Apocalypticism also eschews prophetic eschatology's portrayal of God working through human agents in favour of God's reliance on supernatural forces to end history as we know it.[8] As will be shown, the fictions in this study, with the notable exception of Atwood's "Hairball," invoke prophetic eschatology to challenge the apocalyptic belief that redemption cannot be brought about on Earth by an earthly community. In Ondaatje's novel, characters like Kip, the Asian sapper who risks his life to defuse bombs, do not wait for the world to end; instead, they feel charged with "a map of responsibility" to prevent apocalyptic disaster (195). In keeping with Ondaatje's reference to maps in the discussion that follows, this study demonstrates how prophetic and apocalyptic eschatology are linked to two distinct approaches to mapmaking.

Finally, in contrast to prophetic eschatology, which is delivered in

plain language to the community as a whole, apocalypse is usually
esoteric in nature and constitutes a secret reserved for a select few,
chosen by God. "The words of the prophets," Scholem writes, "which
in their original context appear so clear and direct, henceforth
become riddles, allegories, and mysteries which are interpreted – one
might say, deciphered – by an apocalyptic homiletic or an original
apocalyptic vision" (6). Thus, the initial chapters of this study focus
on the encrypted, allegorical nature of apocalyptic hermeneutics:
Headhunter's secular prophets, who utter and interpret apocalyptic
riddles and allegories, are spiritualists and schizophrenics. And in
The English Patient's post-apocalyptic landscape of fragments and
ruins, everyone, including the reader, must assume the role of the
seer, linking isolated fragments to create meaning.

Having distinguished apocalyptic from prophetic eschatology, there
remains a need to consider the specific features that characterize apocalypse. One of the easiest ways to become acquainted with apocalypse's
distinctive political, structural, and thematic features is to consider Revelation, the biblical text on which all of the fictions in this study rely. As
the title "Revelation" suggests, the apocalyptic paradigm is "revela-
tory"; that is, "the author claims to have received a divine revelation"
and this revelation is "usually in the form of a dream or vision and is
mediated by or interpreted by an angel" (Reddish 21). Apocalypse –
and Revelation is no exception – concerns itself with the unveiling of a
secret, a divine plan, which inevitably involves the destruction and
judgement of the old, earthly world and the creation of a new, heavenly
paradise. Revelation, however, is not merely "an eschatological tract
satisfying the curiosity of those who wanted to know what would happen in the future"; instead, its purpose is "to reveal something hidden
which will enable readers to view their present situation from a completely different perspective" (Rowland 46). In the often ironic and self-
reflexive treatments of apocalypse examined in this study, the secret frequently concerns the traumatic violence at the heart of apocalypse. In
keeping with Rowland's insight, by graphically depicting the violence
directed at women, children, minorities, and nature itself, the texts
invite readers to consider the impact of apocalypse from the "different
perspective" of the victimized non-elect. In *Obasan*, for example, the
non-elect are personified by the Japanese Canadians interned during
the Second World War, "the despised rendered voiceless, stripped of
car, radio, camera, and every means of communication, a trainload of
eyes covered with mud and spittle" (119).

Revelation does not simply unveil "something hidden"; the secret revealed is part of an overarching, politically inflected text. Written during the last decade of the first century CE by John of Patmos,[9] an early Christian, Revelation's fundamental aim lies in challenging its readers to resist the Roman empire and to remain faithful to the teachings of Christ: "Here is a call," John proclaims, "for the endurance and faith of the saints" (13:10). John begins his testimony by explaining that, while he was on the island of Patmos, he heard "a loud voice like a trumpet" telling him to write down all the visions that he sees in a book and to send these visions to the seven churches (1:10). By repeatedly directing his message to the members of the churches persecuted and oppressed by the Romans, John's testimony highlights a central feature of apocalypse's ideological and political dimensions. Simply put, early apocalypses are disaster narratives registering the impact of Roman imperialism and colonialism – a feature that resonates with Canadian writers. To borrow Mitchell Reddish's words, apocalyptic literature is "crisis literature," writings produced "during a time of perceived crisis to offer hope to oppressed and beleaguered individuals by giving them an alternative picture of reality" (24). Apocalyptic literature, then, functioned as "a form of protest against society. It was resistance literature, whether the 'enemy' was political, military, social, or theological" (25). By describing "the eventual destruction of Rome and the other forces of evil and by assuring the readers of eschatological rewards for the faithful," Reddish argues, John "offered hope and encouragement to Christians who were being persecuted (or at least perceived the possibility of persecution)" (30). As this study demonstrates, the apocalyptic narratives fashioned by Canadian writers at century's end also function as "crisis literature," identifying a variety of oppressive political and social forces. Findley's novel concentrates on corporate executives who, like the rapacious colonizers before them, stop at nothing to satisfy their greed and ambition, while Ondaatje's, Atwood's, King's, and Kogawa's fictions depict evil deeds committed both by individuals and nation-states. But in all of the texts, the legacy of imperialism and colonization looms large, with Britain, the USA, and even Canada assuming the role of Babylon – the decadent, oppressive locus of Roman might featured in Revelation.

Owing to the emphasis on testimony in the biblical apocalypse, many of the contemporary anti-apocalyptic fictions in this study understandably reflect on the act of bearing witness. However, unlike

John, who tells the story from the perspective of the elect, the works considered here typically offer the testimony of apocalypse's traumatized victims. In *Obasan*, for example, Aunt Emily self-consciously adopts the role of witness and cites the Lord's command to Habakkuk: "Write the vision; make it plain upon tablets, so he may run who reads it" (Habakkuk 2:2). Yet, as *Obasan* demonstrates, it is difficult and perhaps even impossible to fulfill this commandment because traumatic testimony is fundamentally ambivalent. On the one hand, such testimony attempts to recall and represent the event – "to write the vision and make it plain." On the other hand, it also demonstrates the inability or refusal to work through the traumatic impact of the event. Indeed, some critics wonder whether, ethically speaking, apocalyptic violence should be rendered comprehensible because this would bring what should remain fundamentally incomprehensible and an affront to reason within the grasp of the intellect and therefore normalize it (Caruth, *Trauma* 154–6).

The ethics of bearing witness is also a factor in King's novel, which likewise conveys traumatic testimony but introduces complications specific to Native cultures. Within most Native cultures the accepted process of bearing witness effectively violates three traditional ethics of Northern Native peoples (Fagan 109–10). To offer testimony without contravening Native ethics, King's text, like many other works by Native writers, relies on humour. A comic approach allows *Green Grass, Running Water* to represent the "hidden," to bear witness to the traumatic impact of imperialism and colonization while respecting Native ethics. As will be seen, many of the texts adopt covert means of bearing witness.

Indeed, structurally and stylistically, Revelation's message is covert. As suggested earlier, Revelation conveys its secret message and politically charged vision by adopting a fundamentally allegorical and intertextual design. John crammed his politicized vision of catastrophe and redemption with surreal, allegorical images, including the Son of Man, from whose mouth issues a two-edged sword, the four horsemen, and the ten-horned, seven-headed beast that rises from the sea.[10] The author of Revelation "took up the concepts, phrases, and imagery of Isaiah, Daniel, and other Jewish prophecies and eschatologies, adapted them to Christian Messianism, and developed them into the intricately ordered symbolism of the most awesome and influential of all apocalyptic visions" (Abrams, *Natural Supernaturalism* 40). Many passages are "simply translated from the

Hebrew Bible, and in addition, there are more than 300 references to Daniel, Isaiah, Second Isaiah, Jeremiah, Ezekiel and Zechariah" (Cohn, *Cosmos, Chaos, and the World to Come* 212).[11] Thus, Revelation is intricately recursive; that is, it "represents the present and future by replicating or alluding to passages in earlier biblical texts, especially in Genesis, Exodus, the Old Testament prophets, and the apocalyptic visions in Daniel" (Abrams, "Apocalypse" 9). The allusive and fragmentary nature of the text led Bloom to describe Revelation as "a jigsaw puzzle in which nearly all the pieces are torn away from their contexts" (1). Although all of the works in this study are intertextual – Findley's *Headhunter*, which opens in the Metro Toronto Reference Library; Ondaatje's *The English Patient*, which includes fragments of canonical texts including Herodotus's *The Histories*; and King's *Green Grass, Running Water*, which presupposes an encyclopaedic knowledge of US literature and history – they self-reflexively signal their debt to apocalypse's densely intertextual and recursive design. As critics have observed, Canadian writers are particularly drawn to intertextuality and frequently parody canonical narratives, often by playfully locating them within a Canadian setting, to subvert their power (Söderlind 18).

Given apocalypse's emphasis on intertextuality, one might ask what is the effect of this allusive structure? According to Northrop Frye, the seer fashions this intertextual and allegorical design to create an overarching vision of "all of history from beginning to end, conveying the impression of temporal unity" ("Typology" 70). This panoramic vision is yet another fundamental characteristic of apocalyptic literature; in rewriting the past, apocalyptic texts forecast the future. As this study argues, the apocalyptic plot can be understood as providing readers with a temporal and spatial map that emphasizes divine unity. The unified vision afforded by Revelation inscribes the temporal trajectory of past, present, and future, as well as the location of the final contest between good and evil and of the New Jerusalem.[12] It is important to stress the temporal and spatial cartographic features of John's vision because virtually all of the fictions under consideration engage with apocalypse's obsession with producing a unified vision of space and time in the form of a map. As the analysis of Ondaatje's and King's novels will demonstrate, both apocalyptic and prophetic eschatology provide readers with two very different maps. Whereas the apocalyptic map relentlessly directs readers to the future and inscribes the features of the New Jerusalem,

the prophetic map grounds itself in the present and traces important
connections between the present and the past.[13]

Moreover, Revelation adopts a transcendent perspective to demonstrate, in accordance with the apocalyptic genre, that "God had all
things under control": "In spite of how events might appear to those
on earth, who were living in the midst of chaos, destruction, and confusion, the universe was not out of control. God had predetermined
the nature of the universe and the course of world history. At the
appropriate time – which was very soon – God would bring history
to a climax, and the rewards and punishments seen by the writer
would become reality" (Reddish 21–2). Typically, the apocalyptic
prophet carefully locates his or her vision "in a near future and just
before the end of time" (Frye, "Typology" 70). A number of texts,
most obviously *Headhunter*, adopt this temporal perspective, locating
their narrators' visions prior to an imminent catastrophe. In contrast
to Revelation, the impression afforded by the use of intertexts in
these novels undermines the assurance that God has "all things
under control." And unlike the biblical apocalypse, contemporary
Canadian fiction does not rely on intertexts and allegory to establish
an overarching, divine vision. Instead, the texts invoke these tropes
to highlight the fragmentation generated by the apocalyptic storms
that continually threaten to destroy all traces of human history.

According to Revelation, during the apocalyptic storm, the non-
elect, like "earthen pots," will "be broken in pieces" (2:27). Parallel-
ing the emphasis on fragmentation and ruin in the biblical paradigm,
works such as *The English Patient*, "Hairball," and *Obasan* explicitly
grapple with the implications of this irrevocable fragmentation.
Ondaatje's novel embarks on an extended analysis of the topos of the
ruin or fragment and ultimately adopts Walter Benjamin's view of
the fragment and allegory. According to Benjamin, it is the task of the
allegorist to construct meaning from the fragments of apocalyptic
catastrophe. In keeping with his views, *The English Patient* uses fragments of prior narratives and images of fragmentation to create an
emblem of apocalypse that challenges the biblical apocalypse's representation of divine order and control. Ondaatje's novel specifically
recalls Benjamin's belief that the destruction of the body in allegorical narratives "prepares the body of the living person for emblematic
purposes" (*The Origin of the German Tragic Drama* 216). In *The English
Patient*, the patient's body serves as an allegorical fragment – an
emblem of catastrophe. Similarly, in Atwood's short story "Hairball,"

the body is also used for emblematic purposes; in this case, the fragment used to create an emblem of catastrophe is a cyst removed from the protagonist's uterus, dubbed "Hairball." Atwood's story, like *The English Patient*, invokes the apocalyptic image of the fragment to prompt readers to grapple with the violence of its apocalypse and its impact on the non-elect. Finally, in *Obasan*, the body once again serves as an emblem of apocalypse; in this case, it is the body of the protagonist's mother, burned beyond recognition by the atomic blast at Nagasaki. In keeping with Walter Benjamin's writings, *The English Patient*, and "Hairball," *Obasan* ultimately champions an aesthetics and politics of brokenness and woundedness over that of wholeness, order, and control.

Referring to the biblical paradigm's overarching vision of order and control, Stephen O'Leary argues further that apocalypse's ultimate goal is to establish a "unique temporal and teleological framework for understanding evil" by claiming that God has permitted evil to grow in power until the appointed endtime when evil will be punished and good rewarded (6). It is also this facet of apocalypse, namely, its capacity to provide a "framework for understanding evil" that unites all of the writers considered in this study – writers who felt compelled to analyze and challenge the apocalyptic paradigm in the wake of the Second World War. In their texts, evil typically springs from an uncritical reliance on the apocalyptic narrative, which divides the world into the elect and the non-elect, and seeks to exterminate the latter.

To grasp how the works in this study subvert the apocalyptic paradigm, it is essential to draw a distinction between apocalyptic and non-Christian teleologies in order to further pursue the notion of apocalypse as a kind of spatial and temporal map. M.H. Abrams explains: "As against Greek and Roman primitivism and cyclism (the theory of eternal recurrence), the biblical paradigm attributes to earthly history a single and sharply defined plot with a beginning (the *fiat* of creation), a catastrophe (the fall of man), a crisis (the Incarnation and Resurrection of Christ), and a coming end (the abrupt Second Advent of Christ as King, followed by the replacement of the old world by 'a new heaven and new earth') which will convert the tragedy of human history into a cosmic comedy. This historical plot, furthermore, has a divine Author, who planned its middle and end before the beginning, created the great stage and agents of history, infallibly controls all its events, and guarantees its ultimate consummation" ("Apocalypse" 9). Both Ondaatje's *The English Patient* and King's *Green Grass, Running Water* self-consciously invoke maps and mapmaking to illustrate that there are different ways of plotting human history. In effect, both works champion treating maps in accordance with prophetic eschatology as sites of communal, earthly knowledge with strong ties to the past. King's novel argues further that differences between modes of plotting – cyclism versus the linear biblical apocalyptic paradigm – lie at the heart of the clash between Native and non-Native peoples.

During an interview, Native Canadian author Tomson Highway illustrated the difference between the cyclical Native and linear apocalyptic worldviews by drawing a circle on a piece of paper: "Whereas the Indian system ... is a circle, a never-ending circle ... the European system is a straight line, what I call the Genesis to Revelations line: progress, progress, progress from point A to point B, until the apocalypse comes. As a result, the circle was shattered and got stretched open to a straight line and the impact psychologically and spiritually was devastating" (8). Highway's decision to pick up a pencil and draw lines and circles reinforces the idea that the apocalyptic plot can function as a spiritual map and explains why Native peoples suffered and continue to suffer when they are forced to accept a non-Native, linear, apocalyptic worldview. The linear Christian model does not make sense, according to Highway, because Native teleology does not include a notion of messianic redemption: there was no Fall; thus, there is no need to anticipate the violent purgation and destruction of the world. Highway explained further that at the centre of North American Indian mythology is not an agonized figure, like Christ, who was sacrificed on the cross, but a magical being known as "Trickster." In contrast to the masculine, tragic figure of Christ, Trickster is an androgynous shapeshifter, essentially a "comic, clownish sort of character ... [whose] role is to teach us about the nature and the meaning of existence on the planet Earth; he straddles the consciousness of man and that of God, the Great Spirit" (10).

In a similar departure from the apocalyptic plot, the maps fashioned by Ondaatje's melancholy protagonists look to the past and pay homage to the lost cities and the dead, rather than celebrate the future and the creation of the unified holy city. King's novel likewise invokes maps and mapmaking to reject Revelation's linear trajectory – what Highway describes as "the Genesis to Revelations line." For King, as for Highway, the Native North American model of the circle provides a vital alternative to apocalypse's destructive, linear, future-oriented map. In contrast to King's celebration of an alternative to apocalypse symbolized by the circle, Kogawa's novel (echoing Ondaatje's and Atwood's fascination with the fragment) invokes a cartography of ruin to explore what is described here as an aesthetics and politics of brokenness.

Canadian writers are particularly drawn to the map image because, as critics have observed, this image "is the mainstay" of Canadian writing, particularly contemporary Canadian writing (Huggan 34). In her book on Canadian literature, Gail McGregor describes the map as "probably *the* iconic artifact in the Canadian's conceptual vocabulary" (350). The prominence of the metaphor of the map in Canadian literature can be credited, in part, to the fact that the development of Canadian literature coincided with the age of discovery. The sheer immensity of the country "needed to be brought down to size – made amenable (in a standard colonialist move) to human settlement" (Huggan 34). Yet critics and creative writers have continued to rely on the image of the map to articulate "a cartography of difference constructed on the principles of cultural diversity that are more appropriate to the heterogenous nature of postcolonial societies/cultures" (147–8). In the fictions under consideration here, the image of the map relates both to the Canadian preoccupation with mapping and to the mythic cartography of Revelation. But rather than adopt the future-oriented stance of the elect and dispense with the maps of the earthly world in favour of John's map of the New Jerusalem, contemporary Canadian writers privilege earthly, historical maps.

It is not surprising that these fictions draw attention to prophetic maps that concentrate on this world rather than the next, in the light of Canadian writers' tendency to side with the non-elect, whose gruesome fate is outlined in the biblical apocalypse. Revelation inscribes a fundamental opposition between the elect and the non-elect – an opposition that each of the fictions in this study interrogates. Apocalyptic eschatology relies on binary opposition:

Apocalyptic narrative and prophecy is a chiaroscuro history, in which the agencies are the opponent forces of light and of darkness and there is no middle ground between the totally good and the absolutely evil. On the negative side are ranged Satan, the Beast, and the Great Whore, "Babylon the Great, the Mother of Harlots and Abominations of the Earth," together with the

earthy agents of iniquity ("the kings of the earth" and their armies), to whom
exegetes soon applied the collective term "Antichrist." Opposed to them are
God, Christ, the "new Jerusalem ... prepared as a bride adorned for her husband," and the company of earthly saints. The consummation of history, as
noted earlier, occurs not by mediation between these polar opposites, but
only after the extirpation of the forces of evil by the forces of good. (Abrams,
"Apocalypse" 11)

In keeping with apocalypse's "chiarascuro history," the texts considered in the initial chapters portray a moral landscape without a middle ground between good and evil. While all of the texts invoke these
oppositions – elect/good, non-elect/evil – they take pains to illustrate their complexity and instability; ultimately, whether one is with
or against the elect depends on one's perspective. For instance, Findley's elect – his "Saints of God" as Cohn (*The Pursuit of the Millenium*)
would call them[14] – led by a psychiatrist named Marlow, battle an
oppressive and corrupt social order, incarnated in Marlow's evil
employer, aptly named Kurtz, who perversely believes that he is one
of the elect working on behalf of humankind. Ondaatje's novel, set
during the Second World War, explicitly aligns the four central characters who oppose the war with the elect. From the start, the English
Patient is likened to a "despairing saint," and the Asian sapper, Kip,
who befriends him, is repeatedly described as a "warrior saint."
Unlike Ondaatje's novel, which preserves the apocalyptic notions of
the elect and the Saints of God, *Headhunter* calls these apocalyptic
motifs into question, demonstrating how fascism's belief in inher-
ently inferior and superior people, and its plans to exterminate the
former, mirror apocalypse's absolute opposition between the elect
and the non-elect. In effect, fascism adopted the myth of apocalypse
and applied it to the real world. By focusing on the unsavoury
aspects of apocalypse's division between absolute good and evil, and
by positing an alternative, Findley's novel, like the other works in
this study, emphasizes the distinction between prophetic and apocalyptic eschatology. These works champion pre-exilic, prophetic
notions of the elect inclusive of the entire community, and reject post-
exilic, apocalyptic views of the elect comprising only a small, privileged subset of the community.

   The distinction between pre-exilic and post-exilic beliefs about the
fate of the elect and the non-elect is central to all of the works under
consideration. In prophetic eschatology, the suffering and trial of the

endtime was understood to "have an effect on the entire nation, including those who were the oppressors, for through repentance and purification the nation would once again be made whole" (Hanson 396). In apocalyptic narratives, no hope exists for a national repentance that could lead to purification; only "a bloody purge whereby the wicked would be exterminated, leaving those who were destined to be recipients of the salvation to come" (396).[15]

While all of the works grapple with apocalyptic violence, Atwood's short story "Hairball" and several other stories in *Wilderness Tips* focus on the gendered nature of the violence at the heart of apocalypse, revealing the rage unleashed on the non-elect, expressed most graphically in the fate of Jezebel and the Whore of Babylon. According to Revelation, the Whore's flesh is devoured and burned up with fire (Rev. 17:16). Atwood's focus on the specifically gendered and cannibalistic nature of apocalyptic violence confirms what many critics have observed about the treatment of the Woman/Other in the biblical apocalypse. In *Death and Desire*, Tina Pippin explains that the story of Revelation figures the "ultimate release of a colonized people," but this release is effected by the murder and consumption of a powerful female (28). Similarly, there is "an important strand of apocalyptic imagining that seeks to destroy the world expressly in order to eliminate female sexuality" (Berger 11).

It was suggested at the outset that Revelation, in keeping with its name, unveils a secret, and that its hidden message, predicated on violence and absolute destruction, is politically charged. More precisely, contemporary Canadian writers, recalling the visions of apocalyptic writers at mid-century, most notably MacLennan, Mitchell, and Watson, stress the links between apocalyptic violence and the creation of the Canadian nation-state. The fictions in this study demonstrate what remains primarily latent in the earlier fictions, namely, that the originary apocalyptic violence that engendered the nation-state typically involved the subordination and commodification of women, Native peoples, ethnic minorities, and the landscape. For instance, Atwood's fiction draws on Native Wendigo stories – tales of flesh-eating monsters. Yet, rather than presenting these tales as exotic artifacts of a primitive culture, the stories in *Wilderness Tips* remind us that they should be more properly understood as apocalyptic disaster narratives that register the impact of imperialism and colonization. Indeed, Findley's Kurtz, Atwood's protagonist in "Hairball," and the ironically named J. Houvagh in King's novel embrace apocalypse's promise of redemption through violence. Moreover, their greed, selfishness, and pursuit of future gain are explicitly tied to strategies initially used by imperial and colonial powers. In this way, these texts demonstrate the ongoing legacy of apocalyptic thinking in Canada.

The silence that surrounds apocalyptic violence also raises an important question: is it a coincidence that people remain ignorant of the gendered and racialized violence at the heart of apocalypse? The texts in this study demonstrate, however, that forgetting to remember is, in fact, a constituent feature both of apocalypse and the origin of the nation. In his study of shell-shocked veterans of the First World War, Freud observed that there was typically a delayed response to trauma, a period of latency, during which the memory of the traumatic event remained inaccessible to the conscious mind. Freud's concept of latency helps to explain the amnesia that obscures the often violent creation of nation-states. As Homi Bhabha, following Ernest Renan, observes, to establish the new nation as natural and essential, the "violence involved in establishing the nation's writ" must be forgotten; it is "this forgetting – a minus in the origin – that constitutes the *beginning* of the nation's narrative" (310). Despite the effects of this creative amnesia, traces of apocalyptic violence – the fragments and ruin generated by the ongoing catastrophe – remain visible.

Ironically, Revelation hints at the traumatic nature of apocalypse from the start when John, the impossibly stoic narrator, confesses that when he first saw the Son of Man he fainted, falling at Christ's feet "as though dead" (1:12–17). Christ subsequently commands John to wake from his faint and write down the catastrophic events that await humankind (1:17–19). Preoccupied as he is with the fate of the elect, John never emotionally engages or empathizes with the far more traumatic experience of the non-elect. Indeed, the goal of this study is to show how, in their rewriting of apocalypse, contemporary Canadian authors give voice to the trauma of the non-elect.[16]

Moreover, by countering apocalypse's progressive structure, the fictions in this study allow for a retrospective analysis of apocalypse's traumatic impact. *Headhunter*, for instance, aims at uncovering who or what traumatized a group of children to the point that they lost the ability to speak. Similarly, *The English Patient* features a man so badly injured both physically and psychologically that he suffers from amnesia and cannot remember his own name. The study concludes with *Obasan*, a firsthand account of Canada's betrayal of the Japanese Canadians during the Second World War, which graphically illustrates the impact of trauma on the individual, the community, and the nation. Focusing as it does on the internment and insisting on the connections between the betrayal of the Japanese Canadians and the genocide of the Native peoples, *Obasan* fashions a distinctly Canadian apocalypse. More precisely, in its interrogation of apocalypse, *Obasan* reveals that apocalypse is structurally engineered to resist difference or alterity by expressing "a desire for closure in the final 'truth' represented by a single, male deity" (Woodland 51). Ultimately, by exposing the pervasiveness of the apocalyptic paradigm and by analysing its ruthless exclusion of difference, the fictions under consideration invite readers to reconsider apocalypse from an ex-centric, Canadian perspective.

The End(s) of Myth:
Apocalyptic and Prophetic Visions
in *Headhunter*

The dreams of apocalypse, if they usurp waking thought, may be the worst dreams.

Kermode (The Sense of an Ending 108)

In Timothy Findley's first novel, *The Last of the Crazy People* (1967), an eleven-year-old boy becomes convinced that the end of the world is fast approaching. His belief in the world's imminent destruction is instilled by the prophetic visions of a drunken servant. In her booming voice, she warns him: "'No one knows, 'cept they knows it's coming. Arm'geddon ... Like for a moment it's gonna be real, real, terrible, hon ... But for those of us in this perdition *now*, it will surely be bless'd relief'" (98–9). The power of the apocalyptic narrative works on the child's imagination, and at the end of the novel he realizes the prophecy by gunning down his entire family, transforming the narrative of the end from a fantastic biblical fiction into a tragic lived experience.

What are readers to make of this tragedy? Is it simply the result of an insane conflation of the biblical fiction and the text's reality? Or does the text imply something far more disturbing, namely, that apocalyptic dreams have a way of resisting strategies of containment, of blurring the boundaries between art and life?

In the process of examining the apocalyptic narrative, the post-Second World War texts in this study convey the sobering awareness that the violent biblical myth has never been restricted to the literary realm. Similar eschatological concerns appear in Findley's subsequent works, including *The Wars* (1977), *Famous Last Words* (1981), and *Not Wanted on the Voyage* (1984). However, while *Headhunter* (1994) invokes virtually every facet of the apocalyptic paradigm, rather than remain complicit with that, the text challenges the quest for transcendent revelation. Whereas the protagonist of *The Last of the Crazy People* acts out the apocalyptic plot to its grisly conclusion, in *Headhunter*, a significant number of characters, although caught up in the apocalyptic plot, resist and ultimately subvert the traditional apocalyptic perspective, which calls for the destruction of the world in favour of the world to come. Although at times *Headhunter* seems to convey an uncompromising apocalyptic vision, it simultaneously counters this radical vision with a more earthly and historically oriented perspective. As a result, the novel never fully embraces the apocalyptic perspective; ultimately, it champions a perspective with strong ties to pre-exilic prophetic eschatology – a prophetic perspective that stresses humanity's responsibilities in the here and now.

By tracing allusions to apocalyptic discourse in the novel, this chapter shows how the text paradoxically signals the imaginative tenacity, the untrustworthiness, and the limitations of the apocalyptic vision – a vision that represents transformation as absolute destruction. More specifically, this chapter examines how Findley's novel adopts and adapts some fundamental apocalyptic motifs: its intertextual design, its transcendent temporal perspective, its promise of the New Jerusalem, its status as deviant or secret knowledge, and its concepts of the elect and of the enemies of the elect, the latter embodied by the Antichrist. Written by an "ex-centric" Canadian who grew up during the apocalyptic horrors of the Second World War, Findley's novel does not simply reinscribe the biblical paradigm. Instead, in keeping with Canadian writers' concern for the "beautiful losers," the novel rewrites the myth of the end to give voice to the victims of apocalyptic disasters. The narrative's principal tactics for destabilizing the myth of apocalypse entail disclosing the permeable boundary between the elect and the non-elect and implying that the apocalyptic paradigm has horrifically shaped events in the real world: Findley's texts repeatedly link apocalyptic visions of perfection with the horrors perpetrated by Nazi Germany. These tactics enable *Headhunter* to destablize the apocalyptic paradigm and to promote an alternative to apocalypse based on prophetic eschatology.

In keeping with what Harold Bloom called apocalypse's "jig-saw puzzle" design (1), Findley's novel signals its intertextual structure immediately: *Headhunter* opens in the Metro Toronto Reference Library. Seated on a bench, the schizophrenic ex-librarian Lilah Kemp reads Conrad's *Heart of Darkness* and accidentally conjures the horror-meister Kurtz from page 92, setting him loose in the streets of Toronto. Retooled for the times, Kurtz has become a modern-day headhunter, a "shrink," who wields seemingly limitless power as the head of his empire, a psychiatric institute.

From the start, the novel posits a mysterious link between Kurtz and a group of catatonic children at the Queen Street Mental Health Centre. The trauma suffered by these children constitutes the enigma at the heart of the text. Following Kurtz's escape, a host of characters (including Charlie Marlow), based on familiar figures from canonical texts, make their appearance in Findley's work. As one might expect, the task of uncovering the root of the children's trauma falls to Marlow. In the light of the abundant allusions to Conrad's novel, the initial scene, which establishes *Heart of Darkness* with its critique of imperialism as a primary intertext, can be taken as emblematic. Like Revelation, whose numerous intertexts direct readers to earlier books in the biblical archive, Findley's apocalyptic novel also functions as a reference library. However, whereas Revelation directs the reader to the New Jerusalem and provides assurance that "God had all things under control," *Headhunter*'s intertextual design refuses this consoling fiction.

In addition to its debt to Conrad's novel, *Headhunter* relies heavily on two other classic works: Fitzgerald's *The Great Gatsby* and Flaubert's *Madame Bovary*.¹ But not all of *Headhunter*'s literary allusions are as overt and intricately developed as these. Often the novel makes only a fleeting reference to a canonical work; the title of a book or the name of a character usually suffices to signal the connection to a well-known intertext. Early on, for instance, we learn that Lilah marches around the city pushing a baby carriage. Under the blankets is a copy of *Wuthering Heights*. Later on, readers are introduced to Dr Shelley, a psychiatrist who conducts sadistic experiments involving animals and whose name forges a connection with Mary Shelley and her gothic novel *Frankenstein*. This link is reinforced by a comment made by an important character in Findley's novel, Lilah Kemp's beloved teacher, Nicholas Fagan, the learned professor of literature from Trinity College, Dublin.² Lilah recalls that, in one of his lectures, Fagan proclaimed: "If I were to propose a text for the twentieth century, it would be Joseph Conrad's *Heart of Darkness*. As subtext, I would nominate Mary Shelley's *Frankenstein*" (139). In choosing *Madame Bovary*, *Heart of Darkness*, and *The Great Gatsby*, Findley acknowledges the founding novels of Continental, British, and US modernism. Moreover, by confronting readers with this barrage of intertextual material – specifically works such as *Heart of Darkness* and *Frankenstein* that repeatedly focus our attention on the intersections among dreams of transcendence and technological control – the text both reveals its debt to the allusive structure of apocalyptic discourse and highlights the implications of its persistent hold on our imagination.[3]

Rather than invoke intertexts to promote faith in a fixed system in the tradition of apocalyptic writings, however, the novel's reliance on canonical works demonstrates Findley's belief that it is crucial to examine the plots that have shaped human culture: "As writing itself is a flowing from the pen, so literature is a part of the flowing process. Thornton Wilder urged young writers to be familiar with the works of those who had preceded them so they might *know where they enter*. Literature is never done with. Neither what was, nor what is, nor what will be. It is all one voice – it is the voice of humankind – noting, annotating, witnessing, and recording the progress of its species" (Findley, "Turning Down the Volume"; quoted in Bailey 215). As his comments suggest, Findley links the future of the species with literature – a future that, in his view, specifically entails coming to grips with the Second World War and the Holocaust. Findley entered an age that came *after* Auschwitz – an age that underwent "a complete re-evaluation of cultural and human progress ... Thus Findley's post-Holocaust vision concerns ... humanity's relation to itself, to its culture, and to its texts" (Bailey 215).

In keeping with other Canadian authors on the margins of empire, Findley uses intertexts to acknowledge and contest "the canonical myths and forms of European and American literatures" (Hutcheon, *The Canadian Postmodern* 6). He challenges these myths and forms by parodically altering them to reflect a Canadian perspective. In *Head-hunter*, for instance, Kurtz is "not the leader-in-waiting, hidden in the African wilderness, but is the head of the most important psychiatric institution in Canada and is known for his research throughout the world ... Conrad's Marlow may have had trouble seeing Kurtz in the fleeting light of jungle bonfires, but Findley's Marlow has even more difficulty seeing Kurtz in the blinding light of social and academic brilliance" (Bailey 183). Findley's treatment of these canonical texts thus paradoxically reflects both a reverence for the canon and an urge to challenge its status and power by rewriting and relocating canonical texts in a Canadian setting.

Findley's more fundamental reliance on the biblical intertext of apocalypse is also marked by the same urge to acknowledge and challenge the biblical myth of the end; "many critics – from Northrop Frye to D.G. Jones – have argued for the importance of the Bible and biblical structures in Canadian literature, but novels such as Cohen's *Beautiful Losers* or Findley's *Not Wanted on the Voyage* parody those structures and narratives in a typically postmodern way, both exploiting and subverting their undeniable cultural authority" (Hutcheon, *The Canadian Postmodern* 7). *Headhunter* may also be added to this list, for by gesturing toward apocalypse's intertextual design, Findley's narrative seemingly invokes Revelation's characteristic temporal vision, but with the striking omission of the promise of the New Jerusalem.

In contrast to biblical prophetic writings, which involve a narrower set of temporal events, the ancient apocalyptists offer a vision of all of history from beginning to end, conveying the impression of temporal unity.[4] The creation of this type of panoramic vision is a fundamental characteristic of apocalyptic discourse; apocalyptic prophets carefully locate their vision "in a near future and just before the end of time" (Frye, "Typology" 70). In addition, whereas prophecy confirms that "this world is God's world and that in the world His goodness and truth will yet be justified," apocalyptists promote a more pessimistic view of the world: "their optimism, their hope, is not directed to what history will bring forth, but to that which will arise in its ruin" (Scholem 10). Moreover, the catastrophic character of apocalyptic redemption manifests itself in signs of terror and decadence: "in world wars and revolutions, in epidemics, famine, and economic catastrophe; but to an equal degree in apostasy and the desecration of God's name, in forgetting of the Torah and the upsetting of all moral order to the point of dissolving the laws of nature" (12).

In *Headhunter*, we can discern the same transcendent temporal perspective and the familiar catalogue of catastrophic signs, including the forgetting of the Torah. In Findley's futuristic universe, the world has "begun to fracture and to fragment, nation by nation," rival gangs of Moonmen and Leatherheads stalk the streets, and AIDS has been joined by another plague called sturnusemia (34). But the narrator asserts that sturnusemia and AIDS are not the only plagues: "Civilization – sickened – had itself become a plague. And its course ... could be followed by tracing the patterns of mental breakdown ... Psychiatric case loads, everywhere, carried alarming numbers. Broken dreamers, their minds in ruin. This was the human race" (388). Findley's literary critic Nicholas Fagan confirms this diagnosis and condemns his culture's fascination with disaster: "*Nothing better illustrates than these two books [Heart of Darkness and Frankenstein] the consequence of human ambition. On reading them again, I fell away from my complacent view that nothing could be done to stop us, and took up my current view that the human race has found its destiny in self-destruction*" (139).[5] Despite the gruesome novelty of some of *Headhunter*'s apocalyptic signs, familiar landmarks confirm that the world hurtling toward catastrophe represents a spatial and temporal extension of our own.

For the most part, the characters remain confined to their historical moment. But, like the seer of Revelation, the third-person, extradiegetic narrator offers the reader proleptic insights, which suggests that he has transcended the world of time and history as we know them. Commenting on people's response to the plague, the narrator states: "Most were sceptical – others were incredulous ... The truth was, most eyes would open too late on a world without birds and a city under siege. But that was not now – that was later, much later, after Kurtz and after Lilah Kemp" (10). Later, remarking on Marlow's first, misguided impression of Kurtz, the narrator says: "Within weeks, Marlow ... would laugh at his own innocence. But that was not now. That was later" (199). Throughout the text, the catalogue of signs and dark pronouncements concerning a future known only by the visionary narrator reinforces the novel's reliance on the apocalyptic paradigm.

Far from completely embracing apocalyptic eschatology, however, by selecting aspects of this discourse and rejecting others in favour of prophetic eschatology, the novel launches its critique. Although the narrator assumes a transcendent position, he does not promote an apocalyptic vision that points beyond the end to a new paradise. Instead, he gestures relentlessly to the nontranscendent destruction of the world. As a result, the absence of the topos of the New Jerusalem, the keystone of the biblical apocalypse, comes to haunt the narrative.[6] In this way, rather than simply mobilizing desires for paradise, the figure of the end serves as an imaginative vantage point from which western culture's lethal fascination with apocalypse may be interrogated.

Quite often *Headhunter* strikes a precarious balance between the presentation of what Paul Hanson describes as visionary and realistic elements, common to both prophetic and apocalyptic eschatology. According to Hanson, the visionary element, more pronounced in apocalyptic eschatology, entails a "vision of a divine order that transcends all mundane institutions and structures" (30). By contrast, the element of realism, a stronger component in prophetic eschatology, involves a concern "with the day-to-day maintenance of those same mundane institutions and structures, and with preserving continuity so as to assure a context for the continued life of the community" (30). When separated from realism, the vision leads "to a retreat into the world of ecstasy and dreams and to an abdication of the social responsibility of translating the vision of the divine order into the realm of everyday earthly concerns" (30). Alternatively, when separated from the vision, the realism "becomes a sterile preserver of the status quo which absolutized and eternalized the existing order together with all of its inequities" (30).

This type of oscillation recalls Catherine Hunter's arguments concerning Findley's ambivalence about the act of narration itself: the desire "to narrate the story seems matched by a desire not to narrate it, a desire to keep the story somehow transcendent, as if it were above or beyond narration" (2); she notes that his texts "display an ambivalence toward self and story – both a nostalgic desire for stable absolutes and a desire for the fragmentation, or even destruction, of them" (4). In keeping with Hunter's observations, Findley's ambivalence has an equally strong impact on his approach to his intertexts and the biblical myth of apocalypse. An awareness of his painstaking negotiations between visionary and realist elements also helps to explain more precisely why *Headhunter* rejects the apocalyptic indifference to social responsibility, yet, nevertheless, consistently draws on apocalyptic discourse. Findley's ambivalence in this regard is characteristic of the treatment of the Bible in the works of many contemporary Canadian writers who rely on parody to acknowledge the Bible's authority and, at the same time, undermine its authority and its claim to offer "a single and final meaning" (Hutcheon, *The Canadian Postmodern* 7).

The text's reliance on a visionary narrator is only one of many elements adopted and adapted from biblical apocalyptic discourse. In

addition to offering a panoramic temporal structure and glaring
images of destruction, apocalypses are also characterized by the private, transcendent content of their visions. Whereas Jewish messianism addresses the entire nation and sets forth images of natural and
historical events through which God speaks, apocalyptic prophecy is
revealed solely to the individual and its declarations involve "special
'secret' knowledge gained from an inner realm not accessible to every
man" (Scholem 5). Leonard Thompson goes so far as to describe the
knowledge contained in Revelation as "deviant knowledge" because
it is gained by "esoteric means apart from larger communal, institution validation" (181). Although this "deviant" knowledge is based
on personal revelation, the possibility of considering this revelation
to be "a partisan, idiosyncratic view of the world is minimized by the
narrative style" (178).

In *Headhunter*'s realistic displacement[7] of apocalypse, the biblical
prophets' sacred visions have become the property of secular spiritualists and schizophrenics such as Lilah Kemp and Amy Wylie.[8] Just
as Revelation's narrative style prevents the listener from dismissing
the information on the grounds that it is idiosyncratic, Findley's narrative likewise controls and transforms the reader's response to the
character's visions. For example, most readers initially reject Lilah's
fantastic claim that she has released Kurtz from Conrad's *Heart of
Darkness*. But their reaction to Lilah is tempered and manipulated by
the text in at least two ways. First, the narrator's dispassionate treatment of Lilah's condition undercuts a measure of the readers' skepticism. Second, and, more importantly, after this opening scene, readers learn that the man who stood before Lilah in the Reference
Library is indeed Kurtz. The narrative's matter-of-fact validation of
Lilah's vision (and others that follow) dissuades readers from interpreting her illness as a disease that generates nonsensical, eccentric
visions. Instead, the text portrays her madness, which connects her to
a myriad of famous persons from the past and literary characters, as
a visionary gift *"for cutting through time"* (365). Although her visions
constitute "deviant knowledge," in accordance with the apocalyptic
paradigm, they are nevertheless accorded legitimacy. Moreover,
Findley's choice of Lilah – a powerless, alienated woman on the margins of society – reflects a trend in Canadian literature. As many critics have argued, the marginalized female voice "politically and culturally personifies Canada" (Irvine 11).

Headhunter refigures the sacred scriptures as the secular canon of Western literature. Those who are prepared to become "familiar with the works of those who had preceded them so they might *know where they enter*" constitute the elect, whereas the apostates desecrate and forget their "Torah." Although *Headhunter* avoids simply reversing centre and margin, the narrative subtly identifies the marginalized Lilah as a member of the elect. In this way, the narrative turns the reader's attention to the permeable boundary between the elect and the non-elect – a tactic that ultimately destablizes the apocalyptic paradigm. Anne Bailey argues that Findley writes "in a post-Holocaust world, a fact which pervades all his works, filling them with a profound skepticism, not only of technology, but also of romanticism, modernism, and elitism" (216). Thus, while *Headhunter* invokes the idea of the elect, the narrative does not subscribe to the apocalyptic vision of the category.

Again, a distinction must be drawn between pre-exilic, prophetic notions of the elect – which encompasses the entire community – and post-exilic, apocalyptic view of the elect, which includes only a small subset of the community. With her "evangelical passion for literature" (*Headhunter* 11), Lilah represents the contemporary incarnation of Revelation's Saints of God. Like a priestess welcoming initiates into the temple, in her role as librarian, she eagerly turned toward the "bright unwritten faces of the young," enjoining them to "Read! Read! Read!" (364). Rather than preach to an isolated, elite group, Lilah, in keeping with the pre-exilic prophetic tradition, addresses the entire community and implicitly suggests that a sacred encounter with literature potentially awaits anyone.

Despite her passion, Lilah considers herself a mere student, a humble disciple, whereas Nicholas Fagan, whose "voice was the voice of English literature itself," is a god (40, 266). Fagan, who is clearly a member – if not the leader – of the elect, consistently describes the function of literature, using language that recalls the rituals of religious worship. In the New Testament, toward the conclusion of his sermon on spiritual gifts, Paul describes the way in which prophets should ideally conduct a service of worship, which includes, among other things, the singing of hymns and the proclamation of apocalypses. Prophets can use any one of several forms of worship: a prayer, a hymn, a revelation, or even a teaching (Cor. 14:26). According to Paul, every prophet should be permitted to give his revelation, so that all may learn and all be comforted. As far as Fagan is concerned, literature itself constitutes a hymn or song that offers comfort and instruction. At one point, Lilah recalls his words: "[a] *book is a way of singing ... A way of singing our way out of darkness. The darkness that is night – and the darkness that is ignorance – and the darkness that is ... [fear]*" (138).[9] The link Fagan implicitly draws between literature and religious worship is reinforced when Lilah visits the University Bookstore on College Street, which once served as the home of the Toronto Reference Library. She walks "[r]ound and round the islands of shelves ... with a measured pace, reciting the titles under her breath, as one might utter prayers in a cloister" (270). Drifting through her mind is a phrase uttered by her teacher – a playful allusion to the famous Shakespeare quotation. But Fagan's alteration infuses the phrase with spiritual overtones: "*All the words are prayers...and all the men and women merely pray-ers ...*" (271). Lilah and Fagan are not alone in their reverence for literature; others, including Marlow and Amy Wylie, join the ranks of the elect. Marlow, who met Fagan at Harvard, finds Fagan to be an enthusiastic supporter of his use of literature as a tool in psychiatric research (365).

On the whole, however, devotion to literature is not sufficient to qualify one for membership to the elect. The characters' reverence for literature is tempered by a sobering awareness shared by those who come after Auschwitz and thus "can no longer believe that people who read and listen to great works of art will be morally, intellectually, or politically superior" and "can no longer romanticize the cult of literature, nor the cult of literary genius" (Bailey 215). As a result, in Findley's novel, the criteria for inclusion into the realm of the elect does not simply entail a passion for literature, it is also practical and humanitarian. In essence, the elect differ from the apostates on the basis of the former's willingness to rage against a corrupt empire that dismisses culture as well as environmental and social concerns in favour of a ruthless pursuit of economic gain.

In his study *The Book of Revelation: Apocalypse and Empire*, Leonard Thompson counters the prevailing view of the apocalyptists as a desperately oppressed minority. He argues that John writes not as a beleaguered outcast but as "a true cosmopolitan" who is nevertheless unequivocal in his negative attitude toward Asian society and the empire (5). According to Revelation, the political order of Rome is "wholly corrupt, belonging to the Satanic realm," and the economic order "belongs to the same corrupt realm" (Thompson 175). Buying and selling require the "stamp" of the beast (Rev. 13:16–17). Thompson goes on to explain that, "[i]n contrast to the writings of Paul or to 1 Peter, the seer of Revelation rejects any recognition of the empire as a godly order. In both style and content the writer of the Book of Revelation sets his work against the public order" (192).

This same rage against a corrupt empire informs *Headhunter*'s primary intertext *Heart of Darkness*, which charts the exploitation of the Congo by Belgium's King Leopold II. In his essay on the subject, Conrad describes the Belgian empire's activities in the Congo as the "vilest scramble for loot that ever disfigured the history of human conscience and geographical exploration" (187). According to one critic, Conrad's work "is not merely a reflection of the modern temper; it is an active revolt against it" (Erdinast-Vulcan 19). In keeping with the rejection of empire in Revelation and *Heart of Darkness* – a rejection that is not restricted to social outcasts – the members of Findley's elect include characters from all walks of life. What they have in common is not their status as outcasts (Marlow can hardly be described as marginalized) but their rage and their belief that they must battle against a decadent and brutal social order. In keeping with many apocalyptic narratives fashioned by contemporary Canadian writers, *Headhunter* serves as "crisis literature," unveiling a range of oppressive political and social forces. In Findley's Canadian rewriting of Conrad's text, evil is not located in far off Africa, but in Toronto, where Dr Kurtz perpetrates horrific deeds in the name of science rather than empire, furthering his ambition and reaping lucrative rewards from the government and transnational drug companies.

Using the familiar language of election and images of a Manichean struggle, Lilah claims responsibility for overthrowing the demonic power. Two days after she releases Kurtz, she clutches the shoes of Peter the Rabbit, her talisman, and utters the following prayer: "*Dear shoes ... I require some news of Kurtz. I have released him out of Heart of Darkness. He has disappeared and I am afraid. Kurtz, if he puts his mind to it, can destroy the world – and only I can prevent him. I have been chosen to be his Marlow – and must begin my journey – but I don't know where to start ...* " (39). Unlike Lilah, who wholly embraces her mission, the "real" Marlow only reluctantly assumes the job of uncovering Kurtz's nefarious use of experimental drugs on children – drugs that render them the pliant, silent victims of their fathers' perverted appetites. In keeping with Lilah's outlook, Marlow views his task as a battle (499). And he continues to invoke martial imagery when he describes Fagan's attitude toward society. According to Marlow, Fagan rejects pessimism in favour of "the stabilizing influence of his anger. He fought back. He drew a bead with his aging eyes and fired at human pride and wilful ignorance – not with a fusillade, but with a single bullet" (381).

In the case of Amy Wylie, the battle between good and evil becomes an all-out war against reality. A schizophrenic poet, Amy crusades on behalf of the animals slaughtered in a misguided attempt to prevent the spread of the plague. According to her sister, Amy is "never at rest – never making peace with reality. War was more like it" (346). Along these lines, Marlow's colleague, the psychiatrist Austen Purvis, also distinguishes himself as a soldier in the war against reality. In a skirmish with Doctor Shelley who "was overly fond of somnificating her patients," Purvis yells, *We are not here to drag* [the insane] ... *willy-nilly back into our world! We are here to drag our perceptions forward into theirs!*" (189). Unable to win his fight, Purvis shoots himself; but, before he dies, he enjoins Marlow to continue the war against the tyrannous power and save the children (402). The motley crew of Findley's crusaders would not be complete without Orley, the black maid in the Berry household, whose innocent husband was shot by police. Ever since the incident twelve years ago, Orley has nurtured rage at social injustice; her rage was "still a source of satisfaction. She had vowed that she would foster it until the day she died – and up until now – including now – she had succeeded" (240).

Taken together, Findley's elect – based on the prophetic notion of the elect that encompasses the entire community – wage war against the oppression and exploitation of groups marginalized and, in some cases, traumatized by society. In keeping with the Canadian interest in focusing on the losers rather than the winners of history, Findley's narrative examines the silencing of a range of victims of apocalyptic violence. In contrast to fully developed apocalyptic eschatology, however, Findley's humanitarian elect do not anticipate that their struggle will end in earthly destruction and secure the salvation of a privileged few. Instead, in keeping with prophetic eschatology, they fight to eradicate suffering on this Earth. As a result, the restored community will exist not in Heaven but in the historical realm – the realm of the here and now.

In this way, Findley's narrative maintains a delicate balance between prophetic and apocalyptic eschatology. Furthermore, although the text stresses the need to ensure continuity, particularly the continuity of the literary archive, the prophetic tradition seemingly shifts toward the apocalyptic in the novel's depiction of Kurtz, the chaotic and immoral force bent on destroying the community. In Findley's anti-apocalyptic narrative, Kurtz appears as evil because he wholeheartedly embraces the myth of apocalypse and believes that the world and its inhabitants deserve to perish, so long as a select few ascend into a new world. Yet, rather than maintain apocalypse's division between good and evil in its depiction of the demonic host, the text subverts the biblical paradigm by blurring the boundaries between the elect and their foe: in a poignant scene toward the conclusion, the narrative reveals that Kurtz himself was a victimized child.

In the apocalyptic paradigm, the righteous anger of the elect is directed at an enemy who is personified by the Antichrist (see Abrams's definition quoted on pages 23–4 of this book), a pseudo-messiah, portrayed as a gigantic embodiment of "anarchic, destructive power" (Cohn, *The Pursuit of the Millenium* 20), who is "allowed to make war on the saints and to conquer them" (Rev. 13:7). When Lilah discovers that the man she conjured directs the Parkin Institute, she knows that she has unleashed the Antichrist. After reading the marble panel outside his door, she concludes: "Rupert Kurtz was God" (53). Like the biblical force of evil, Kurtz is prone to exalting himself. In his infamous research paper, he boasts, "*We psychiatrists … must necessarily appear to the mentally ill as being in the nature of gods. We approach them with miracles up our sleeves. 'Save us!' they cry – and we do …* " (603). To clarify the difference between good and evil, between true and false gods, the text juxtaposes Fagan and Kurtz.[10] Each man has his followers; Lilah's devotion to Fagan is mirrored by Julian Slade's affirmation of Kurtz's divine status. By Kurtz's own admission, the "bedeviled" Slade – a schizophrenic, moribund artist – had been "something of a disciple as well as a patient" (265). Slade had "believed in what Kurtz was doing at the Parkin"; and the latter found it "exhilarating" to have "a believer at his feet" (265–6).

As noted earlier, Fagan likewise attracts believers, and espouses a quasi-religious view of literature that conceives of books as a way of singing our way out of the darkness that is fear (138). When asked to sing his favourite songs, Fagan begins "roaring out all the names of all the men and women, all the dogs and all the cats and all the children who came forth from books" (138). In contrast to Fagan's communal orientation and insistence on the need to escape fear, Kurtz adores Slade's art – whose subject matter is always terror – precisely because it "verified his fears" and "informed him that fear was wonderful" (102). Not surprisingly, Kurtz's favourite painting, a canvas filled with mutilated male bodies, is dubbed "a depiction of hell" (455). Rather than join in Fagan's choir, Kurtz remains isolated, mesmerized by his disciple's masterfully executed "hymn to violence" (203).

Like his fictional predecessor, Findley's Kurtz knows no bounds in his quest to establish his transcendent empire. In pursuit of this goal, he sanctions the activities of the pedophiliac Club of Men and willingly sacrifices children to their fathers' carnal desires. What Kurtz and the Club of Men do not understand or simply choose to dismiss – and this is made clear in the text – is that children are the future.[11] By agreeing to their deaths, Kurtz assumes the apocalyptic stance of the post-exilic visionaries, who, like the author of Revelation, dismissed the claims of all earthly institutions and structures, abdicating themselves completely from any social responsibility.

In the end, Marlow learns that Kurtz's corrupt nature was shaped by Kurtz's tortured relations with his sadistic father; this information intimates that the division between good and evil is permeable. All his life, Kurtz wanted to please an utterly selfish man whose "criterion...was money – not achievement," but his father "simply laughed at ...[his] efforts. Laughed at them, and died still laughing" (620). In its relentless depiction of the abuse and, in some cases, infanticide, *Headhunter* once again draws on the traditional apocalyptic paradigm, where the world is seen in terms of a mortal struggle "waged by good parents and good children against bad parents and bad children" (Cohn, *The Pursuit of the Millenium* 69). In the popular eschatology of the Middle Ages, the elect saw themselves as good children. Their leaders perceived themselves as incarnate gods, who combined the fantastic images of the divine Father and His Son, the risen Christ. In reward for following the Messiah, the elect shared in their saviour's supernatural power; in opposition to the "armies of the Saints, and scarcely less powerful than they, there appears a host of demonic fathers and sons" (71). The concern for good children left at the mercy of bad parents remains a long-standing motif in Findley's corpus.[12] In *Headhunter*, however, it assumes mythic and apocalyptic proportions. Viewed within the context of Canadian literature, the motif recalls

Canada's postcolonial status. In keeping with the narrative's parodic appropriation of European and US canonical texts, the figure of the dominated child battling against an evil parent underscores the ex-centric Canadian desire to examine and challenge the centre's power and control.

The battle between good and evil is integral to prophetic and apocalyptic eschatology. Findley, however, mobilizes apocalypse in order to defuse it; ultimately, he promotes a community-oriented vision characteristic of prophetic eschatology. The novel repeatedly demonstrates that an effective way to challenge the apocalyptic paradigm involves revealing the permeable boundary between the elect and the demonic host. The line between good and evil is much traversed in Findley's texts: "By persistently attacking the oppressive and limiting tactics of various cultural authorities, Findley attempts to include and give voice to the silenced, continually expanding our notions of the human community. However, the 'silenced' in Findley's novels ... are often seduced by their increasing empowerment into authoritative, oppressive roles as well, re-enacting the very violence that once silenced them" (Bailey 219). This type of seduction is perhaps most evident in an episode featuring Charlie Marlow. In this scene, Marlow feels alienated while attending a dinner party in honour of Nicholas Fagan. Part of his discomfort stems from the ostentatious show of wealth and power at the party. But he is also uncomfortable because his hosts have likely not read any of the expensively bound paperbacks (379) in their library. Initially, Marlow ponders whether it matters that they are not readers, and he tries to dismiss the importance of reading, by reminding himself that books are just "cultural artifacts and, if found in some vault a thousand years hence, could probably not be deciphered" (380). At one point, he asks himself "what it was that drove him to think so badly of people who had found a way ... to live without the support of books. To live, in their way, entirely without the support of culture" (380). Gradually, however, he gives way to despair; it is at this point that Marlow admits to feeling "deeply uncomfortable" – a feeling which is linked to "the fact that he was a snob, an elitist and – against his wishes – a believer in that most dangerous of concepts, the concept of men and women who were superior" (380).

By emphasizing Marlow's belief in "that most dangerous of concepts," the novel highlights the radical shift that occurred after the Second World War, when Canadian writers began to self-consciously explore the violence of the biblical myth and to probe why it escapes the bounds of literature. As one of the first civilians to view photographs from Dachau, taken by the first official photographer allowed through the gates of the Nazi concentration camp, Findley's friend Ivan Moffatt (Roberts, *Timothy Findley: Stories from a Life* 38), Findley was well aware that the belief in "superior men and women" allowed the Nazis to justify murdering six million Jews and other so-called undesirables.[13]

Marlow's preoccupation with the waning of high culture and his belief in superior men and women is clearly linked to the biblical apocalypse's faith in the elect. But these biblical ideas, in turn, informed the late-nineteenth-century European doctrines that espoused a belief in the powers of superior individuals – a belief that was given practical application during the Second World War. Carlyle's "hero" and Nietszche's "superman," in conjunction with the writings of Vilfredo Pareto, Gaetano Mosca, and the literature produced by the movement known as the Action Française also directly influenced modernist writers such as Yeats, Lewis, Pound, Eliot, and Lawrence. Like Marlow, these writers believed that the masses required the guidance of a higher, responsible, conscious class (Harrison 27).

Findley's post-Holocaust novels repeatedly explore how educated and kind individuals are seduced by apocalypse's belief in the right of the powerful to silence and dismiss the powerless. Findley understood that "we are all capable of being seduced by the power and glamour of the elite" because "'the seeds of fascism lie dormant within us all"; more important, "the realization of this fact is our best defence against it" (Findley quoted in Roberts, *Timothy Findley: Stories from a Life* 73).

Earlier novels, including *The Butterfly Plague, Famous Last Words* and *Not Wanted on the Voyage*, also underscore the connection between apocalyptic discourse and the visions of heavenly perfection that inspired totalitarian movements in the first half of this century.[14] From his research on modernism, Findley was likewise familiar with the apocalyptic sentiments of writers such as Pound and Yeats. In anticipation of the end of his age, Yeats "filled his poems with images of decadence, and praised war because he saw in it...the means of renewal" (Kermode, *The Sense of an Ending* 98). At one point, Yeats proclaimed that the "'danger is that there will be no war ... Love war because of its horror, that belief may be changed, civilization renewed'" (quoted in Kermode, *The Sense of an Ending* 98). Perhaps Kermode puts it best when he says, "[w]hat we feel about these men at times is perhaps that they retreated into some paradigm, into a timeless and unreal vacuum from which all reality had been pumped" (113).

In *Headhunter*, the links between this strain of modernist elitism and Marlow's belief in the concept of superior men and women emphasize the difficulty of drawing neat divisions between good and evil. Even benevolent men like Marlow err on occasion and maintain views that other people, with a more practical and sinister bent, have used to justify holocausts of one kind or another.[15] Viewed in this light, *Headhunter* demonstrates that, like it or not, everyone has the capacity to be lured by apocalypse's promise of redemption through violence. This realization dawns on Marlow at the end of the novel, when he tries on a gang member's abandoned glove. After placing the glove on his left hand – the sinister hand – Marlow thinks, "We all could be Moonmen ... My hand in this glove – a perfect fit. Kurtz too in all of us. All of us in Kurtz" (622). In his study of apocalypse, Thompson likewise argues that, for all its apparent Manichean divisions, Revelation nevertheless conveys the indeterminacy between good and evil.[16]

In Findley's novel, Marlow's identification with the Moonmen and with Kurtz signals an awareness that apocalyptic pessimism concerning existing structures and institutions, together with desires for radical change are not restricted to crazed, evil individuals. At issue in the text is not the apocalyptic vision of perfection, but the implication of severing this vision from the realm of everyday earthly morality. Whereas *The Last of the Crazy People* demonstrates the translation of apocalyptic discourse into reality, *Headhunter* contests the view that the existing order is so tainted that it cannot be redeemed and that the new order must be preceded by the extermination of all that came before. The text's resistence to apocalypse's unifying geographic, demographic, and ideological logic – a logic that reduces the entire world to the new heaven, its diverse inhabitants to a privileged elect, and many faiths to Christianity – reflects what many critics view as a particularly Canadian response. Postmodern Canadian writers share "a concern for the different, the local, the particular – in opposition to the uniform, the universal, the centralized" (Hutcheon, *The Canadian Postmodern* 19).

In the end, what separates Fagan's group from Kurtz's entourage

is merely the latter's more fervent and active embrace of the apocalyptic paradigm and its promise of radical, unifying transformation.
For instance, at the opening of Slade's exhibition, Kurtz encounters
Griffen Price. The wealthy owner of a host of factories churning out
souvenirs, Price makes a mockery of art and culture; in the novel,
such behaviour is the mark of the beast. Price, who fancies "himself
as something of a social critic," seizes the opportunity to expound his
theory that the human race "needs another Mengele to bring it up to
date" (86–7). He goes on to explain that, when he was visiting his factory in Prague, he stood in the glassworks and had the following
vision: "'There were all these men with mechanical buffers polishing,
polishing bits of crystal. Turning them, turning them, making them
perfect. And I thought: if only we could do that to ourselves; shape
ourselves that way ... [M]y vision was that we are ready for another
version of the human race. The final honing ... And this is where you
come in – the king of psychiatry. I mean – if there are new forms of
human beings, then it follows there must be new forms of madness'"
(87–8); "the allusions here to the Holocaust are unmistakable and
telling" (Bailey 195), and although Kurtz "does not want to commit
himself" to what Price is saying, from his behaviour it becomes clear
that he shares Price's vision.

   Like Price, Kurtz has his own radical plans for the human race.
Later, in his office overlooking the University of Toronto, he attests to
his faith in the imminent end of the earthly world, and he mocks so-
called intellectuals for their inability to grasp radical, apocalyptic
change: "Naming. Defining. Quantifying. Quantumizing. Everyone
preparing for the past to repeat itself – as if the past was a continuum
and that now did not exist ... *And when the past has been defined...not
one of them will have the courage to say: it is over*" (209). Kurtz expresses
similar views at the close of the novel. On his deathbed, he refers to
the present as being a *"long-dead civilization"* (615). Gesturing to the
world below, he encourages Marlow to hasten its destruction: "*It is all
changed now ... There will be a new social contract ... All those fires beyond
the windows ... There is nothing down there for us, Marlow. Not any longer.
Go out and light more fires. If everyone did that, we would have the stuff of
a new world ready for the making*" (616). Kurtz's faith in the radically
new – as opposed to restoration or renovation – aligns him with
apocalyptic thinkers such as Price: both men are seduced by apocalypse's and fascism's promise of perfection. But these men omit a
fundamental aspect of the eschatological vision, namely, the recogni-

tion that the final condition of humankind rests on the idea that "history is a *moral* process, with a goal toward which it is moving" (Salmond 734; emphasis mine). By stripping their visions of any vestige of morality, the narrative sharpens the focus on the dangers of an unqualified attraction to the formal, aesthetic elegance of beginning, middle, and end that informs the biblical narrative and served as a beacon for fascism. In this way, readers are reminded of the disasters that potentially ensue when the apocalyptic dreams are projected onto the world.

The texts in this study reflect an increasing awareness that the influence of apocalypse is pervasive and that the myth never functioned solely as a discrete literary genre but has always shaped philosophical and political thinking as well as historical events. Theorists such as Paul Ricoeur and Frank Kermode have attempted to explain the tendency of apocalypse to exceed the bounds of literature, and for this reason it is useful to consider Findley's novel in light of their insights. The projection of this narrative onto the world – the translation of a theological narrative structure to a historical-political model for praxis – is facilitated by the fact that, in the Bible, the end of the world and the end of the book are concurrent: "the idea of the end of the world comes to us by means of a text that, in the biblical canon received in the Christian West, at least, concludes the Bible. Apocalypse can thus signify both the end of the world and the end of the book at the same time. This congruence between the world and the book extends even further. The beginning of the book is about the beginning and the end of the book is about the end" (Ricoeur 23). In his study of narrative, Ricoeur discerns a gradual transformation of the apocalyptic paradigm; as he explains, crisis now replaces the end (24). In the contemporary novel, he argues, one can best observe "the decline of paradigms ... the ruin of the fiction of the end" (24).

By contrast, Kermode, who likewise sees a shift from end to "crisis," maintains that humanity cannot do without apocalypse. He argues that its elegant linear form fulfills an incontrovertible human need to see the world as ordered and meaningful. Novels, he suggests, must have beginnings and ends "even if the world has not" (*The Sense of an Ending* 138). By telling lies, novels convert the otherwise meaningless chaos of existence into meaningful patterns (135). These lies only get out of hand, according to Kermode, when people lapse into literary primitivism and treat fictions, which are consciously false, as if they were empirically true; thus "the world is changed to conform with a fiction, as by the murder of the Jews. The effect is to insult reality, and to regress to myth" (109). Although he maps the intersections among the apocalyptic visions of the modernists and fascist ideology, Kermode intimates that this was merely an unfortunate lapse and that what is needed is simply a more vigilant policing of the border between reality and fiction.

It is at this point that Kermode's theory and Findley's novel part company. As a Canadian who self-consciously inhabits a post-Holocaust, atomic age, Findley is deeply concerned with ways to neutralize the myth of apocalypse, but, unlike Kermode, he does not believe that this violent story can be safely locked away inside the pages of a book. The myth's refusal to be contained in this fashion is graphically illustrated in the opening scene of Findley's novel, in which Kurtz bursts forth from the pages of *Heart of Darkness*. Although *Headhunter* affirms Kermode's view of literature as a vital lie, it nevertheless erodes the very foundation of his argument: his assumption of a clear-cut boundary between reality and fiction. For Lilah, literature and life are indistinguishable; she wheels *Wuthering Heights* around in her buggy and treats it as her child. Despite the fact that she is schizophrenic, readers learn, to borrow Kurtz's words, that there is nothing "in the wide world of madness that was not the property of sanity as well" (102). Her behaviour, then, merely exaggerates our acceptance of the everyday interpenetration of art and life. Indeed, this is characteristic of postmodern Canadian novels – "novels that admit openly they are fiction, but suggest that fiction is just another means by which we make sense of our world ... and that, as such, it is comparable to historiography, philosophy, physics, sociology, and so on" (Hutcheon, *The Canadian Postmodern* x–xi).

In an effort to distinguish the *as if* of fiction from the *is* of reality, critics such as Kermode look to literature for concordance and a disingenuous assurance of simplicity – the lie of apocalypse. But Findley's postmodern text emphasizes that this vision of the boundary between art and life and of a world – in which fiction can be identified and contained, thereby neatly ridding the world of fiction – is itself a fiction.[17] To borrow Fagan's metaphor, books may be a way of singing, but they do not always offer simple harmonies. This view is confirmed by Marlow, who uses literature as psychotherapy. He believes in literature's "healing powers – not because of its sentiments, but because of its complexities." As he says: "No human life need ever be as knotted as Anna Karenina's life had been" (186).

Rather than simplify the chaos of life, Marlow implies that books offer us complexity, maybe of a similar or, perhaps, different sort. The impulse to pit the complexity of life against the reductiveness of art is likewise undercut by Fagan's view of literature: the *"characters drawn on the page by the makers of literature ... are distillations of our thwarted selves. We are their echoes and their shadows"* (138).

The reader's awareness of the permeable membrane between fact and fiction – an awareness that precludes any faith in a simple "cure" for the spread of apocalyptic dreams – becomes even more apparent when Findley makes an appearance in his own novel. He emerges as the character "Timothy Findley," a writer who is Marlow's patient. "Findley" complains to his psychiatrist that most people spend their time lying (203). Here we have a fictional representation of a real-life author insisting that people (in fiction and/or everyday life) make a habit of lying. The episode confronts readers with the paradox of the Cretan liar. But there is no need to wiggle through the logical convolutions to recognize that "Findley's" reflexive appearance and his comments underscore the idea that we cannot help but narrate our lives and that we are all caught in the grip of a host of plots, which, like language itself, existed before we were born.[18]

The text's insistence on our complicated and inextricable connection to apocalyptic discourse may well be the primary revelation conveyed by the novel. As Cohn and other critics illustrate, the apocalyptic paradigm, since its inception, has been repeatedly projected onto history; to pretend that we have outgrown it is foolish and dangerously myopic. Precisely because we have inherited this plot, hope lies not in rejecting the paradigm but in working through it and exploring less radical alternatives such as prophetic eschatology. Findley's text intimates that part of the process of working through our obsession with apocalypse involves reinterpreting the term, which has traditionally been identified with the promise that fiction will be stripped away and truth revealed. Findley's answer to apocalypse, then, is to adopt and adapt the biblical narrative, bringing it in line with prophetic eschatology, which is content to wrestle with the truths found in this world rather than use violence to attain the truth in the New Jerusalem.

Many of the texts in this study draw attention to spirituality's obsession with this "edge" – an obsession energized by the belief that beyond the edge is divine truth. These texts demonstrate, however, that tearing away the veil does not disclose God's truth. Indeed, the act of unveiling exposes that both the edge and what supposedly lies beyond it are human constructs. Etymologically, the term "apocalypse" suggests an unveiling (*apo* [from or away], *kalupsis* [covering] from *kalupto* [to cover] and *kalumma* [veil]). As a site of unveiling, apocalypse becomes "largely a matter of *seeing*; and what one sees by imagining an apocalypse depends chiefly upon how one conceives of the veil" (Robinson xiii). If we perceive fiction as a veil obstructing a revelation of the truth or a transcendent realm, then the impulse will be to try to tear it away. The futility of tearing away the veil becomes apparent in the scene where John Dai Bowen tries to take a photograph of Emma Berry's perfect face, which she hides behind her veil (103). Although he manages to take a picture, the text clarifies that the perfection he captures on film, far from God's handiwork and the truth, is actually the handiwork of her husband, the famous surgeon, Maynard Berry. After Emma was burned in a fire, the surgeon refashioned her face, without her permission, according to his desires. This episode suggests that tearing away the veil will disclose, not the truth, but merely human notions of perfection, which are repeatedly inscribed onto the world and people's flesh. By emphasizing the futility and destructiveness of this gesture, *Headhunter* demonstrates that we are far better off if we recognize the veil's constructed nature and play with its potential to serve as a screen or mirror.

This alternative is highlighted in the scene where Kurtz asks his friend and patient Fabiana Holbach to write an essay in answer to the question "Who do you think you are?" Fabiana begins the essay by insisting that there can be no unveiling of an essential truth because identity itself is nothing more than a fiction – a performance: "It's a drag act – men pretending to be men – women pretending to be women – but only the artists will tell us that. The rest of us cannot bear the revelation" (341). Rather than continue the futile search for this elusive, essential identity, Fabiana turns her attention to the boundary between art and life and criticizes others (save her friend, the writer) for not doing the same, essentially, for not interrogating the nature of our inventions: "The whole damn world is a mirror. But no one sees anyone else. We only – all of us – see ourselves – AND TURN AWAY ... My writing friend has looked in the mirror and what he sees is the whole world staring back. And he has the gall to say: that is not me – it's you" (341). In the end, rather than author the truth about herself, she gives Kurtz a fiction – an insightful sketch of herself composed by her "writing friend" (342). Although Fabiana invokes the traditional image of art as a mirror, her use of the metaphor proves more complex than the standard interpretation of "reflexive" fiction as a mirror, the surface of artifice that reflects a freestanding reality apprehended by a coherent, stable, and knowable self.

In contrast to those critics who argue for the utter separation between the word and the world, relegating reflexive fiction to the funhouse of art-for-art's-sake, Findley's novel repeatedly undermines attempts to separate world and word. Like many Canadian postmodern authors, Findley uses intertextuality to bring about a direct confrontation with the issue of the relation of art to the world outside it – to the world of "those social, cultural, and ultimately ideological systems by which we all live our lives" (Hutcheon, *The Canadian Postmodern* 9). By self-consciously foregrounding that narratives or, to use a semiotic model, "code systems" – textual or otherwise – shape knowledge, *Headhunter* denaturalizes apocalypse's entrenched codes and the knowledge it helps to constitute, and demonstrates that the biblical paradigm can be challenged from the margins. At the end of the novel, Fabiana, who has loved Kurtz all along, asks Marlow if Kurtz mentioned her before he died. Marlow replies, "Yes... He wanted me to tell you he was sorry" (621). In accordance with the conclusion of *Heart of Darkness*, Marlow tells Kurtz's "intended" a lie. But he does not view his behaviour as an unfortunate breach in the wall separating fact from fiction, an infelicitous leakage of falsehood into truth. Instead, he takes it as a given that people rely on fictions to map out their existence: "This way, he thought, we write each other's lives – by means of fictions. Sustaining fictions. Uplifting fictions. Lies. This way, we lead one another toward survival. This way we point the way to darkness – saying: come with me into the light" (622). If, as Marlow claims, people write each other's lives by means of fictions, then it is essential to interrogate and rewrite apocalypse. Accordingly, Findley's narrative installs and challenges apocalypse's key tropes: its recursive and intertextual structure, its overarching temporal perspective, its emphasis on the heavenly city, its status as deviant knowledge, and its concepts of the elect and the non-elect. By drawing attention to the permeable boundary between the elect and the non-elect and by demonstrating how the myth of apocalypse refuses to be contained in the imagination, *Headhunter* ultimately destabilizes the apocalyptic paradigm. In the process of launching its critique of the biblical story of the end, the text also outlines an alternative vision – one that in keeping with prophetic eschatology rejects isolated, transcendent fantasies in favour of the need for responsible action in a communal context.

At the end of the novel, Lilah surmises that no one will believe what has happened. "It's only a book, they would say. That's all it is. A story. Just a story" (625). By this time, however, readers will have recognized that, in Findley's eyes, stories represent the collective unconscious of the culture we have inherited and we ignore them at our peril. As Findley himself stated, it is essential for people to *know where they enter* because literature "is never done with" ("Turning Down the Volume"; quoted in Bailey 215) So long as we deny that Kurtz is in all of us and that we are all informed by eschatological narratives, dreams of apocalypse will continue to usurp waking thought.

Allegories of Ruin and Redemption: Michael Ondaatje's *The English Patient*

There is no document of civilization which is not at the same time a document of barbarism.

Benjamin (Illuminations 256)

Timothy Findley's *Headhunter* invokes virtually all of the topoi of apocalypse, including the narrative's recursive and panoramic structure, its preoccupation with representing the signs of terror and decadence, and its Manichean division between the elect and the non-elect. Of course, Findley's text gives the biblical story a contemporary twist by mapping the corrupt, ancient empire of Babylon onto a well-known Canadian city, Toronto the Good, and by emphasizing the permeable boundary between the elect and the non-elect. As the novel demonstrates, Toronto has been tainted by the legacy of imperialism – a legacy vividly depicted by the novel's central intertext, *Heart of Darkness*. To counter the corrupt influence of this evil empire and its demonic leader, Findley's narrative turns to the salutary powers of art. Functioning as a secular Torah, art, according to the novel, can forge a communal vision that, in keeping with prophetic eschatology, stresses humanity's responsibility in the here and now.

Ondaatje's novel *The English Patient* mirrors Findley's treatment of apocalypse in a number of ways. First, *The English Patient* draws on readers' familiarity with the apocalyptic paradigm by introducing the characteristic images of terror, decadence, and ruin. Second, it challenges Western culture's obsession with apocalypse by echoing *Headhunter*'s skepticism of models of progress predicated on an apocalyptic break with the past. Third, the narrative articulates a

profound distrust of individuals who, like Findley's Kurtz, turn res-
olutely toward the future, equating their absolute rejection of the past
with a Nietzschean "will to power." And finally, like *Headhunter*,
Ondaatje's novel demonstrates the traumatic impact of apocalyptic
violence and champions a stance akin to prophetic eschatology as an
antidote to apocalypse's preoccupation with a future predicated on
terror and destruction. In a bid to resist the apocalyptic paradigm,
both novels celebrate art's capacity to forge bonds among individuals and link a community to its past.

While the novels share certain features, they differ in crucial ways.
For one, Ondaatje's text offers a far more extensive exploration of the
topos of the ruin or fragment. Whereas Findley's *Headhunter* refers to
a civilization of "[b]roken dreamers, their minds in ruin" (388), *The
English Patient* uses the image of the ruin to inform the narrative's
content and structure, functioning, on the one hand, as the visible
sign of contemporary society's decadence and destructive impulse
and furnishing, on the other, the building blocks of a positive aesthetic of the ruin. By relying on fragments (and thereby refusing to
provide images of wholeness) and by resisting apocalypse's sequential teleology, Ondaatje's novel launches a profound attack against
the formal structure of the apocalyptic plot.

In addition to its emphasis on the image of the ruin, Ondaatje's text
differs from Findley's novel by broadening the latter's valorization of
the discourse of art to include the discourses of science and religion.
The English Patient repeatedly demonstrates how these discourses
intersect and how, by virtue of their intersection, they can mitigate
against apocalyptic disaster. As portrayed in the novel, these discourses serve as tools "for cutting through time" (Findley, *Headhunter*
365), establishing a vital sense of temporal continuity. In contrast to
the temporal and spatial map of apocalypse, which aims relentlessly
toward the future, the discourses of art, science, and religion are discursive maps containing allegorical fragments that, according to
Headhunter, gesture toward the past.

The most profound difference between *Headhunter* and *The English
Patient* lies in the latter's conception of apocalyptic timing. In contrast
to Findley's portrayal of apocalypse as an imminent event,
Ondaatje's text (in accordance with Paul Ricoeur's insights concerning the transformation of the apocalyptic paradigm in which "crisis
now replaces the end") figures the catastrophe as immanent, thus
portraying apocalypse as an ongoing disaster.

Most of Ondaatje's novels explore the fate of the outsider. His fascination with history's beautiful losers is a Canadian preoccupation. In earlier works, Ondaatje conveys the perspective of marginalized historical figures, including Billy the Kid, a criminal, and Buddy Bolden, a famous black coronetist who went mad. In the novel *In the Skin of a Lion*, Ondaatje turns his gaze to the anonymous men and women who risked their lives to build the city of Toronto. Published in the final decade of the twentieth century, *The English Patient* also fixes its gaze on the past and traces the lives of four traumatized individuals who are caught up in the Second World War: a badly burned man who may or may not be English; his shell-shocked young nurse, Hana; the wounded thief, Caravaggio; and Kip, the South-Asian sapper. Together, they find temporary asylum in a bombed-out Tuscan villa during the final months of 1945. By the time they gather, the explosive forces of the conflict have already shattered their minds, their bodies, and the opulent Villa San Girolamo, which they inhabit. The novel concludes with an examination of the devastating impact of the bombing of Japan, emphasizing Kip's horrified response to this event. In keeping with the other works in this study, *The English Patient* focuses relentlessly on the devastation wrought by apocalyptic thinking on the disenfranchised and gives voice to their trauma.

The English Patient's obsession with the fragment, allegory, and the view of apocalypse as an ongoing crisis is perhaps best understood in the light of Walter Benjamin's apocalyptic theory. Benjamin's writings are particularly germane to an apocalyptic reading of Ondaatje's text because Benjamin was deeply interested in the concept of revelation and wrote "hundreds of pages on the allegorical transformations of the Bible" (Britt 25). While Benjamin accorded the Bible the status of sacred text, he was, like Findley and Ondaatje, equally concerned with secular literature that exhibited "the scriptural function" – literature whose "content or context participates significantly in a religious or sacred tradition" (Britt 30). Finally, Benjamin shared Canadian writers' concern for the victim and repeatedly called attention to the suffering experienced by "history's anonymous losers" (Honneth 128).

As it turns out, Benjamin himself was a victim of history. The son of affluent Jewish parents in Berlin, Benjamin chose to die by his own hand rather than face death in a concentration camp during the Second World War. After experiencing the First World War, Benjamin was convinced that the next war would be fought with gas and bring

about the extinction of civilization. At the outbreak of the Second
World War, Benjamin found himself in Paris. When the German
troops stormed into Paris in 1940, Benjamin attempted, with a group
of other refugees, to enter Spain by an unmarked route over the
mountains, with the goal of escaping to the United States. However,
his group was apprehended by border guards who allowed them to
spend the night in Spain but told them they would be taken back
across the border the next morning. That night, Benjamin committed
suicide by swallowing morphine tablets. The guards were so shaken
by this that they allowed his companions to proceed (see J. Roberts
19). Taken together, Benjamin's experiences as a Jew in Germany and,
later, in occupied France and his eccentric status as an intellectual
who "had no proper career and published little except short articles
and book reviews" (J. Roberts 1) mark him as an ex-centric figure –
one of history's beautiful losers.

Ondaatje's debt to Benjamin is most apparent in *The English
Patient*'s subversive approach to two characteristic features of apocalyptic narratives, the fragment and allegory. By outlining the novel's
debt to a Benjaminian view of contemporary ruin and the non-progressive character of human history, this chapter analyzes the extent
to which the novel portrays apocalyptic catastrophe as irrevocable.
Hope is not entirely absent, however, because the novel portrays the
discourses of science, art, and religion as maps exhibiting the "scriptural function." These discursive maps participate in a sacred tradition because they contain allegorical fragments that can challenge the
temporal map of apocalypse and convey crucial knowledge; if properly charted and interpreted, these maps have the power to forestall
disaster.

By tracing the emphasis Ondaatje places on the fragment or ruin,
this chapter demonstrates how *The English Patient* adopts Benjamin's view of human history as non-progressive, a process of
decline. The chapter argues further that Ondaatje's text, in keeping
with Benjamin's understanding of the importance of the fragment
in the creation of allegorical art, mirrors Revelation's allegorical
structure with subversive intent. Ondaatje's text invokes fragments
of prior narratives and foregrounds images of fragmentation to
create an emblem of apocalyptic disaster that opposes Revelation's
portrayal of divine order and wholeness. In keeping with Canadian writers' characteristically ex-centric perspective, *The English
Patient* emphasizes the trauma of the non-elect and challenges

the logic of apocalypse by promoting an alternative based on prophetic eschatology.

Like Findley's *Headhunter*, Ondaatje's text raises fundamental questions about apocalypse, namely, what role does human knowledge play in instigating apocalypse? What are the most profound losses associated with apocalyptic thinking? And, finally, what is the status and power of the elect? In keeping with Findley's novel, Ondaatje's fiction emphasizes that it is not human knowledge itself that ushers in apocalypse but a specific approach to knowledge – one that is ruthlessly future-oriented and self-interested. (Margaret Atwood's short story "Hairball" offers a detailed characterization of this approach.) Yet, far from viewing human knowledge as the root of the problem, both Findley and Ondaatje rely on and promote a thorough grounding in art. Whereas Findley views art as a secular Torah capable of helping humanity to resist apocalyptic thinking in favour of prophetic eschatology, Ondaatje's narrative broadens the category to include the discourses of art, science, and religion. Furthermore, in *The English Patient*, these discourses serve as allegorical maps containing traces of past generations' utopian spiritual dreams – what Benjamin describes as "a secret agreement between past generations and the present one" (*Illuminations* ii) – that reinforce the commitment to prophetic eschatology. Both *Headhunter* and *The English Patient* repeatedly promote prophetic eschatology as an alternative to the apocalyptic paradigm. Indeed, for both Benjamin and Ondaatje, the continuity between past and present and the vast wealth of knowledge afforded by the past are threatened by apocalyptic thinking, which, in the name of progress, transforms the earthly world into a landscape of ruins.

In section nine of the "Theses on the Philosophy of History," Benjamin envisions the angel in Klee's painting "Angelus Novus" as the "angel of history": "His eyes are staring, his mouth is open, his wings are spread. This is how one pictures the angel of history. His face is turned toward the past. Where we perceive a chain of events, he sees one single catastrophe which keeps piling wreckage upon wreckage and hurls it in front of his feet. The angel would like to stay, awaken the dead, and make whole what has been smashed. But a storm is blowing from Paradise; it has got caught in his wings with such violence that the angel can no longer close them. This storm irresistibly propels him into the future to which his back is turned, while the pile of debris before him grows skyward. This storm is what we call progress" (*Illuminations* 257–8). Benjamin's interpretation of Klee's painting, which provides the foundation for his apocalyptic conception of history, remains both striking and enigmatic for several reasons: first, in a profoundly anti-modern gesture, the angel turns to the past, only to be unwillingly blown into the future; second, its melancholy gaze accurately discerns not a series of triumphs but a single unending catastrophe that piles "wreckage upon wreckage" – an image of ruin; and, finally, the angel's desire to repair what has been broken is paradoxically frustrated by nothing other than progress.

Like the "angel of history," who mournfully surveys a landscape of ruins, Ondaatje's narrative maps a wounded geography – the architectural, bodily, and psychic wreckage caused by the war. In keeping with Canadian writers who offer the story and storytelling of the losers, Ondaatje's novel does not dwell on the elect's triumphant entry into the heavenly city. Instead, the narrative addresses the plight of the traumatized victims and considers what, if anything, can be meaningfully constructed from the ruins of the earthly world. Although each of the writers in this study approaches this situation differently, the task of extracting meaning from the traces of an apocalyptic disaster is of fundamental importance to contemporary Canadian authors intent on conveying the perspective of those barred from Paradise. For Ondaatje and Benjamin, it is the task of the allegorist to construct meaning from the fragments of apocalyptic catastrophe. To this end, then, Ondaatje's novel draws on allegory, one of apocalypse's most striking formal features. Revelation conveys its cryptic messages through allegory, a form of extended metaphor in which objects, person, and actions in a narrative "are equated with meanings that lie outside the narrative itself" (Holman). And, as many of its allegorical images are drawn from earlier apocalypses and prophecies, Revelation is also densely intertextual. But rather than rely on allegory and intertextuality to support apocalypse's vision of a unified path from destruction to the New Jerusalem, Ondaatje's anti-apocalyptic use of these features emphasizes brokenness, parallelling Benjamin's understanding of allegory and its relation to the fallen and fragmented character of human history.

In *The Origin of German Tragic Drama*, Benjamin advances his theory of the fragment in the context of a thorough-going analysis of allegory. As Peter Burger notes, Benjamin's study outlines a four-fold concept of allegory; the first two aspects outline its production aesthetics and underscore its relation to the fragment: "1. The allegorist pulls one element out of the totality of the life context, isolating it, depriving it of its function. Allegory is therefore essentially fragment and thus the opposite of the organic symbol: 'In the field of allegorical intuition, the image is a fragment, a rune ... The false appearance (*Schein*) of totality is extinguished'(*Origin* 176). 2. The allegorist joins the isolated reality fragments and thereby creates meaning. This is posited meaning; it does not derive from the original context of the fragments" (Burger 69). For Benjamin, allegory depends on the removal of elements from their organic context. But the work of the allegorist lies both in depriving the element of its function and in joining fragments to posit another meaning; the technical term that describes these activities is "montage" (see Burger 73–82).[1] Having experienced fascism, Benjamin was deeply suspicious of the appeal of the beautiful symbol. For this reason, he opposed the "organic symbol" in favour of coded meanings of allegory that required the application of the intellect. Findley, who was equally horrified at attempts on the part of the powerful to dictate the fate of the powerless, also relies on a process similar to montage to acknowledge and contest canonical European and US fictions. But whereas *Headhunter* uses montage playfully to deconstruct these fictions, Ondaatje's melancholy narrative treats the fragmentation of the West's master narratives as a far more tragic loss.

In Ondaatje's *The English Patient*, the image of the ruin predominates. From the start, the text portrays the patient, burned to the bone, with his "black body" and "destroyed feet," as a physical ruin. The first section clarifies that this human wreck is mirrored by the architectural wreckage that surrounds him. Referring to the villa, the narrator explains that some rooms "could not be entered because of the rubble. One bomb crater allowed moon and rain into the library downstairs ..." (7–8). The second section, which bears the title "In Near Ruins," focuses on Caravaggio, the thief whose thumbs were brutally cut off during a torture session. The title of the section is drawn from the narrator's comment that Caravaggio was "in near ruins" when he was brought to the hospital for care (27). In this same section, the narrator goes on to compare Hana to a ruin: "Nurses too became shell-shocked from the dying around them. Or from something as small as a letter ... They broke the way a man dismantling a mine broke the second his geography exploded. The way Hana broke in Santa Chiara Hospital when an official ... gave her a letter that told her of the death of her father" (41). Not only are minds, bodies, and geographies broken and reduced to ruins, but the narrative structure itself is seemingly marked by the explosive forces of war. Like *Head-hunter*, populated with "broken dreamers, their minds in ruin," who inhabit an apocalyptic wasteland, *The English Patient* portrays the ruin of the earthly world and conveys the trauma of the non-elect. But, in contrast to *Headhunter*, which, for the most part, retains a linear, narrative structure, *The English Patient* fragments its own narrative to highlight the impact of apocalyptic disaster and offer a concrete example of the fracturing of linear narratives.

Examples of the text's fragmented structure abound, but perhaps the most telling concerns the events that lead to Caravaggio's arrest and torture. Rather than offer an organic, chronological account, the text forces readers to contend with a series of non-sequential fragments that must be pieced together in order for them to make sense (35–9). In much the same way, the books that Hana reads to the patient have "gaps of plot like sections of a road washed out by storms, missing incidents as if locusts had consumed a section of tapestry, as if plaster loosened by the bombing had fallen away from a mural at night" (7). Narrative fragmentation is also the principal feature of the book that the patient brought with him through the fire, "a copy of Herodotus that he had added to, cutting and gluing in pages from other books or writing in his own observations" (16).

Ondaatje's text not only relies on the production aesthetics of allegory, a fundamental feature of apocalypse, but, in a subversive, anti-apocalyptic gesture, also exploits the fact that allegory and, more specifically, montage, can stress the autonomy of the individual parts as opposed to the work as a whole; in montage the "negation of synthesis becomes a compositional principle" (Adorno 232). Generally speaking, the novel's emphasis on montage supports Benjamin's view that, in certain historical periods, when society's relation to absolutes has become uncertain, "the production of 'perfect' works of art is given over to epigones, and the creation of authentic works assumes the form of fragments or ruins" (see Wolin 59). As the examples cited above demonstrate, and in contrast to an apocalyptic narrative that relies on an intertextual and allegorical design to create an overarching vision of "all of history from beginning to end, conveying the image of temporal unity" (Frye, "Typology" 70), Ondaatje's novel, like *Headhunter*, repeatedly uses images of destruction to convey the fragmentation of an organic whole.

In addition to the prominence of the fragment or ruin in *The English Patient*, the narrative also promotes the view that a series of apocalyptic disasters have already occurred. Both the historical period in which the action takes place and the novel's treatment of the past reflect a debt to apocalypse's recursive structure – Revelation fashions its vision of the future by replicating or alluding to passages in earlier biblical texts – and to Benjamin's recursive and pessimistic conception of history. For both Benjamin and Ondaatje, the Second World War serves as a vantage point from which to survey humanity's precarious position in what both authors envision as an apocalyptic storm that threatens to erase all traces of the past. While revelations of the Holocaust and the impact of fascism also contribute to Findley's apocalyptic sensibility, Benjamin and Ondaatje conceive of the Fall as having already and irrevocably taken place. The storm is already "blowing from Paradise," and humankind, exiled from the Garden, inhabits a profane world.

Ondaatje's reliance on what Benjamin describes as an allegorical way of seeing – which rests on an apocalyptic conception of history – makes the novel a study of catastrophe; as such, it raises several important questions. First, what is the nature of apocalypse according to Ondaatje, an ex-centric Canadian writing at the turn of the new millennium? Second, what exactly has been lost as a result of the catastrophe? Third, is this loss truly irrevocable or can it somehow be redeemed? Fourth, what is the relationship between humanity's quest for knowledge – specifically, the discourses of science, art, and religion – and redemption? Finally, how faithfully does the text invoke the apocalyptic paradigm? Are there, as we saw in *Headhunter*, an elect capable of rising up, embracing a community-oriented, prophetic eschatological tradition, and overthrowing the Antichrist?

From the start, readers gain a sense of Ondaatje's conception of apocalypse as a series of ongoing catastrophes. When *The English Patient* opens, the patient has fallen from a burning plane with "his head on fire" (5). Like Milton's Satan, hurled "headlong from th' ethereal sky," the patient is described as simply another casualty of "the war in heaven" (5). An outcast from Paradise, he takes consolation in the *trompe l'oeil* of a garden created by human hands and finds refuge in a room with "trees and bowers painted over its walls and ceiling" (3–4). Here, the painting of the garden functions as an

allegorical emblem that signals the loss of Eden and humanity's separation from "genuine, immediately accessible, *immanent* meaning"
(Spencer 63). While Ondaatje's narrative, like Findley's, is densely
intertextual, in contrast to *Headhunter*, *The English Patient*'s apocalypse is not a catastrophe that awaits humanity in the not-too-distant
future: it is an event that has already taken place and continues
unabated.

According to *The English Patient*, the apocalypse is not an isolated,
singular event. Therefore, while allusions to the Fall in Ondaatje's
novel link the patient to Milton's Satan, subsequent references to *Paradise Lost* and Piero della Francesca's frescoes identify the patient
with Adam, whose decision to eat from the Tree of Knowledge
brought death into the world (70, 143). According to *The English
Patient*, the fall into sin constitutes an ongoing phenomenon; even
death itself is not final. On several occasions, characters insist that the
patient is not simply wounded but is, in fact, dead, referring to him
as a "corpse" and a "ghost" (28, 45). The emphasis on wounded bodies and corpses once again reveals the text's connection with Benjamin's version of allegory, where the corpse and the fragmented, tortured body play crucial roles. As Benjamin argues, in contrast to
representations of the body's wholeness and perfection, the destruction of the body in allegorical narratives "prepares the body of the
living person for emblematic purposes" (*The Origin of German Tragic
Drama* 216). In *The English Patient*, the patient's body functions as an
allegorical fragment – an emblem of catastrophe.

The text's overarching emphasis on death and decay follows what
Benjamin sees as allegory's representation of history as "decline"
(*The Origin of German Tragic Drama* 166); the observer of allegorical
works "is confronted with the 'facies hippocratica' (the deathmask)
of history as a petrified primordial landscape" (166). Only this type
of unrelenting insistence on decline, according to Benjamin, could
challenge modernism's faith in progress. The deathmask of history
hovers over Ondaatje's entire text, which opens with the patient's fall
and concludes with the nuclear bombing of Japan. Its non-progressive structure – coupled with its use of biblical and Miltonic allusions, which stress death, fire, and destruction – unmasks the idea of
modern progress and implicitly aligns it with catastrophe. In *The
English Patient*, catastrophe, associated with the war and the rise of
fascism, is tied to humanity's faith in civilization and progress, a
paradox also observed in Findley's *Headhunter*. When Hana explains

that Kip is involved in the war because he believes in "a civilized world. He's a civilized man," Caravaggio announces bitterly, "First mistake" (*The English Patient* 122).

In this way, history, as envisioned by Canadian writers dedicated to tracing the fate of the non-elect barred from the New Jerusalem, is portrayed as a series of devastating losses. Just as Findley, with *Headhunter,* and Ondaatje, with *The English Patient,* show themselves suspicious of civilization and progress, Benjamin, in his writings, and perhaps most eloquently in the "Theses," argues that fascism, one of his era's prime evils, owes its success to humanity's stubborn faith in human progress because, in the name of progress, the opponents of fascism treat it "as a historical norm" (*Illuminations* 257). To correct this distorted and dangerous view, Benjamin advocates a radical re-evaluation of progress: "The idea of progress must be based on the idea of catastrophe. That things have gone this far is the catastrophe. Catastrophe is not what threatens to occur at any given moment but what is given at any given moment. Strindberg's conception: Hell is nothing that stands ahead of us – rather, *this life in the present*" ("Central Park" 50). Adopting the characteristically Canadian perspective of apocalypse's traumatized victims, Ondaatje's novel, like Findley's, often shares Benjamin's perspective and frequently undercuts the reader's unquestioning belief in progress: section three opens with the narrator's ironic comment that the "last mediaeval war was fought in Italy in 1943 and 1944" (69).

Because the narrative does not simply focus on an isolated disaster, but forges connections among seemingly disparate catastrophes, it thereby reinforces Benjamin's view of human history as a "single catastrophe which keeps piling wreckage upon wreckage." As noted above, the patient's fall recalls the Miltonic account of the Fall of Satan and Adam. But both the literal and the biblical disasters ultimately prefigure the nuclear holocaust unleashed at the end of the war (and the end of the text). By deploying this recursive structure, the text adopts the analeptic gaze of Benjamin's "angel of history" and intimates that the nuclear fires that erupt in Hiroshima and Nagasaki can be traced back to the storm blowing from Paradise.

In an anti-apocalyptic bid to dispel the fascist illusion of progress, the novel illustrates the connections among catastrophes through the use of related imagery, as when Kip learns about the attack on Hiroshima and Nagasaki and feels as if "all the winds of the world have been sucked into Asia" (287). If he closes his eyes, he "sees the

streets of Asia full of fire. It rolls across cities like a burst map, the
hurricane of heat withering bodies as it meets them, the shadow of
humans suddenly in the air" (284). Although, on one level, the novel
portrays the bombing as a uniquely catastrophic event, references to
wind and fire also surface in earlier descriptions and, thus, identify
the nuclear holocaust with other apocalyptic events in human history. In an earlier episode, the patient uses the images of wind and
fire to describe the medieval Bonfire of the Vanities, which likewise
engendered destruction and signalled the end of peaceful, civilized
relationships (57–8). Both events are conceived of in apocalyptic
terms. When Caravaggio considers the bombing of Japan, he speaks
of the "death of a civilisation" (286) and echoes Benjamin's belief that
the war would bring the extinction of civilization. Similarly, in her
letter to her stepmother, Hana writes that "it feels like the end of the
world" (292). The Second World War instigated a radical change in
Canadian writers' conceptions of apocalypse; the atomic bomb – the
symbol of Western technological prowess – haunts *The English Patient*
and also Joy Kogawa's *Obasan* (the subject of chapter 5).

Adopting the melancholy view of the non-elect, Ondaatje's text not
only highlights the connection between disasters in human history
but also forges connections between the nuclear attack and the biblical apocalypse by juxtaposing the bombing of Japan with the apocalyptic prophecy of Isaiah. The first seemingly innocuous reference to
Isaiah occurs when Kip recalls entering the Sistine Chapel. Using his
rifle telescope, he surveyed the famous ceiling until his eye "reached
the great face and was stilled by it, the face like a spear, wise, unforgiving" (77). When Kip asked whose face he was looking at, a fellow
soldier explained that it was the "great face" of Isaiah. After the
bombing, as the novel draws to a close, Kip's thoughts once again
return to Isaiah. Finding himself unable to live among members of
the nations that sanctioned the bombing, he flees San Girolamo on his
motorbike. During his flight, he recalls several of Isaiah's prophecies
concerning the dreadful Day of the Lord.

In this remarkable scene, Ondaatje conveys the absolute loss instigated by humanity's most recent apocalyptic catastrophe by con-
structing a tableau that echoes Benjamin's account of the "angel of
history": Kip "feels he carries the body of the Englishman with him
in this flight. It sits on the petrol tank facing him, the black body in
an embrace with his, facing the past over his shoulder, facing the
countryside they are flying from, that receding palace of strangers on

the Italian hill which shall never be rebuilt" (294). In this revised emblem, the English patient assumes the angel's position, while the villa and the fragile community it housed function as synecdoches for every fragile human community destroyed by the ongoing catastrophe – the fire that rolls across "cities like a burst map."

The novel's emphasis on catastrophe raises a question cited earlier that also surfaces in Findley's *Headhunter*: is humanity's quest for knowledge responsible for instigating apocalypse or is apocalyptic disaster linked to a particular approach to knowledge? Although in Ondaatje's text "Satan" is the name of a four-thousand-pound bomb and the plot leads inexorably to the nuclear attack on Japan, the narrative does not simply conflate catastrophe and the biblical Antichrist with humanity's quest for knowledge. Indeed, the text precludes readers from viewing the discourses of science and technology as unequivocally evil, although they clearly pave the way for the nuclear bomb. Rather than condemn scientific discourses and the desire for knowledge that fuels them, the text invites readers to explore very different approaches to the acquisition and deployment of knowledge; at least two distinct models for the gathering and transmission of knowledge are presented in the novel – models that recall the distinction between prophetic and apocalyptic eschatology. Thus, in keeping with Findley's novel, *The English Patient* challenges apocalypse by turning toward a prior prophetic, community-oriented eschatological tradition.

Before an analysis of these models for transmitting knowledge is offered, it is worth noting that the text prevents readers from treating the discourses of science, art, and religion as autonomous entities. In what may well be a strategic move to facilitate a more accurate and synthetic understanding of the relationship among these discourses and their scriptural function, the narrative frequently portrays the discourse of science as complemented by and interwoven within the discourses of Western religion and art. On several occasions, the text highlights the vivid intersection among these discourses. For example, in a scene previously mentioned, Kip uses his military equipment (a product of technology) to light the Sistine Chapel (a religious site) so that he can gaze on the "wise" and "unforgiving" face of Isaiah (an artistic rendering by Michelangelo) (77).

The repeated emphasis on these intersections performs the important task of negating the false semblance of autonomy and self-sufficiency that typically characterizes readers' perceptions of these discourses and the discourse of art in particular. Simply put, the prevalence of episodes that bring art into play with science and religion makes it difficult for readers to treat works of art as beautiful and consoling, but largely irrelevant, cultural commodities. Instead, art is endowed with a profound sociopolitical and religious significance – together with the discourses of science and religion, art serves as a map that can challenge the apocalyptic plot. Yet, whereas Findley's novel focuses primarily on the scriptural function of art, Ondaatje's narrative links the discourses of art, science, and religion, treating them as a secular Torah that can strengthen the bonds of the earthly community and therby resist apocalyptic eschatology.

The privileged status of artistic discourse in *The English Patient* recalls Findley's belief that it is essential for people to familiarize themselves with the plots that have shaped human culture – "to know where they enter." Ondaatje's emphasis on art extends Findley's belief in the significance of art by recalling Benjamin's later understanding of the importance of art and tradition, which is specifically linked to a notion of redemption. For Benjamin, a survey of historical existence reveals a state of perpetual disintegration or "irresistible decay" (*The Origin of German Tragic Drama* 178). However, he felt that exceptions were to be found in the realm of aesthetic experience, specifically, in allegorical works of art. According to Benjamin, one of the strongest impulses in allegory is "an appreciation of the transience of things, a concern to rescue them for eternity" (223). What survives in the allegorical ruin is "the extraordinary detail of the allegorical references: an object of knowledge which has settled in the consciously constructed ruins" (182).

In section 2 of the "Theses," Benjamin elaborates on his rather cryptic statement about the "object of knowledge" and explains that embedded in the past is an index or map that, if read properly, can guide humanity: "The past carries with it a temporal index by which it is referred to redemption. There is a secret agreement between past generations and the present one. Our coming was expected on earth. Like every generation that preceded us, we have been endowed with a *weak* Messianic power, a power to which the past has a claim" (*Illuminations* ii). Axel Honneth argues that what is meant by "claim" here is "a kind of moral right that past generations have vis-à-vis those living, because the latter draw advantage from the sufferings and toils which the former had to endure and which were not atoned for" (127). Honneth argues further that, in Benjamin's view, every historical process is "pervaded by a chain of moral entanglements, one in which every unatoned suffering of the past further increases the objective debt of the present generation" (127). This suffering was experienced by "history's anonymous losers," whose "cries for help, silent revolt, or their loud protests were not listened to by their contemporaries" (Honneth 128).

For Benjamin, the "secret agreement between past generations and the present one" is specifically embedded in artifacts and traditions that have the power to convey crucial information. Perhaps Richard Wolin best explains what this "index" contains: Benjamin "recognized the decline of traditional life forms ... as an irreparable loss; for the meaning potentials objectified in the cultural products of traditional societies contain a promise of transcendence; they are the objects in which past ages have deposited their collective dreams and longings, their aspirations for a better life, aspirations which adverse historical conditions have heretofore frustrated, and it falls due to future generations to preserve such hopes for a better life, if not to redeem them outright" (217). Benjamin's belief in humanity's ability to extract crucial knowledge from the past – to "blast a specific era out of the homogenous course of history" – leads him to an important re-evaluation of artifacts and tradition. This same faith in humanity's ability to appreciate the index of the past and to repay the debt to "history's anonymous losers" informs all of the works in this study and plays a central role in Ondaatje's novel.

When Kip finds himself at the intersection of the three discourses – science, art, and religion – he concludes that "there was no order but for *the great maps of art* that showed judgement, piety, and sacrifice" (70; my emphasis). His statement, which aligns art with cartography, sheds light on the novel's reverence for historical artifacts and helps answer the question posed earlier; namely, what does humanity forfeit when apocalyptic fires roll across "cities like a burst map"? The cartographic imagery in the text allows the discourses of science, art, and religion to function as temporal indexes, as maps containing traces of "a secret agreement" between past generations and the present one concerning catastrophe and redemption. Moreover, these are maps with strong ties to prophetic eschatology. For Ondaatje, the desire to map and the quest for knowledge alone do not usher in apocalypse. Instead, catastrophe springs from a particular orientation toward knowledge, characterized by an orientation toward the future rather than the past and by a desire to possess and reify or, worse, eradicate maps altogether.

From the start of the novel, readers are made aware that the patient's elite status and the reverence he elicits from others stems from the fact that he is a repository of information about the past. He upholds an approach to mapping that recalls prophetic eschatology and stresses its communal nature and its orientation toward the past. This human ruin has internalized a host of maps from different centuries. As he confesses to Hana, all he needed "was the name of a small ridge, a local custom, a cell of this historical animal, and the map of the world would slide into place" (19). After he falls from his plane, the Bedouins keep him alive because of his knowledge; as payment for having saved him, he draws his rescuers "maps that go beyond their own boundaries" (21).

The English Patient's valorization of geographical and scientific maps also informs the scene in which Kip first meets the patient. The sapper delights in his newfound older friend, who embodies a "reservoir of information about Allied and enemy weaponry": "The Englishman knew not only about the absurd Italian fuzes but also knew the detailed topography of this region of Tuscany. Soon they were drawing outlines of bombs for each other and talking out the theory of each specific circuit" (88–9). In both of these episodes, the patient transmits his knowledge by drawing maps for others. These scenes also introduce readers to very different ways of approaching the acquisition and deployment of knowledge.

As suggested earlier, the patient's behaviour outlines one possible approach, which involves treating maps as sites of communal knowledge that should travel from hand to hand, from one place to another. Often, as in the scene in which he sketches with Kip, the maps travel across generations. Ondaatje's text reinforces this communal and intergenerational approach to maps and mapmaking in the subsequent conversation between the patient and the sapper. At one point, the patient inquires about Kip's teacher, and the latter fondly recalls his mentor, Lord Suffolk. Kip's account of his teacher once again highlights an intergenerational approach to the exchange of knowledge.

From Kip's description, readers learn that the older Lord Suffolk, a gentle, reclusive man, led a team of sappers fondly known as the Holy Trinity during the war. Suffolk and his team taught Kip a number of valuable lessons. On the one hand, he learned about the potentially catastrophic, explosive forces of progress and technology that informed each new bomb that he struggled to decode. On the other, he also learned about the existence of communal forces that bind individuals.

Kip first becomes aware of these communal forces in the scene in which he visits Lord Suffolk's country home. Inside the stone cottage, Kip notices a map on a roller. One morning, he pulls it down and reads the inscription: "Countisbury and Area. Mapped by R. Fones. Drawn by desire of Mr. James Halliday." Charmed and intrigued, he repeats the phrase "drawn by desire," and decides that "he was beginning to love the English" (190). Owing to his repetition of the phrase, readers become aware that it affords multiple interpretations. Taken literally, the phrase suggests that someone has drawn a map because it was desired *by* another. But it also suggests that one creates a map because one is drawn by desire *for* another. In the latter case, the knowledge encoded and transmitted by the map could thus be said to testify to a "secret agreement" between individuals – an agreement based on desire which could potentially span generations. The text underscores this type of secret agreement when, after a lethal and unfamiliar bomb murders the Holy Trinity, Kip risks his life to decode the solution. After completing the arduous process of defusing the bomb, he draws a map of the zvs-40 problem and signs it: "Drawn by desire of Lord Suffolk, by his student Lieutenant Kirpal Singh, 10 May 1941" (198).

To summarize, through the portraits of Kip, his beloved teacher, and the patient, the text highlights a communal and intergenerational approach to the transmission of knowledge, which is encoded in maps of one sort or another. These maps are drawn by individuals who, to borrow Benjamin's words, aspire to making "whole what has been smashed." Like Benjamin's "angel of history," and in contrast to those who embrace apocalyptic eschatology, these individuals typically face the past and offer their maps out of respect and love for the dead. In keeping with prophetic eschatology, both the communal nature and the orientation toward the past constitute fundamental characteristics of this approach. They are evident when the patient discusses his reasons for mapping the desert and insists that he and his fellow members of the Geographical Society were interested in how their lives "could mean something to the past. We sailed into the past. We were young. We all slept with Herodotus" (141).

In contrast to this approach to the transmission of knowledge, the text confirms that maps are also drawn in an attempt to isolate mapmakers and to render them immortal. Distinguishing between these two approaches, the patient explains that mapmakers who wish to immortalize themselves do not engage in a dialogue with the past; instead, in accordance with apocalyptic eschatology with its emphasis on the elect, these mapmakers stress their individuality and orient themselves toward the future: "When we are young we do not look into mirrors. It is when we are old, concerned with our name, our legend, *what our lives will mean to the future*. We become vain with the names we own, our claims to have been the first eyes, the strongest army, the cleverest merchant. It is when he is old that Narcissus wants a graven image of himself" (141–2; my emphasis). In Benjamin's conceptual framework, the goal of this type of mapping is "the *possession* of objects and not their emancipation" (see Wolin 93). For this reason, this form of mapping is associated with reification, idolatry, and the construction of a "graven image." As Wolin explains, for Benjamin, this type of approach to knowledge, "indistinguishable from the Nietzschean 'will to power,' will stop at nothing to reach this end, and its preferred technique ... has been the imperious assertion of the primacy of the knowing subject over the object to be known" (93). This is the apocalyptic and elitist approach adopted by Findley's Kurtz.

In contrast, the communal and historical approach, which plays such an important role in Ondaatje's novel, mirrors Benjamin's awareness of a very different attitude toward truth, characterized by an "intentionless state of being" and "total immersion and absorption" (*The Origin of German Tragic Drama* 46). During his career as an explorer, the patient devoted himself to this type of intentionless approach. In a frequently cited passage, he describes having immersed and virtually erased himself in the construction of a shifting, communal map:

There were rivers of desert tribes, the most beautiful humans I've met in my life. We were German, English, Hungarian, African – all of us insignificant to them. Gradually we became nationless. I came to hate nations ...

The desert could not be claimed or owned – it was a piece of cloth carried by winds, never held down by stones, and given a hundred shifting names long before Canterbury existed, long before battles and treaties quilted Europe and the East ... We disappeared into landscape. Fire and sand. We left the harbours of oasis. The places water came to and touched ... Ain, Bir, Wadi, Foggara, Khottara, Shaduf. I didn't want my name against such beautiful names. Erase the family name! Erase nations! I was taught such things by the desert. (138–9)

Later, the patient makes a similar proclamation:

I believe in such cartography – to be marked by nature, not just to label ourselves on a map like the names of rich men and women on buildings. We are
communal histories, communal books. We are not owned or monogamous in
our taste or experience. All I desired was to walk upon such an earth that had
no maps. (261)

In *Territorial Disputes*, Graham Huggan argues that this emphasis on erasure represents a Canadian concern. As he says, many contemporary Canadian writers "seem less interested than their immediate or more distant predecessors in evoking a sense of place than in expressing a kind of placelessness through which the notion of a fixed location, and the corresponding possibility of a fixed identity are resisted" (56).

In addition to emphasizing a postcolonial, Canadian perspective, the distinction drawn in *The English Patient* between a communal and intergenerational approach to mapmaking and an approach that isolates and attempts to render the elite mapmaker immortal recalls the two antithetical approaches to eschatology outlined earlier; accordingly, Ondaatje's text, like Findley's, repeatedly rejects apocalyptic eschatology in favour of prophetic eschatology.[2]

As mentioned earlier, in comparison to Findley's text, *The English Patient* focuses more broadly on the intersections between art, science, and religion, endowing these discourses with a scriptural function and the power of prophetic eschatology to forestall disaster. Although all of the communal and intergenerational maps analyzed thus far pertain to geography and science, the text's extensive references to maps are not restricted to these discourses. The novel also forges important connections between the acquisition and transmission of knowledge in the form of mapmaking and the discourses of art and religion.

To appreciate how art and religion can function as maps, readers must understand Kip's pronouncement: "there was no order but for the great maps of art" (70). This statement will remain unintelligible unless readers determine what maps and art, specifically religious art, have in common. The narrator hints at a possible connection when he outlines the similarities between the effects of morphine and the properties of a map. Referring to the effects of the drug on the patient, the narrator explains that it "races in him, imploding time and geography the way maps compress the world onto a two-dimensional sheet of paper" (161). It is this capacity to implode time and geography that is the common denominator linking mapmaking to the discourses of art and religion.

Throughout the text, these discourses compress history and geography and transmit crucial information from the past to the present. Like the geographical and scientific maps drawn by the patient, Kip, and Lord Suffolk, artistic and religious artifacts serve as communal and transgenerational maps. In several scenes, these discourses effect the implosion or compression of space and time. For example, when Kip and his fellow soldiers enter the Gothic church at Arezzo, they look up with their service binoculars. As the narrator explains, the twentieth-century soldiers came "upon their contemporary faces" in the Piero della Francesca frescoes of the Queen of Sheba, King Solomon, and Adam (70). These frescoes function as maps because they "implode" time and geography, enabling the soldiers to forge connections between past and present and read in these medieval tableaus "their contemporary faces."[3]

Apocalyptic eschatology insists on the radical break between this world and the next. By contrast, in both Ondaatje's novel and Benjamin's philosophical writings, the ability to recognize (particularly, in moments of danger) relationships between past and present eras emerges as one of humanity's most crucial tasks:

To articulate the past historically does not mean to recognize it 'the way it really was' (Ranke). Instead, it means to seize hold of a memory as it flashes up at a moment of danger. Historical materialism wishes to retain that image of the past which unexpectedly appears to man singled out by history at a moment of danger. The danger affects both the content of the tradition and its receivers. (Benjamin, *Illuminations* 255)

An individual's relationship to history, according to Benjamin, should not be sequential – the "telling the sequence of events like the beads of a rosary" (263). Instead, an individual must grasp "the constellation which his own era has formed with a definite earlier one. Thus he establishes a conception of the present as the 'time of the now' which is shot through with chips of Messianic time" (263).

In Ondaatje's novel, the discourses of science, art, and religion are invested with such "chips of Messianic time" – that is to say, they constitute maps that encode the utopian, spiritual dreams of past eras. The necessity of grasping the knowledge afforded by such maps is urgently conveyed by Benjamin, who understood that in a society obsessed with apocalyptic eschatology, "every image of the past that is not recognized by the present as one of its own concerns threatens to disappear irretrievably" (*Illuminations* 255). In Benjamin's eyes, the danger threatens both the past and the present: "Only that historian will have the gift of fanning the spark of hope in the past who is firmly convinced that *even the dead* will not be safe from the enemy if he wins" (*Illuminations* 255). For Benjamin, Ondaatje, and Findley, the enemy is anyone who acts on the apocalyptic desire to eradicate the earthly world and its inhabitants in anticipation of the New Jerusalem.

The English Patient exposes the temporally double-sided nature of the apocalyptic threat in the scene prior to the nightmarish account of the nuclear attack. Moments before he learns about the bombing of Hiroshima, Kip recalls a particularly terrifying mission, in which he was sent to Naples to determine whether the enemy had planted a bomb that would, if detonated, have razed the entire city. After attempting unsuccessfully to locate the bomb, Kip makes his way to the Church of San Giovanni a Carbonara. Curling up beside a tableau featuring a woman and an angel, he reasons that "if he is going to explode he will do so in the company of these two. They will die or be secure" (281). For him these terracotta figures are not simply lifeless artifacts; instead "they are company," and he "walks within the discussion of these creatures that represent some fable about mankind and heaven" (279). If he dies, these artifacts and the knowledge contained in their otherworldly discussion will "die" along with him.

Although it is never explicitly stated, this vital, allegorical tableau under siege portrays the Annunciation – one of Christianity's clearest promises of redemption. Thus, in keeping with Benjamin's view, Ondaatje's novel highlights that both life in the present – represented by Kip and the entire city of Naples – and the image of redeemed life embedded in the indexes of the past are threatened. By responding to the artistic and religious artifact as a fellow creature – essentially, responding to the work's aura – Kip fulfills Benjamin's understanding of the task of the ideal historian, who, in a moment of danger, grasps "the constellation which his own era has formed with a definite earlier one" and thereby establishes "a conception of the present as the 'time of the now' which is pregnant with the promise of transcendence" (*Illuminations* 263). When Kip safely awakens the next morning, it is as if a miracle has taken place – a miracle in which the angel, covered in the dust of antiquity, yet animated by the contemporary wonder of electricity, clearly participates: "Under the thin layer of dust the angel's face has a powerful joy. Attached to its back are the six light bulbs, two of which are defunct. But in spite of that the wonder of electricity suddenly lights its wings from underneath, so that their blood-red and blue and goldness the colour of mustard fields shine animated in the late afternoon" (281). Again, in contrast to apocalyptic eschatology, which celebrates the destruction of the world and every trace of human civilization, in both Ondaatje's and Benjamin's writings, religious artifacts attain significance because they remind humankind of the promise of redemption by providing the foundation for a dialectical leap that blasts "a specific era out of the homogeneous course of history" (*Illuminations* 263).

For Benjamin, in keeping with prophetic eschatology, redemption involves experiencing the continuity between past and present. In his later writings, he credits diverse diverse objects and cultural practices, ranging from artifacts to religious rituals, with the power to forge this sense of temporal continuity. In a memorable episode in *The English Patient*, a religious ritual serves as the foundation for this type of dialectical leap. At one point, Kip watches the Marine Festival of the Virgin Mary at Gabicce Mare through his rifle telescope. Although he is a Sikh from the Punjab, he recognizes that an urgent necessity compels the adults and children of the besieged town to ignore the war or, more precisely, to suspend historical time and imaginatively enter sacred time. As he says: "These were not romantic people. They had survived the Fascists, the English, Gauls, Goths and Germans. They had been owned so often it meant nothing. But this blue and cream plaster figure had come out of the sea, was placed in a grape truck full of flowers, while the band marched ahead of her in silence" (79). Likely because they had been "owned so often," these oppressed people turn to the "collective desires of unfree humanity" embedded in these rituals (Wolin 262). For his own part, while surveying the plaster figure of Mary through his rifle telescope, Kip is struck by the fact that he sees "someone he knew. A sister. Someday a daughter" (*The English Patient* 80). In this episode, as when Kip's fellow soldiers contemplate the discursive maps of religious art, time and geography implode. As a result of their compression, and in keeping with prophetic eschatology's emphasis on human history, Kip resists the future-oriented logic of apocalypse and is granted a communal vision of himself, his family, and his earthly future.[4]

In light of the text's valorization of prophetic eschatology and, by extension, artifacts and tradition, owing to their ability to compress time and geography and thereby strengthen communal ties, it is not surprising that the novel aligns catastrophe with the apocalyptic breaking of the bonds between past and present, the explosion of bridges, and the destruction of invaluable, historical discursive maps.[5] As noted earlier, the patient alludes to several important features of apocalyptic catastrophe in his discussion of the Bonfire of the Vanities. He informs Hana that the Villa San Girolamo was very likely known as the Villa Bruscoli in 1483, when it was owned by Poliziano. A poet and translator of Homer, Poliziano was friends with such luminaries as Pico della Mirandola and Michelangelo. Reflecting on these ancient times, the patient explains:

Yes, I think a lot happened here ... Pico and Lorenzo and Poliziano and the young Michelangelo. They held in each hand the new world and the old world ... They sat in this room with a bust of Plato and argued all night.

And then came Savonarola's cry out of the streets: "Repentance! The deluge is coming!" And everything was swept away – free will, the desire to be elegant, fame, the right to worship Plato as well as Christ. Now came the bonfire – the burning of wigs, books, animal hides, *maps*. (57; my emphasis)[6]

In relating the story, the patient stresses the most salient features of the catastrophe: "[The] great maps lost in the bonfires and the burning of Plato's statue, whose marble exfoliated in the heat, the cracks across wisdom like precise reports across the valley as Poliziano stood on the grass hills smelling the future." In this description, the nightmare images of attempts at purification through violence, specifically fire and burning, foreshadow the nuclear fires portrayed at the end of the war. Past and present implode, as contemporary gunshots – "precise reports" – echo in the sound of Plato's sculpture cracking. The exfoliation of the marble "in the heat" also prefigures the effects of the bomb, whose "hurricane of heat wither[s] bodies as it meets them" (284). Temporal compression also informs the text's description of Poliziano's reaction to the catastrophe – a reaction that prophesies subsequent responses to apocalyptic disasters. Like Benjamin's "angel of history," Poliziano perches on the Tuscan hillside as the smoke-filled winds of progress rush past. Together with the more recent inhabitants of the villa, and with readers of the text, he inhales the apocalyptic stench of progress. The same smoke-filled winds of progress accompany the bombing of Japan. As Kip tells his former friends: "I'll leave you the radio to swallow your history lesson ... All those speeches of civilisation from kings and queens and presidents ... such voices of abstract order. Smell it" (285). By juxtaposing the Bonfire of the Vanities with the bombing of Japan, *The English Patient* demonstrates the violence of apocalypse as well as the fundamental futility of apocalyptic thinking that seeks to replace the earthly world with a heavenly paradise but merely piles "wreckage upon wreckage."

Thus far, this chapter has emphasized how *The English Patient* both identifies and demonstrates how different discursive maps, in accordance with prophetic eschatology, create bridges between past and present ages; it also illustrates what happens when these maps are destroyed as a result of apocalyptic thinking. In a characteristically Canadian fashion, these bridges enable individuals in the present to redeem history's anonymous losers and their unfulfilled, spiritual dreams – dreams often encoded in allegories. It is still necessary, however, to consider the repercussions of what Benjamin terms "an allegorical way of seeing" in order to appreciate the melancholy approach of the allegorist and allegory's reductive aspects – features related both to Benjamin's anti-apocalyptic view of history and to Canadian writers' preoccupation with the victims of history.

Standard definitions of allegory explain that it is present in narrative fictions "in which the agents and actions, and sometimes the setting as well, are contrived to make coherent sense on the 'literal,' or primary, level of signification, and at the same time to signify a second, correlated order of agents, concepts, and events" (Abrams, *Glossary of Literary Terms*); "Most allegory in order to function at all depends on the reader's grasp of an interpretative *context* not given (although it may be referred to) in the text itself. A high degree of optical awareness, and the implication of a hierarchy of values, and a stable, hierarchised organisation of existence are common features of familiar allegories" (Spencer 62). Ondaatje's narrative frequently invites readers to adopt an allegorical way of seeing, as suggested by the following passage:

The storm rolls out of Piedmont to the south and to the east. Lightning falls upon the steeples of the small alpine chapels whose tableaux reenact the Stations of the Cross or the Mysteries of the Rosary. In the small towns of Varese and Varallo, larger-than-life terra-cotta figures carved in the 1600s are revealed briefly depicting biblical scenes ... The Villa San Girolamo, located where it is, also receives such moments of light ... Kip will walk with no qualms under the trees in his patch of garden during such storms ... The naive Catholic images from those hillside shrines that he has seen are with him in the half-darkness ... Perhaps this villa is a similar tableau, the four of them in private movement, momentarily lit up, flung ironically against this war. (277–8)

In this description, the two basic elements in the production of allegory are evident: the removal of elements from their context (the four characters in "private movement") and the joining of fragments to form a "tableau" (the isolated characters "momentarily lit up, flung ironically against this war"). Unlike the surrounding biblical tableaux, however, the allegorical scene Kip perceives and in which he participates is ironic and anti-apocalyptic. Although it is apparent that the text reflexively constructs an ironic, anti-apocalyptic, allegorical tableau, readers must still consider the implications of adopting an allegorical way of seeing.

Readers might presume that allegorical narratives, which typically refer to "a hierarchy of values, and a stable, hierarchised organisation of existence," would, in keeping with apocalypse, reaffirm the existence of absolutes. In Revelation, this hierarchy is portrayed as God's plan and the revelation of the New Jerusalem. However, as Benjamin explains in his study of Baroque German drama, allegory can also profoundly register the anti-apocalyptic dissolution of meaningful existence. For Benjamin, "[T]he evocation of that 'framework' of meaning for allegory – and especially the forced, deliberate or ostentatious evocation of such a framework – is itself symptomatic of a significant loss of a sense of genuine, immediately accessible, *imminent* meaning. Allegories, even those which proclaim the stability and fullness of meaning in the (hierarchised) universe can thus be seen as deconstructing themselves" (Spencer 63). Not only is allegory inextricably connected to an awareness of loss, but the success of the allegorist's creation depends on the strength of the artist's unwavering, melancholy gaze.[7] The allegorist's melancholy, in keeping with the melancholy expressed by a range of contemporary Canadian fiction, springs from a recognition of the absence of divine truth, the illusory nature of progress, and, most importantly, the trauma and loss sustained by history's anonymous victims. The allegorist's eye, like Klee's angel, remains fixed on the victims of history. As Benjamin explains: "If the object becomes allegorical under the gaze of melancholy, if melancholy causes life to flow out of it and it remains behind dead but eternally secure, then it is exposed to the allegorist, it is unconditionally in his power. That is, it is now quite incapable of emanating any meaning or significance of its own: such significance as it has, it acquires from the allegorist ... [T]hrough it he speaks of something different and for him it becomes a key to the realm of hidden knowledge; and he reveres it as the emblem of this" (*The Origin of German Tragic Drama* 183–4). Benjamin goes on to argue that the human body "could be no exception to the commandment which ordered the destruction of the organic so that the true meaning ... might be picked up from its fragments" (216). He admits that the work of allegory is crude and sadistic because it "betrays and devalues things in an inexpressible manner" (185).

Nowhere is this melancholy and sadistic translation of the body into an allegorical emblem portrayed more forcibly than in the episode in which the patient assumes the role of allegorist and transforms his dying lover into an artifact. After she is mortally injured in a plane crash, the patient takes paint from the walls of the Cave of Swimmers and covers her wounded body in "bright pigment. Herbs and stones and light and the ash of acacia to make her eternal" (260–1). This episode starkly identifies the brutality involved in witnessing catastrophe and shaping it into art. There is a high price to be paid for wresting meaning from death and decay. This explains why the patient identifies with the disturbing and ambiguous Egyptian god of death, Anubis. Endowed with a man's body and a jackal's head, the deity's office, as the "opener of the ways" (258), was to take the souls of the dead before the judge of the infernal regions.

In keeping with Benjamin's understanding of the dialectical relationship between the decline of profane existence and divine redemption, the text identifies the patient, a man who demonstrates a profound understanding of the past, with both the angel's countenance and history's deathmask. As he tells his dying lover: "I have lived in the desert for years and I have come to believe in such things ... The jackal with one eye that looks back and one that regards the path you consider taking. In his jaws are pieces of the past he delivers to you, and when all of that time is fully discovered it will prove to have been already known" (259). The patient clearly understands his role as one who grasps "the constellation which his own era has formed with a definite earlier one."

Thus far, this chapter has explored the text's use of both allegory and the allegorical way of seeing to foreground the allegorist's melancholy approach and allegory's reductive nature. Without this information, readers of the novel might leave it with a false sense of optimism and hope for reconciliation. To a certain extent, some optimism seems warranted, especially in the light of the tremendous emphasis placed on the efforts of a host of individuals (including Hana in her role as a nurse and Kip in his capacity as a sapper) who assume the role of the elect and dedicate themselves to "making whole what has been smashed." Ultimately, however, although *The English Patient* counters the destructive forces of the Antichrist by the elect (or, the Saints of God), the narrative refuses to provide hope that anyone can extinguish apocalyptic thinking – an outcome that, ironically, would conform to the logic of apocalypse.

At this point, we are in a position to explore important questions: who are Ondaatje's Saints of God, and are they, in their twentieth-century incarnations, able to overthrow the Antichrist? In what also appears to be a gesture of supreme optimism, virtually every member of the group who adopts the villa as a refuge is identified with sainthood. As in *Headhunter*, in *The English Patient*, the elect are united by a reverence for art and by a commitment to rage against a corrupt empire that sacrifices individuals in pursuit of political and economic gain.[8] From the start, we are told that Hana views the patient as her "despairing saint" (3). When Caravaggio accuses her of tying herself to a corpse, she insists that the patient "is a saint. A despairing saint." (45). Later, Hana herself is compared to a saint; after they become lovers, Kip takes comfort at night in "the way she crawls in against his body like a saint" (128). Of all the characters, however, Kip is most closely identified with sainthood, particularly when Hana and the patient describe him as a "warrior saint" (209). As she listens to Kip speak "of warrior saints," Hana comes to feel that "he is one, stern and visionary, pausing only in these rare times of sunlight to be godless" (217). In associating the patient, Hana, and

Kip with sainthood, the text not only recalls the apocalyptic paradigm and its Saints of God but also demonstrates the power of reve-
latory allegory and communal and historical maps.[9]

Although Kip is identified with the warrior saint, the text does not
intimate that he operates in a world of absolutes and organic wholes.
When Hana thinks of her lover's dangerous work, she conceives of
his precarious existence in terms of a mural that she saw in Siena: "A
fresco of a city. A few yards outside the city walls the artist's paint
had crumbled away, so there was not even the security of art to provide an orchard in the far acres for the traveller leaving the castle.
That was where, she felt, Kip went during the day. Each morning he
would step from the painted scene toward the dark bluffs of chaos.
The knight. The warrior saint" (273). In Ondaatje's narrative, the
warrior saint operates in a ruined landscape, a world in chaos.

The text's final and perhaps most important reference to the warrior saint surfaces in the scene discussed earlier, in which Kip, unable
to prevent the destruction of Naples, not to mention himself, sleeps
beside the tableau featuring a woman and an angel. Before he drifts
off to sleep, we are told that he sees "a new toughness in the face of
the angel he didn't notice before ... the angel too is a warrior" (280).
However, in this episode, Kip does not so much internalize the image
of the warrior saint as enter into allegory:

He is sprawled out with a smile on his face, as if relieved finally to be sleep-
ing... The palm of his left hand facedown on the concrete. The colour of his
turban echoes that of the lace collar at the neck of Mary.

At her feet the small Indian sapper, in uniform, beside the six slippers.
There seems to be no time here. Each of them has selected the most comfort-
able of positions to forget time ... The tableau now, with Kip at the feet of the
two figures, suggests a debate over his fate. The raised terra-cotta arm a stay
of execution, a promise of some great future for this sleeper, childlike, for-
eign-born. The three of them almost at the point of decision, agreement.
(280–1)

Given Benjamin's understanding of the destructive and brutal nature of
allegory, readers should remain skeptical of Kip's transformation; after
all, people must die before they are canonized as saints. By positioning
Kip as a saint, in the ostentatious fashion of allegory, the text reduces the
complexity of Kip's character and prepares him for his emblematic role
and his "great future" as the critic of Western civilization.

This future, primarily an allegorical narrative conceit, manifests itself when Kip delivers his speech condemning the privileging of Western society's dominance over nations – a dominance secured by its discursive maps. Virtually inarticulate with rage, he turns on his former companions and states: "My brother told me. Never turn your back on Europe. The deal makers. The contract makers. *The map drawers* ... In my country, when a father breaks justice in two, you kill the father" (284–5; my emphasis). On the whole, it is difficult to know what to make of Kip's emergence as a warrior saint and his violent renunciation of European order. His condemnation seemingly entails an outright rejection of Western discourses, including the great maps, which he previously saw as guaranteeing order. Yet, if readers take Kip's message seriously and accept that Europeans cannot be trusted because their so-called civilized maps have always been documents of brutality, then what does this say about the status of Ondaatje's novel?

Novels are also maps, as readers have likely inferred.[10] As Huggan observes, in Canadian literature, during the second half of the twentieth century, "the map topos came to feature less as the abstract representation of the external environment than as a structural – and, by its very nature, restricted – metaphor for the creative act" (46). However, Kip's attack on Western maps emphasizes that every human artifact is suspect; even Ondaatje's novel cannot claim exemption from the chaos and decay that characterizes human history. In what can be taken as an attempt to account for his own fragmented, allegorical map, Ondaatje's narrator states that "many books open with an author's assurance of order ... But novels commenced with hesitation or chaos" (93). Later, he admits that, typically, the "successful defusing of a bomb ended novels. Wise white fatherly men shook hands, were acknowledged, and limped away, having been coaxed out of solitude for this special occasion" (105). In this novel, however, the fathers have all died, and those who remain alive are deemed untrustworthy. Moreover, as Kip intimates, there is seemingly no hope that anyone, not even the elect, can successfully defuse the threat posed by the nuclear bomb (285).

To its credit, *The English Patient*, in keeping with Findley's *Headhunter*, refuses to soften the blow of its portrait of humanity's ongoing catastrophe with divine images of reconciliation. Whereas Findley's novel outlines the limitations involved in positing the categories of the elect and non-elect by emphasizing the permeable boundary between the two, Ondaatje's novel underscores the violence inherent in creating the category of the elect. This is portrayed most obviously in the narrative's transformation of Kip into a "warrior saint." In keeping with Benjamin, it would seem that Ondaatje also believes that "not optimism, but pessimism is the order of the day": "And that means pessimism all along the line. Absolutely. Mistrust in the fate of literature, mistrust in the fate of freedom, mistrust in the fate of humanity, but three times mistrust in all reconciliation: between classes, between nations, between individuals" (*Reflections, Essays, Aphorisms, Autobiographical Writings* 191). If it is the case, as Benjamin argues, that only an unflinching account of catastrophe can inspire humanity with a longing for redemption, and thereby transform history's "deathmask into the angel's countenance," then the unresolved ending of Ondaatje's novel is apt.[11] In its final pages, the text offers only unreconciled fragments of profane existence, glimpses of Hana and Kip, living in their respective countries of origin, years after the war: "And so Hana moves and her face turns, and in a regret she lowers her hair. Her shoulder touches the edge of a cupboard and a glass dislodges. Kirpal's left hand swoops down and catches the dropped fork an inch from the floor and gently passes it into the fingers of his daughter, a wrinkle at the edge of his eyes behind his spectacles" (301–2). Although wholeness remains elusive, the text confirms that the allegorist's melancholy gaze can still forge connections and shape tableaus that implode space and time. In the text's final emblem, the entropic force of decline and the image of ruin, conveyed by Hana's "regret" and the falling glass that will presumably shatter, are countered not by divine intervention but by human action – a timely, skilful, and compassionate profane gesture.

Thus, Ondaatje, like Findley, perceives the Second World War as a watershed event in human history that necessitates a profound reconsideration of the nature of apocalypse and the traumatized victims of apocalyptic thinking. Although Findley's and Ondaatje's texts do not view the apocalyptic narrative in the same way and they rely on different techniques to subvert it, they share a preoccupation with history's beautiful losers and a belief in prophetic eschatology's ability to resist apocalypse. Indeed, with the exception of Atwood's short stories, the preoccupation with prophetic eschatology's capacity to counter apocalyptic eschatology is a unifying thread among the fictions in this study.

3

Margaret Atwood's "Hairball": Apocalyptic Cannibal Fiction

The previous chapters explored the ways in which *Headhunter* and *The English Patient* invoke a host of characteristic apocalyptic features. Rather than mobilize these features to recreate a full-blown apocalypse, however, both fictions rely on familiar apocalyptic topoi to launch a critique of apocalyptic eschatology. *Headhunter* challenges the apocalyptic narrative by blurring the boundary between the elect and the non-elect, thereby calling into question apocalyptic notions of perfection as well as the category of the Saints of God. While *The English Patient* maintains the latter category, it subverts the logic of apocalypse by adopting and adapting allegory, another of its key tropes. In contrast to the biblical apocalypse, which relies on allegory to promote the belief that God has everything under control, Ondaatje's novel uses allegory to highlight the devastation and ruin wrought by apocalyptic thinking. Although their strategies for subverting apocalypse differ, both Findley's and Ondaatje's anti-apocalyptic fictions stress the traumatic results of apocalyptic thinking and champion an alternative to apocalypse based on prophetic eschatology. This alternative approach looks to the past rather than to a future ushered in by violence and honours the earthly world and its inhabitants rather than destroying them in pursuit of the New Jerusalem.

This chapter focuses on Margaret Atwood's short story "Hairball," from her collection *Wilderness Tips*, and offers a more detailed examination of yet another aspect of apocalypse touched on in the earlier chapters, namely, the relationship between apocalypse and violence. While *The English Patient* and *Headhunter* reflect on apocalyptic violence, "Hairball," in contrast, excludes virtually all references to prophetic eschatology and, ultimately, any alternatives to the brutal logic of apocalypse. As a result, her apocalyptic story may well be the bleakest of all the works considered here because it demonstrates what happens when ruthless, future-oriented apocalyptic thinking goes unchallenged.

For Findley and Ondaatje the enemy is anyone who acts on his apocalyptic desires to destroy and consume this world to pave the way for the heavenly city. In "Hairball," Atwood portrays this enemy and emphasizes the rage unleashed on the non-elect, expressed most graphically in the fate of the Whore of Babylon. It is this largely over-looked aspect of apocalypse – the violent, cannibalistic feast and pur-gation of the non-elect – that Atwood's stories never let us forget. Furthermore, as her stories illustrate, in the case of the North Ameri-can settler-invader society, the apocalyptic violence that engendered Canadian nation-space legitimized the conquering of the Native peo-ples, the subjugation of women, and the commodification of the land-scape. Put somewhat differently, the Canadian nation was founded by establishing citizenship as a legal and political category for white males that historically excluded non-whites and women and that guaranteed the rights of those white male citizens over non-whites and women.

Although, according to Homi Bhabha, evidence of the violence that attends nation-building "must be forgotten," traces nevertheless remain. In Findley's *Headhunter*, Marlow literally finds traces (pho-tographs) of the children abused by the Club of Men, which lead him to Kurtz. Similarly, in Ondaatje's text, shattered geographies and bodies attest to the brutality of the seemingly unending wars launched to secure the nation-state – wars that culminate in the bombing of Japan. Referring to the events that led Joseph Conrad to pen *Heart of Darkness* (one of Findley's central intertexts), Kip specif-ically denounces the imperial powers that sanctioned this disaster: "'American, French, I don't care. When you start bombing the brown races of the world, you're an Englishman. You had King Leopold of Belgium and now you have fucking Harry Truman of the USA. You all learned it from the English'" (286). Whereas Findley's and Ondaatje novels forge links between apocalyptic eschatology and the Second World War, the fictions by Atwood, King, and Kogawa adopt a broader historical approach and link apocalypse to the formation of the nation-state and, more precisely, the violent appropriation of First Nations lands and cultures.

To refresh her readers' memories concerning the repressed violence at the beginning of Canadian history, Atwood's fiction draws on native Wendigo stories – tales of flesh-eating monsters. Rather than treat these tales as exotic artifacts of a primitive culture, "Hairball" invokes elements from Wendigo tales to highlight parallels between the settler-invader society's treatment of the non-elect – the Native peoples – and its treatment of women. At bottom, Atwood's stories underscore the connections among apocalypse, the legacy of imperialism and colonization, and the predatory and consumptive nature of apocalypse's gender politics. Indeed, parallels between violent events in "Hairball" and the biblical story Revelation show how women, like Native peoples, are viewed as figures of abjection to legitimize their marginalization and ultimate consumption.

The fate of promiscuous women looms large in the various stories collected in *Wilderness Tips*, a concern that also surfaces in Atwood's novel *The Robber Bride* (1993).[1] In Revelation, The Whore of Babylon's death stages an even more gruesome cannibal feast than the fate of Jezebel. As the angel says to John: "Come, I will show you the judgement of the great harlot who is seated upon many waters, and with whom the kings of the earth have committed fornication, and with the wine of whose fornication the dwellers on earth have become drunk" (17:1). The angel goes on to tell John: "the ten horns that you saw, they and the beast will hate the harlot; they will make her desolate and naked, and devour her flesh and burn her up with fire" (Rev. 17:16). Later, John hears "a great multitude in heaven, crying, 'Hallelujah! The smoke from her goes up for ever and ever'" (19:3). In addition to describing the cannibalistic orgy reserved for the Whore, the angel also describes the "great supper of God" in which "the flesh of kings, the flesh of captains, the flesh of mighty men, the flesh of horses and their riders, and the flesh of all men, both free and slave, both small and great" will be eaten (Rev. 19:17–19).

Atwood's focus on violence raises an important question: what exactly are readers to make of apocalypse's emphasis on violence and consumption? In *Death and Desire*, Tina Pippin concludes that Revelation is a misogynist, cannibal narrative, focusing on the "desire for and death of the female" (16). In the apocalyptic story, the body of woman "is marginalized ... or violently destroyed ... What is considered unclean and dangerous by the male hierarchy has to be placed outside the camp. Those on the inside ... in this cultural system are all male" (50). Only the 144,000 men "who have not defiled themselves with women" can enter the New Jerusalem (Rev. 14:4).

In her study, Pippin comments specifically on the famous mid-sixteenth-century Brussels Tapestry of the apocalyptic marriage that shows the marriage supper, "with a beautiful, smiling Bride with her arm around the Lamb ... [and] directly above the Bride's head lies the burning Whore, surrounded by flames with a look of horror on her face" (107). In the light of its treatment of women, Pippin concludes that Revelation is "the 'writing of the disaster' of the history of women in male-dominated societies" (79).

Mary Wilson Carpenter also explores the gendered nature of apocalyptic violence. She finds it disturbing that "even recent twentieth-century 'representations of apocalypse' have consistently overlooked [the fact]... that the violence of Revelation is *male* violence, and that it is a violence *between* men and *to* women" (110). "I would suggest," she asserts, "that it is the foregrounded and yet denied reference of the Whore to the female body that confers power on the spectacle of the destruction and consumption of 'Rome/Babylon'": "In the narrative of male sexual paranoia, 'Woman' must be constructed as that known object to which male anxiety can be transferred, either to secure male power or to be utterly destroyed – and consumed. Marilyn Frye notes that 'masculinist literature is abundant with indications of male cannibalism, of males deriving essential sustenance from females.' That image of the phallic 'horns' devouring the naked body of the Whore is surely one of these instances of 'male cannibalism'" (Carpenter 117). According to Revelation, John observes that on the forehead of the Whore "is written a name of mystery" (17:4). Steven Goldsmith argues that the Whore functions as a figure of indeterminacy; for this reason, she must be stripped naked, "unveiled in the ordinary sense of the word of apocalypse, and given a determinate meaning that allows the text to dismiss her and advance toward a vision of community centred on the Logos" (62). In keeping with these critics' insights, Atwood's use of the Wendigo story, with its theme of violent consumption, intimates that in contemporary Western society it is typically women who are demonized and consumed.

The links between apocalyptic violence, specifically metaphoric cannibalism, and women are evident throughout Atwood's corpus, beginning with her first novel, *The Edible Woman* (1969). More recently, in what the magazine *Saturday Night* playfully describes as her "Cannibal Lecture," Atwood professes her ongoing fascination with cannibalism and ponders how a "culture so boring as ours" has come to embrace the notion of the flesh-devouring Wendigo ("Cannibal Lecture" 81). In her lecture, given as part of the Clarendon Lecture Series at Oxford in 1991, she outlines the features of the Wendigo, the cannibal monster who stalks the northern Canadian wilderness and haunts the legends and stories of the Woodland Cree and the Ojibway. All accounts confirm that the Wendigo is "a giant spirit-creature with a heart and sometimes an entire body of ice"; endowed with "prodigious strength," it can travel "as fast as the wind" (Atwood, *Strange Things* 66). In stories featuring this creature, the fear generated by the Wendigo is twofold: "fear of being eaten by one, and fear of becoming one" (67). Ultimately, becoming one is the real horror, because, "if you go Wendigo, you may end by losing your human mind and personality and destroying your own family members, or those you love most" (67).

In a discussion of the portrait of the Wendigo found in longer literary narratives, Atwood offers a psychological explanation for its appearance and suggests that, in some cases, this otherworldly creature represents "a fragment of the protagonist's psyche, a sliver of his repressed inner life made visible" (*Strange Things* 74). In these narratives, the creature that the characters fear or dream about "splits off from the rest of the personality, destroys it, and becomes manifest through the victim's body" (74). In her subsequent analysis of Wayland Drew's novel *The Wabeno Feast* (1973), she argues that the monster offers a tangible illustration of your fate if you succumb to the desire to be superhuman – a desire that results in "the loss of whatever small amount of humanity you may still retain" (84).

Although readers may be unfamiliar with the Wendigo, nevertheless, its features are familiar: Findley portrays Kurtz as a Wendigo, a man who sacrifices children to fulfill his desire to rule his empire in a godlike fashion. Moreover, the Wendigo's status as a "fragment" that becomes "manifest through the victim's body" recalls Benjamin's approach to allegory "Hairball"'s reliance on bodily fragmentation mirrors Benjamin's understanding of the allegorist's use of "the body of the living person for emblematic purposes" (*The Origin of German Tragic Drama* 216). Viewed in this context, the Wendigo serves as an emblem of apocalyptic disaster.

At the conclusion of Atwood's lecture series, which repeatedly returns to the theme of the Wendigo, she states: "A number of you have asked me ... whether any of this stuff is connected at all with my own work. The answer, in a word, is Yes" (*Strange Things* 114). Although she is not known for penning folktales featuring monsters as swift as the wind who gobble up unsuspecting victims in the Canadian north, the stories in *Wilderness Tips* introduce themes of apocalyptic violence, specifically, the ruthless translation of individuals into commodities – metaphoric cannibalism – by adopting and strategically adapting many of the attributes associated with the Wendigo. Whereas non-Native readings of the Wendigo tend to categorize this figure as the fanciful product of an alien culture, Atwood must be credited for rejecting this approach. Instead, she takes the features of the cannibal monster and applies them to her characters. In doing so, she emphasizes that the forms of violence and greed associated with the cannibal monster are not restricted to Native culture but arise, more generally, in social systems in crisis. Atwood's emphasis on the Wendigo figure and on depictions of violence remind readers that the formation of the nation-state was predicated on apocalyptic thinking and entailed the violent subordination of Native peoples, ethnic minorities, women, and the wilderness. Rather than embrace the logic of apocalypse, however, Atwood's fiction, in keeping with Canadian writers' emphasis on history's beautiful losers, demonstrates the horrific legacy of apocalyptic thinking, which sacrifices this world and its inhabitants in pursuit of a heavenly future. This mode of thinking, with its characteristic cannibalistic violence, shapes both the condition of her characters' conflicts and their mode of resolving them. One story in particular – "Hairball" – draws out the central Wendigo characteristics that Atwood uses to delimit a conception of contemporary forms of apocalyptic violence. Although this chapter concentrates intensively on "Hairball," evidence of the relationship between the Wendigo tales and Atwood's stories, of the emphasis on cannibalistic violence, and, finally, of Atwood's view of how apocalyptic thinking affects people's lives is available in all of the stories.

Ironically, although Wendigo stories were initially viewed as illustrative of the violent, primitive nature of their creators, these stories represent Native peoples' response to the apocalyptic violence unleashed on them by non-Natives. In her description of the Wendigo, Atwood offers the standard account of the evil cannibal giant.[2] But this account omits crucial information concerning the meaning of the term and the evolution of Wendigo stories. Without this information, readers cannot fully appreciate how "Hairball" serves as apocalyptic crisis literature, emphasizing the dangers of apocalyptic thinking with its belief in the right of the powerful to silence and eradicate the powerless. Before looking at how the concept of the violent cannibal monster informs her writing, it is important to gain a broader understanding of this widely misunderstood figure.[3]

Basic misunderstandings can occur because the words of Algonkian-speaking peoples are "too often taken as literal (rather than imaginative or symbolic) representations of events" (Preston 112).[4] In the case of the word "Wendigo," Native author and ethnographer Basil Johnston states that non-Native peoples typically translate it as a cannibal monster. However, the word also functions symbolically to connote gluttony and "the image of excess" (*Ojibway Heritage* 66). According to Johnston, "turning Wendigo" is a real possibility because the word refers to the more abstract capacity for self-destruction.[5]

Confusion concerning the term "Wendigo" also arises from errors in translation. One well-known mistake was traced to a compiler of a dictionary, who entered the information regarding the word "Wendigo" and substituted the word "ghoul" for the appropriate word "fool" because he thought that the Native people meant "ghoul." But the correct translation was, indeed, "fool." Among the Northern Algonkians, the word "Wendigo" was frequently used to "denote something like 'a fool,'" namely, "an individual who had lost his or her wits, but never in the sense of 'a ghoul'" (Marano 124).

By far the greatest misunderstanding concerning the Wendigo (which directly relates to Atwood's depictions of violence) involves the belief that the image of the bloodthirsty cannibal monster sprang fully formed from within Native culture. Owing to significant changes in the representation of the monster,[6] a number of anthropologists now believe that "the attribute of cannibalism or the concept of Wendigo as a category or race of non-human entities developed after European contact" (Brown and Brighton 161). In the light of the evidence,[7] anthropologist Lou Marano concludes that the Europeans played a significant role in creating the cannibal monster on which they looked with such revulsion and fascination. Again, while the figure of the Wendigo may seem alien, it symbolizes an attitude that both Findley's and Ondaatje's anti-apocalyptic fictions warn against. In keeping with the mindset of the apocalyptic thinkers in *Headhunter* and *The English Patient*, the Wendigo's selfish greed knows no bounds and dispenses with all social responsibility in its violent, self-destructive quest.

Charles Bishop argues further that the incidence of Wendigo accusations, like the extensive witch trials in the United States, are tied to stress within the community. In the case of Native peoples in North America, this stress was largely brought about by dwindling resources and increased dependence on trading posts.[8] According to Bishop, the extermination of game aroused legitimate fears of starvation, which, in turn, led to increased reports of Wendigo behaviour.[9]

Wendigo tales, passed down from generation to generation, thus attest to the Native people's awareness that the Europeans' apocalyptic thinking posed a threat to the health and well-being of their society. A short fable, told by the Northern Algonkians, illustrates their understanding of the connection between the arrival of the Europeans and the Wendigo: "[Wahpun, the East Wind] saw that the living on this earth, they would require light to guide them through life ... Wahpun would [also] introduce many foreign wares from abroad to support life: food, tools, and raiment. 'Oh!' called out the Rabbit [Wahpus], yes you will introduce many useful things such as you mention, but you will also introduce the Weendigo [*sic*] who will cross the Atlantic and consume human flesh" (quoted in Morrison and Wilson 225). Told by an old man at an Indian feast at York Factory, in the fall of 1823, this story clarifies that the Wendigo is not indigenous, but crosses the Atlantic, arriving in conjunction with the Europeans.

Atwood's adaptation of the violent cannibal figure remains meaningless if Wendigo tales are dismissed as the fanciful product of an exotic culture or treated as so-called empirical facts about Native civilization. Instead, these tales must be read as apocalyptic disaster narratives that register the traumatic impact of imperialism and colonization. The links between the evolution of the violent, flesh-eating Wendigo and the arrival of the Europeans help to explain why Atwood can state emphatically that her stories are informed by Wendigo tales, even though they do not feature cannibal monsters from the Canadian north. This seeming inconsistency is resolved only if we recognize that the stories in *Wilderness Tips*, which span in narrative time from the 1940s to the 1980s, reveal the face of the "white cannibal" and the disastrous outcome of apocalyptic thinking.

By recounting parallel disasters and alluding to canonical disaster narratives of the settler-invader society, including *Frankenstein*, the Franklin Expedition, the Titanic, and Revelation, the stories in *Wilderness Tips* trace the post-contact Wendigo's mirror-image and expose the apocalyptic violence that underpins Western society.[10]

In effect, although their narrative strategies differ, Findley's, Ondaatje's, and Atwood's fictions take pains to expose the face of the white cannibal. This is the face that Marlow sees when he confronts Kurtz on his deathbed and Kurtz tells him to "'go out and light more fires ... [to provide] the stuff of a new world ready for the making'" (616). This is also the face that Kip names the "newly revealed enemy," when he learns about the bombing of Hiroshima and condemns the imperialist white races for their inhuman treatment of "the brown races of the world."

The apocalyptic violence at the heart of the Western and European models of society reaches pathological proportions in Atwood's "Hairball," a story that alludes simultaneously to Wendigo tales and to Revelation as it explores the life of Kat, a young Canadian woman who claws her way to a senior position at an avant-garde magazine in London, England. In Atwood's narrative, Kat, an ex-centric Canadian, initially chooses not to challenge the centre's power and control. Instead, like Findley's Kurtz, Kat is seduced by the centre's power and learns its strategies of competition, violence, and consumption; when "knives were slated for backs, she'd always done the stabbing" (46). Like Findley's Kurtz, Kat also subscribes to apocalypse's promise of redemption through violence. Indeed, her ruthless future-oriented and self-interested behaviour recalls both Kurtz's behaviour and the apocalyptic approach to knowledge outlined in Ondaatje's *The English Patient*. Kurtz dies unrepentant, but Kat lives to experience the disastrous repercussions of her apocalyptic thinking.

Early on, Kat becomes disillusioned with her exhausting life in England. We are told that she "got tired of the grottiness and expense of London" (38), its class divisions, competition, conspicuous consumption, and the English men, who were, according to Kat, "very competitive" and "liked to win" (39). For Kat, London is akin to Babylon – the decadent, oppressive locus of Roman might featured in Revelation. At this point, Kat, the colonial Canadian, has travelled to Rome and internalized the violent, apocalyptic strategies of the imperial rulers.

However, in contrast to *Headhunter* and *The English Patient*, "Hairball" never opposes apocalyptic thinking by prophetic eschatology. Instead, Kat infects others with the apocalyptic desire for perfection and perpetuates the belief that consumption leads to power. Contemplating the basis of her success, she explains: "What you had to make them believe was that you knew something they didn't know yet. What you also had to make them believe was that they too could know this thing, this thing that would give them eminence and power and sexual allure, that would attract envy to them – but for a price. The price of the magazine" (37). The story makes it clear, however, that like the Wendigo who eats and eats but is never sated, apocalyptic perfection is unattainable and, eventually, leaves everyone hungry and their lives in ruin. The people who buy the magazine are never satisfied because, as Kat admits, "it was all photography, it was all iconography ... This was the thing that could never be bought, no matter how much of your pitiful monthly wage you blew on snakeskin" (37). And even though Kat appears to be at the top of the food chain, she, too, remains impoverished and hungry. Unable to "afford many of the things she contextualized so well" (38), she gorges on "the canapes at literary launches in order to scrimp on groceries" (38).

Although initially Kat revels in her power and, like Findley's Kurtz, boasts that "it was like being God" (37), as a colonial in Britain, she is forced to admit that she was "of no class. She had no class" and is deemed to be of "no consequence" (38–9). Thus, despite her efforts to shed her marginal status, Kat remains one of Canada's beautiful losers, and, eventually, like Findley's Kurtz, she succumbs to illness. When Gerald, a scout from a new fashion magazine in Toronto recruits her, Kat, weary of life as an exile, is secretly grateful for the opportunity to escape.

Returning to Toronto with apparent cultural cachet, street smarts, and a heavy dose of imperialist pride, Kat views Canada as an antiquated colonial outpost. Even Gerald, who becomes her boss and lover, strikes her as uniformly harmless and bland. Initially, Kat does not recognize that her Canadian wilderness has tipped and that, in the consumer culture of the 1980s, the relationships between centre and margin, predator and prey, have become ambiguous. As in *Headhunter*, the city is no longer Toronto the Good, and the difference between good and evil is difficult to discern.

The narrative foreshadows the implications of this ambiguity early on, when Kat compares herself to Victor Frankenstein and brags that Gerald is "her creation" (36). But readers familiar with Mary Shelley's gothic tale know that Victor's apocalyptic belief that he is a father figure or creator of a new race is similarly hubristic. Later, after Gerald steals her job at the magazine, Kat identifies herself once again with Victor Frankenstein. She reads Gerald's betrayal as a predictable outcome: the "monster has turned on its own mad scientist. 'I gave you life!' she wants to scream at him" (45). Not only does the *Frankenstein* intertext underscore the basic confusion concerning who is in power, more importantly, it also reinforces Atwood's reliance on the Wendigo theme.

With its Arctic setting and emphasis on the doubled relationship between creature and creator, *Frankenstein* shares basic features of Wendigo stories. To recall Atwood's description of the Wendigo cited earlier, Frankenstein's monster represents a "fragment of the protagonist's psyche, a sliver of his repressed inner life made visible" (*Strange Things* 74). At one point, Victor Frankenstein admits that he considers his creature, the "being whom I had cast among mankind, and endowed with the will and power to effect purposes of horror, nearly in the light of my own vampire, my own spirit let loose from the grave and forced to destroy all that was dear to me" (Shelley 105). Read in the context of Benjamin's approach toward allegory, this monstrous fragment of Victor Frankenstein, which bears his name, is an allegorical "emblem of catastrophe."[11] Taken together, the parallels between Atwood's text, *Frankenstein*, Wendigo tales, and Benjamin's views about allegory signal a related desire to explore the violence – in this instance, specifically cannibalistic violence – that characterizes Western culture.

In her book *Cannibal Culture*, Deborah Root argues that the figure of the cannibal constitutes a powerful, albeit largely "elided and disavowed" metaphor for Western society: "The cannibal seeks human bodies to eat, and the desire for flesh generates escalating desire. This hunger for flesh is generalized into society as a whole when consumption is treated as a virtue and seen as a source of pleasure and excitement in itself. Consumption is power, and the ability to consume excessively and willfully becomes the most desirable aspect of power" (9). Her comments recall the perverse behaviour of Kurtz and the Club of Men in Findley's *Headhunter* – men who derive pleasure

from the slaughter of their own children. Viewed in the context of
Atwood's fiction, Root's insights also shed light on Kat's skill in making the public think that consumption equals power. Root argues further that the figure of the Wendigo offers an accurate picture of the
West because it is, paradoxically, both a hungry predator and something horribly confused and ill (201). In *Headhunter*, Kurtz embodies
this combination of predation and sickness. According to Root, this
predatory attitude and sickness persist because of Western culture's
inability to accept the centrality of its consumptive impulse. This
inability springs from two sources: a failure of reflexivity and a tendency to aestheticize and consume difference (xii).

Atwood avoids the trap of consuming difference and reifying
Native Wendigo stories because her fiction focuses on the presence of
the Wendigo in its European and Western narrative counterparts.
More specifically, the repeated allusions to *Frankenstein*, as well as
accounts of the ill-fated Franklin Expedition, the Titanic, and Revelation facilitate the type of reflexivity that Root argues is missing from
Western discourse because these intertexts remind readers that the
apocalyptic penchant for violence, and greed – metaphorically linked
to cannibalism and an appetite for human flesh – are inextricable elements of our own apocalyptic "cannibal culture." Relying on Western
culture's own canonical Wendigo tales, Atwood's stories underscore
the dangers inherent in apocalyptic thinking. In "Hairball," allusions
to *Frankenstein* warn against the apocalyptic desire to seize power
and transcend the limits of the earthly world – desires predicated on
the commodification of human beings.

In "Hairball," the motifs of violence, consumption, mental instability, and bodily fragmentation and ruin surface with a vengeance.
The story emphasizes the theme of consumption early on. When Gerald first meets Kat, he takes her to an expensive restaurant. After he
entreats her to consider working in Toronto, she coolly surveys the
posh establishment and asks, "Where would I eat?" He assures her
that Toronto is now the restaurant capital of the world and goes on to
enquire about her unusual name. Although the ostensible subject has
changed, they are still talking about consumption. "Is that Kat as in
Krazy?" he asks. She replies, "No ... It's Kat as in KitKat. That's a
chocolate bar. Melts in your mouth" (40). In this brief exchange, Kat
aligns herself with food.

The allusions to the consumption of human flesh in this and subsequent episodes may be read in the light of Northrop Frye's analy-

sis of the dialectical relationship between the Eucharist symbolism of the apocalyptic world and its demonic parody (see *The Anatomy of Criticism* 147–50). According to Frye, in the apocalyptic world we often "find the cannibal feast, the serving up of a child or lover as food" (*The Secular Scripture* 118). Findley's *Headhunter* offers a glimpse of the demonic feast in its portrayal of the Club of Men, fathers who sexually prey on and, on occasion, murder their own children.

An interesting parallel can also be drawn between Kat's remark about her name (which ties in with the preoccupation with chocolate throughout the story) and the Lakota term used for white people, "Wasi'chu," which means "fat-eater," or "greedy one who takes the fat." There are also strong similarities between "Wasi'chu" and the notion of the Wendigo. The Lakota term delineates "a particular mentality, a bizarre obsession that is organized almost entirely around consumption and excess" (Root 10).

In Atwood's fiction, the preoccupation with consumption and the parallels drawn between human beings and food reflect characteristic features of apocalyptic thinking, in which an elect treat the powerless non-elect as fodder to be disposed of or consumed, transformed, as Findley's Kurtz puts it, into "'the stuff of a new world ready for the making.'" In the end, it comes as no surprise in "Hairball" when Gerald, like Frankenstein's monster, usurps Kat's power: while she recovers from an operation to remove an ovarian cyst, Gerald fires her and takes over her job at the magazine. Wendigo legends confirm that it is better to be consumed outright than caught by the creature because the victim who walks out alive becomes a cannibal, totally devoid of individuality (see Columbo 3–4). After his encounter with Kat, Gerald adopts her apocalyptic mentality and emerges as a Wendigo.

Ultimately, it is Kat, like Findley's Kurtz, who epitomizes the sickness at the core of Western culture – a culture that is, paradoxically, both a hungry predator and something terribly confused and ill (Root 201). Much to Gerald's horror, Kat decides to save the cyst she dubs Hairball in a jar of formaldehyde and display it on her mantlepiece. She says that it is no different "than having a stuffed bear's head or anything else with fur and teeth looming over your fireplace ..." (34). Her comment forges a connection between Hairball and other uncanny creatures that haunt the wilderness. Its mysterious nature is also emphasized when Kat's doctor states that, while some people thought "it was present in seedling form from birth, it might also 'be the woman's undeveloped twin'; but, ultimately, what they really were was unknown" (46). His eerie pronouncement highlights the parallels between Kat's relationship to her cyst and the Wendigo's relationship to its victims. When Kat begins to converse with Hairball, it becomes apparent that, like the Wendigo, her cyst represents a fragment of her psyche made visible. In accordance with Atwood's description of the flesh-eating monster, Hairball manifests itself "through the victim's body," splits "off from the rest of the personality, and destroys it" (74).

Kat's treatment of her cyst also recalls Benjamin's understanding of allegory that "depends on the removal of elements from their organic context." In "Hairball," this process entails the actual removal of Kat's cyst from her body. Like the English patient's burned body, the cyst likewise functions as an allegorical fragment – an emblem of catastrophe. Furthermore, Kat's subsequent treatment of her cyst echoes Benjamin's assertion that the human body "could be no exception to the commandment which ordered the destruction of the organic so that the true meaning ... might be picked up from its fragments" (*The Origin of German Tragic Drama* 216). Sitting in front of her cyst, Kat states that Hairball "speaks to her without words ... What it tells her is everything she's never wanted to hear about herself. This is new knowledge, dark and precious and necessary. It cuts" (47).

Like Benjamin's melancholy allegorist who relies on consciously constructed allegories rather than beautiful, organic symbols to promote an intellectual response to history's decline, Atwood's stories force readers to come to terms with apocalyptic violence by fashioning grotesque, allegorical emblems of disaster that promote self-examination. Indeed, as the passage cited above demonstrates, these self-conscious, reflexive moments are embedded within the narrative itself. In another self-reflexive scene, Kat looks at herself in the mirror and ponders her violent, predatory behaviour – the smash-and-grab apocalyptic mentality that guided her every move. In accordance with apocalyptic thinking, she assumed she would attain paradise by engaging in violence. Ironically, paradise recedes, and her life is in ruins or, worse, has been entirely erased: "She's only thirty-five, and she's already losing track of what people ten years younger are thinking. That could be fatal. As time goes by she'll have to race faster and faster to keep up, and for what? Part of the life she should have had is just a gap, it isn't there, it's nothing" (46) . In keeping with allegory's connection to an awareness of loss – a loss tied to the illusory nature of apocalyptic progress and, more importantly, the trauma and devastation experienced by the non-elect – Kat realizes that her quest for power has not enhanced her life but, instead, eradicated it.

Her musings on the rat race, in conjunction with the description of her illness and subsequent infection as a "running sore, a sore from running so hard," also suggest that she has succumbed not to an isolated medical problem but to the diseased, obsessive lifestyle that characterizes Western culture's apocalyptic thinking. Like Findley's Kurtz and the Wendigo, Kat is both "sick *and* predatory" (Root 202). Toward the conclusion of "Hairball," Kat seethes with resentment because she has been consumed and rejected: Gerald fires her. To add insult to injury, after she is fired, she receives an invitation to a party hosted by Gerald and his wife, Cheryl.

Perhaps it is only fitting that Kat, whom the Lakota would view as a greedy "fat-eater," should find herself "crackling inside, like hot fat under the broiler" (47). But the story prevents the reader from deriving any satisfaction from her downfall, by making it clear that there is something horrifically familiar about the way in which this violent game of consumption played by men and women draws to a close. Parallels between this episode and the biblical story Revelation show how women, like Native peoples, are viewed as abject figures to legitimize their subordination and eventual destruction.

Imagining Gerald and his wife preparing for the party, Kat reels from the unfairness of it all: it is a "connubial scene. His conscience is nicely washed. The witch is dead, his foot is on the body, the trophy; he's had his dirty fling, he's ready now for the rest of his life" (47–8). The stark opposition between the death of the witch/whore and the marriage feast specifically recalls Revelation, in which the whore/goddess of Babylon is also murdered and eaten (17:16). Echoing the famous Brussels Tapestry of the apocalyptic marriage, the Bride – here, Gerald's wife – dines at the eucharistic wedding feast. In this case, Atwood's allusions to the marriage supper coupled with references to the Wendigo story, with its emphasis on violence and consumption, suggest that, in Western society, more often than not, it is women who are annihilated.[12]

Kat's position as the lone female entrepreneur forced to work with an all-male board of Canadian businessmen also ironically recalls the fate of the goddess of Babylon. Kat likewise offends the male hierarchy. They "think she's too bizarre, they think she goes way too far" (44–5). Kat's fate recalls Tina Pippin's assertion that the story of Revelation portrays the "ultimate release of a colonized people" – a release figured by the murder and consumption of a powerful female (28). At bottom, Kat threatens the male hierarchy and in keeping with the apocalyptic plot, they place her "outside the camp" (Pippin 50). Only domesticated women – women willing to serve the dominant order's agenda are allowed through the gates.

"Hairball" is particularly intriguing because Kat attempts to challenge the misogynist ideology that informs the biblical cannibal narrative, although the outcome of her challenge remains unclear. In a gesture of defiance (and a most disquieting culinary endeavour), Kat buys two dozen chocolate truffles, nestles her cyst in the box of goodies, and sends the package to Gerald's wife. All along, the text has hinted at the violent and consumptive basis of their relationship, but, with this act, Kat foregrounds a distinctly apocalyptic, cannibalistic element. Again, viewed in terms of Benjamin's theory of allegory, Kat assumes the role of the melancholy allegorist, preparing a fragment of her own body "for emblematic purposes." She is confident that Gerald and his wife will interpret this allegory as an emblem of catastrophe: "Cheryl [Gerald's wife] will open it in public, in front of everyone. There will be distress, there will be questions. Secrets will be unearthed. There will be pain. After that, everything will go way too far" (48).

Afterward, feverish and weak, Kat "foolishly" walks out into the snowfall: "She intends to walk just to the corner, but when she reaches the corner she goes on ... She has done an outrageous thing, but she doesn't feel guilty. She feels light and peaceful and filled with charity, and temporarily without a name" (48). On the one hand, her gruesome gift, coupled with her "foolish" disappearance into the snow, and the erasure of her name (a sign of her humanity) suggest that she has "gone Wendigo."[13] Like the poor souls caught by the cannibal monster, Kat ends up losing her human mind and destroying those she loves. Interpreted in this way, this episode suggests that, in the end, she is merely a victim of her own apocalyptic thinking.

On the other hand, one could argue that by assuming the role of the allegorist and self-consciously treating a fragment of her body as message for public consumption, Kat manages to transform apocalypse's cannibalistic violence into a conscious, Christ-like act of communion.[14] Read in this way, the erasure of her name can be viewed as a liberating gesture that confounds the apocalyptic narrative, akin to the tactics of the intentionless state of being and invisibility championed by the English patient in Ondaatje's text.[15]

In offering her cyst to her lover, Kat forcibly reminds Gerald and, presumably, his guests that their lives, not to mention the nation itself, are predicated on sacrifice.[16] More important, Hairball will remind them that the bodies they degrade, consume, and forget are, in fact, sacred because they ensure the continued existence of the human community. The emphasis on community and communion, in contrast to the greed of isolated individuals, once again recalls the distinction drawn in the previous chapters between prophetic and apocalyptic eschatology. In both Findley's and Ondaatje's novels, individuals battle against apocalyptic thinking by turning toward the past, celebrating the value of earthly communities, and demonstrating that redemption lies in fulfilling the unrealized, utopian dreams of history's beautiful losers. Yet, although Kat gestures toward history's losers, she draws the community's attention to apocalyptic violence through a violent gesture. As a result, the story never proposes a radical alternative to apocalyptic thinking. Instead, with this gesture, Kat invites everyone to do what she has done, and what Atwood has been doing throughout *Wilderness Tips*, namely, to look in the mirror, reflect on our own greedy and violent behaviour – the legacy of the apocalyptic paradigm at the heart of our own disaster narratives – and acknowledge the face of the white cannibal.

To promote this acknowledgement, Atwood essentially relies on a grotesque joke, what critics term "gallows humour." Although some readers might not view Kat's packaging of her cyst in a chocolate box and sending it to her lover's wife as a humourous episode, it does fall under the definition of "trauma humour." Through a structure of partial imitation of the original traumatic violence, "trauma humour allows the indirect expression of repressed traumatic memories" (Fagan 117). This ability to witness apocalyptic violence and respond with a sense of humour ties Atwood's fiction to Tom King's *Green Grass, Running Water*, the focus of the next chapter. But, in contrast to Atwood's story, which includes a single instance of black comedy, in King's novel trauma humour is pervasive. In *Green Grass, Running Water*, characters replay the traumatic impact of the apocalyptic violence unleashed on First Nations' people repeatedly, often in humourous ways. These repetitions are "a form of resistance, but they also continually connect the characters back to their abusive pasts" (Fagan 115). In Atwood's story, Kat's "joke" is also a form of resistance that nevertheless remains complicit, locked in the continual repetition of apocalyptic violence. By contrast, in King's text, humour is far more liberating because it is used in conjunction with the Sun Dance, an alternative to the violent apocalyptic paradigm.

4

Mapping and Dreaming: Resisting Apocalypse in *Green Grass, Running Water*

Contemporary Canadian writers take great pains to emphasize the trauma and devastation instigated by apocalyptic thinking and to demonstrate the necessity of challenging the apocalyptic paradigm, the visionary tool Western culture overtly and covertly uses to establish meaning. Whereas Findley's *Headhunter* and Ondaatje's *The English Patient* champion prophetic eschatology as an alternative to apocalypse, Atwood's "Hairball" offers no such alternative and, as a result, highlights the disaster that ensues when apocalyptic violence goes unchallenged. Owing to the emphasis on the figure of the Wendigo, Atwood's story alludes to the fact that apocalyptic violence was used to pave the way for Canada's creation as a nation-state, a process that involved the genocide of Native North Americans and the appropriation of their land. Whereas the connection between apocalyptic violence and the formation of the nation-state remains latent in Atwood's "Hairball," it is a central and explicit theme in Tom King's *Green Grass, Running Water*.

In effect, all of the works in this study highlight the trauma and loss experienced by those deemed the non-elect. Whereas *Headhunter*, *The English Patient*, and Kogawa's *Obasan* approach these subjects with gravity, "Hairball" briefly demonstrates the possibility of relying on gallows humour to cope with apocalypse's horrific brutality. In *Green Grass, Running Water*, King adopts an entirely comic approach to examine the traumatic impact of apocalyptic eschatology on Native North Americans. Both Atwood's and, to a much greater extent, King's comic approaches raise a fundamental question, namely, why do some writers, particularly North American Native writers, combine the brutal aspect of apocalypse with "the hilarious, the traumatic with the absurd" (Fagan 103). Referring to the bitter humour that pervades contemporary Native writing, Native author Paula Gunn Allen points out that Native humour was transformed by the devastation of European contact: "It's almost gallows humour ... [W]hen you've gone through five hundred years of genocidal experiences, when you know that the other world that surrounds you wants your death and that's all it wants, you get bitter. And you don't get over it. It starts getting passed on almost genetically. It makes for wit, for incredible wit, but under the wit there is a bite" (interview 21–2). In addition to recognizing the link between humour and survival, Kristina Fagan argues that what she terms "trauma humour" is frequently used by Native writers due to the prohibition against bearing witness in most Native cultures. As she explains, the accepted Western process of bearing witness violates three traditional ethics of Northern Native peoples: first, the ethic of non-interference – essentially, the belief that it is wrong to confront people, to give advice, or to interfere or comment on people's behaviour if this information has not been requested; second, the ethic of emotional restraint – simply put, the belief that it is wrong to express anger and grief, especially toward family members; and third, what has been called "The Doctrine of Original Sanctity" – the belief that people are fundamentally good and that emphasis should be placed on promoting the restoration of that goodness, rather than the revealing, prohibition, and punishment of wrongs (Fagan 109–10). An understanding of these ethics helps to explain why King uses a comic approach to tackle traumatic events. Simply put, humour allows Native peoples to respect and evade these ethics or "to communicate the hidden and taboo without openly revealing deep negative emotions and without directly interfering with, criticizing or blaming others" (111–12) .

Although King's novel invokes "trauma humour," it is far more liberating than Atwood's story because King's narrative also emphasizes Native people's capacity to generate alternatives to apocalypse's individualistic, future-oriented maps. In an effort to challenge and, in many cases, to offer alternatives to the apocalyptic paradigm, the fictions in this study, with the exception of Atwood's story, repeatedly turn to the possibilities associated with prophetic eschatology, an approach characterized by its focus on the earthly world and humanity's capacity to work toward redemption. Furthermore, in the texts considered thus far, prophetic eschatology and humanity's ability to avert apocalyptic disaster are linked to the secular discourse of art and, in the case of *The English Patient*, the discourses of science and religion.

In *Headhunter*, for example, Marlow, who "used literature as psychotherapy" because "he believed in its healing powers," suggests that by reading *Anna Karenina* and learning of the tragic end of the heroine, suicidal individuals can avoid replicating the apocalyptic fiction. "Many a suicide had been thwarted because of Anna's death," Marlow asserts, although he goes on to admit that "the trouble was, with books, that no one read any more. That way, trains still claimed many victims" (186). As Atwood's story "Hairball" reminds us, however, the claiming of victims, specifically, the death and dismemberment of the wayward, sexual, mysterious female (including that of Tolstoy's heroine), should not be understood as a random narrative event, but, instead, as an integral feature of Western culture's most cherished visionary tool: apocalypse. Indeed, the route to apocalypse leads "through massacre and terror" (Cohn, *The Pursuit of the Millennium* 125)

What is it, then, that art can do to prevent people from adopting this route? The above quotation from *Headhunter* suggests that art can offer an imaginative context in which to explore the repercussions of the apocalyptic paradigm, thereby obviating the need to act out Armageddon to its grisly conclusion. This is precisely the strategy that Atwood uses in her story "Hairball." But, in addition to offering warnings about the dangers of apocalyptic thinking, *Headhunter* and, to a greater extent, *The English Patient* suggest that the discourses of art, science, and religion can function as a map that may furnish the community with a valuable index to the past and, more specifically, to the wisdom and utopian dreams of history's anonymous losers. By maintaining a focus on this world rather than a heavenly world and by remembering the victims of history and redeeming their unfulfilled aspirations, prophetic eschatology is able to resist apocalyptic eschatology.

In keeping with the works examined thus far, Thomas King's novel *Green Grass, Running Water* also invokes a strategy akin to prophetic eschatology and emphasizes the capacity of art to link a community to its past and to furnish individuals with an alternative to the future-oriented apocalyptic paradigm. However, these fictions differ in their estimation of the timing of apocalyptic disasters. Although all of the fictions allude to the traumatic impact of the legacy of imperialism, colonization, and the creation of the nation-state – the proverbial New Jerusalem – Atwood's and King's fictions specifically link apoc- alypse to the disastrous clash between the settler-invader society and North American Native people. And, like Atwood's "Hairball," King's novel draws attention to this historical moment by inviting readers to consider a particular instance of intercultural communica- tion. Whereas Atwood addresses the portrayal and significance of the Wendigo figure in Western culture, King examines the status of the book in Native culture. Moreover, in keeping with *Headhunter*'s and *The English Patient*'s emphasis on prophetic eschatology and the rev- erence for the discourses of art, religion, and science, King's novel shows how the book, adopted and adapted by Native writers, can function as a communal map that offers an alternative to apoca- lypse's individualistic, future-oriented map. In this way, King's novel elaborates on the intriguing connection between fiction-making and cartography outlined in Ondaatje's novel.

The title of this chapter is drawn from Hugh Brody's *Maps and Dreams*, a text that charts Brody's experience with the Beaver people of the eastern foothills of the Rocky Mountains. In the 1970s, Brody spent eighteen months helping the Beaver people create maps that would indicate the ways in which they had used their lands within living memory. At one point, Brody's Native companions invited him to join them on a hunting trip and, while resting by the fire, they told him that "Indian guys, old-timers, they make maps too" (45). They went on to explain that these maps were revealed in dreams and showed the place where the trails of animals converge and that some of the "really good men" could also see the "dream-trails to heaven" (46). "The dream map was as large as the table top, and had been folded tightly for many years. It was covered with thousands of short, firm, and variously coloured markings ... Abe Fellow and Aggan Wolf explained. Up here is heaven; this is the trail that must be followed; here is a wrong direction; this is where it would be worst of all to go; and over there are all the animals. They explained that all of this had been discovered in dreams. Aggan also said that it was wrong to unpack a dream map except for very special reasons. But the Indians' needs had to be recognized ... Everyone must look at the map now" (267). The men recognized that Brody might find their idea of mapping absurd. "You might say such maps are crazy," they told him. "But maybe the Indians would say that is what your maps are ... Different maps from different people – different *ways*" (45–6).

Brody's experience testifies to the fact that Native American peoples have repeatedly asserted the legitimacy of their own maps and contested European maps and strategies of mapping, which have played a central role in conceptualizing, codifying, and regulating the vision of the settler-invader society. The model of reality afforded by the Western map contributed to the rigidly dualistic philosophy that has enabled Western civilization "to confirm its absolute space of reasonableness, cleanliness, freedom and wealth, precisely by creating equally absolute but sealed-off spaces of madness, dirt, slavery and poverty" (Vernon 17). Chandra Mukerji puts it even more bluntly when she states that "the meaning of land as property to be consumed and used by Europeans was written into the language of maps just as the meaning of the world as sign of God had been in the late Middle Ages" (31). In essence, the Western map replicated apocalypse's division between the elect and the non-elect and legitimized the rights of the former to claim the possessions of the supposed non-elect.

In *Green Grass, Running Water* (1993) Cherokee/Greek/German novelist Thomas King revises inherited apocalyptic maps and replaces them with representations that speak to a Native worldview. But before turning to his text's interrogation of Western culture's apocalyptic maps and mapping strategies, it is necessary to outline the fluid relationship that King and others envision as existing between maps and books. Without this information, readers will be unable to appreciate how King's text champions art and can itself be understood an alternative map that subverts the logic of apocalypse. In his study *Book of the Fourth World*, George Brotherson stresses the importance of viewing Native maps (forms of Native pictorial discourse) and literary texts as closely related and equally legitimate modes of representation. Brotherson notes the problems that arise when Native visual modes of representation, examples of which he terms "classic texts," are not recognized as belonging to the categories of "script" and/or "text": "The concept of the Fourth World text and literature in general has been especially fragmented as a result of having had imposed upon it imported notions of literary medium. For a start, jejune Western pronouncements on what does and does not constitute script, and the categorical binary that separates oral from written, have proved especially inept when applied to the wealth of literary media in native America ... Whole modes of representation have as a result been simply ignored, along with the configuring of space and time whose reason is assumed in the placement and enumeration of every native detail" (4). Brotherson further maintains that, even within the Western philosophical tradition, the overlap between writing and pictorial and/or oral modes of representation has been recognized: "for Derrida [in *Of Grammatology*] 'writing' is in fact present everywhere, in gesture and speech itself, in the traces and paths of landscape" (42).[1]

Green Grass, Running Water adopts this broad understanding of "writing" and opens with an examination of a Native "classic text," namely, the Fort Marion Ledger Art. King's novel underscores how this text affirmed Native people's solidarity in the face of exile and territorial dispossession and recalls how it revised the status of the "book" in Native culture. In King's novel, writing and mapping represent complicitous activities that often serve to secure a Western worldview. Owing to the close relationship he perceives between visual and written forms of codification, and the role they have played in securing the settler-invaders' understanding of "reality," King's project also involves subverting a whole range of Western representational strategies, including the map, the linear narrative (in books – particularly the Bible – but in movies, as well), the stereotype, and literacy itself. The project's ultimate goal is to paralyse the apocalyptic narrative.

Works by other Canadian writers frequently strive toward a "cartography of difference, which endorses a dynamic view of cross-cultural exchange," but their efforts remain primarily directed "toward a de/reterritorialization of Western culture" (Huggan 24). This is precisely what sets King's novel apart from other fictions, including the works discussed in previous chapters. *Green Grass, Running Water* succeeds in articulating a native cosmography, and, as we will see, serves as a map in the traditional, Native sense of the word. More specifically, through its allusions to and depictions of the Sun Dance, the novel counters the traumatic impact of apocalyptic violence by inscribing a radical alternative to apocalypse: the text offers an aboriginal conception of the world, akin to prophetic eschatology, in which the individuals can locate themselves at the centre of a land-based, communal, and non-hierarchial spiritual practice that involves both body and soul.

In this trickster-infused fiction, the incarceration of the seventy-two Indians at Fort Marion in the late 1800s serves as a formal and thematic touchstone that highlights the novel's challenge to the imposition of non-Native boundaries and enclosures and, more generally, to European modes of mapping. King repeatedly alludes to the historical events described by Sidney Lanier, the Southern musician and poet, in a letter to his sister: "I saw seventy two big Indians yesterday: proper men, and tall, as one would wish to behold. They were weary, and greatly worn; but as they stepped out of the cars [of the train], and folded their ample blankets about them, there was a large dignity and majestic sweep about their movements that made me much desire to salute their grave excellencies. Each had his ankles chained together; but managed to walk like a man, withal. They are confined, – by some ass who is in authority – in the lovely old Fort, as unfit for them as they for it. It is in my heart to hope sincerely that they may all get out" (Lanier 115). Readers first become aware of this event's significance in the opening section of *Green Grass, Running Water*, when Dr Alberta Frank, a professor of Native history at the University of Calgary, delivers a lecture on the subject to her students. The novel continues to emphasize the event's centrality by concluding each of its four sections with a portrayal of a variety of mythical protagonists being dragged off to the Fort. The repeated allusions to Fort Marion raise a number of questions, including what led to the Native people's incarceration, and what happened at the Fort. But readers must also consider why King focuses on this particular historical incident and how it informs his novel.

In the summer of 1874, government officials launched a brutal campaign to force the remaining Plains Indian tribes onto reservations. That same year, various tribes, including the Cheyenne, Arapaho, Kiowa, Plains Apache, and Comanche had broken out of their reservations to prevent the extermination of the buffalo. To protect the remnant of the southern herd on the High Plains, these tribes fought engagements at Adobe Walls, Anadarko, and Palo Duro Canyon (see Meredith 92–3). Determined to maintain a traditional life, members of these tribes protested against the slaughter of the buffalo and the limited and artificial boundaries imposed on their people.[2] To forestall their efforts, the military hounded the tribes and burned their camps, one after another. Although the Native people attempted to outrun the army, they had no time to hunt and replenish their supplies. First their horses died of exhaustion and hunger; then, after one of the most severe winters of the decade set in, the Indians themselves began to perish. Finally, starving and freezing, the remaining members of the tribes made their way on foot to the agency and surrendered (see Peterson, chapter 1).

To ensure the complete subjugation of the Plains Indians, the government subsequently rounded up the so-called "notorious hostiles," a total of seventy-two individuals accused of crimes against white settlers and soldiers. After the Indians surrendered to the agency, those considered guilty were imprisoned and "the most hostile were placed in double irons" (Peterson 15). While the rest of their people were sent to reservations, these so-called "hostiles" were chained to wagons and initially transported to Fort Sill, in what is now known as Oklahoma. Shortly after, in April 1875, "without a trial or a hearing," the prisoners were chained to wagons and carried away under guard "to what they believed would be their execution" (Peterson 15). Their journey ended at Saint Augustine, Florida. Sidney Lanier encountered them on 21 May, the day they arrived and were interned in the dank, seventeenth-century Spanish stone fort, then called Fort Marion.

King's text repeatedly and humourously depicts this journey. Here, the use of repetition and humour signal the impact of trauma; humour and trauma both arise "out of the imitation and repetition of previous events" (Fagan 115). In the case of trauma, the experience is repeated again and again "through flashbacks, nightmares, and worst of all, through repetitive, destructive actions" (115). In this way, the body speaks what the mind refuses to know. But, in addition to relying on "trauma humour" to restage the brutal, apocalyptic violence unleashed on the Plains Indian tribes, the novel also alludes to what happened at Fort Marion and highlights the unusual fact that the prisoners became warrior-artists. Although the government's behaviour was brutal, it is unlikely that the fate of the seventy-two prisoners, or the "Florida Boys" as they were called, would have garnered public attention, if their jailer, Lieutenant Richard H. Pratt, had not decided to launch an experiment in penal reform – an experiment that had tremendous repercussions in Canada.[3] Pratt insisted that his charges be taught reading and writing, be given religious instruction, and be assigned to manual labour. More important, Pratt allowed them to earn money and privileges by making items to sell to tourists. The prisoners produced trinkets, such as polished sea beans, bows and arrows, as well as beautifully rendered drawing books filled with autobiographical pictures. Nowadays, these books, which sold in the 1800s for two dollars apiece, have garnered considerable fame. They contain striking images of the Native peoples' life on the Plains, their journey to Fort Marion, and their experience as prisoners, and are known collectively as the Plains Indian Ledger Art.

In the first section of King's novel, Dr Alberta Frank lectures on the Fort Marion episode and the creation of Plains Indian Ledger Art. She relates the gruesome story of the prisoners, including what happened to the Cheyenne Indian Grey Beard, who, after jumping from a window of the train with chains on his hands and legs, was hunted down and shot (against orders) by his captors. She goes on to explain that, when they arrived at Fort Marion, Pratt provided the men with drawing materials, ledger books, and coloured pencils, as "a way to help reduce the boredom of confinement" (15). She then shows her students slides of the inmates' art, but they pay no attention. Even though Dr Frank warns them that the drawings will be on the test, her students remain uninterested. The episode draws to a close after the only attentive pupil, Helen Mooney, asks a simple yet pertinent question:

"Professor Frank," Helen said, "the seventy-one Indians. The ones at Fort Marion. I was wondering."
"About what?"
"Well, for one thing, what happened to them?" (17)

Her question remains unanswered; yet, owing to the emphasis placed on this event, readers sense that they overlook the importance of this history lesson at their peril.

As noted, the text emphasizes the centrality and traumatic nature of this incident by circling back to the fate of the inmates at Fort Marion at the end of each of its four sections. This circular structure has the effect of replaying the abuse over and over, mimicking the structure of a traumatic flashback. In section one, the narrator tells Coyote a story that concludes with soldiers putting the mythical First Woman and Ahdamn on a train to Florida. We are told that "there are a bunch of Indians on that train with chains on their legs. First Woman and Ahdamn have chains on their legs, too" (82). When they

arrive in Florida, they all "sit around and draw pictures" (82).
Although Ahdamn loves having people from "New York and
Toronto and Chicago and Edmonton come down to Florida" to watch
him draw, First Woman refuses to remain imprisoned (82). Disguis-
ing herself as the Lone Ranger, she strolls out of the front gate, leaving Ahdamn behind (83).

In the next section, the narrator tells Coyote a story featuring
Changing Woman; this tale ends similarly with the protagonist being
dragged by soldiers down a dirt road. When Changing Woman looks
around, she sees that there "are soldiers with rifles everywhere. And
there are Indians, too. There are Indians sitting on the ground drawing pictures" (188). In the third section, the narrator's tale featuring
Thought Woman likewise concludes in what is, by now, a familiar
fashion, although to reflect the changing times (presumably the
1960s), the soldiers who arrest Thought Woman have flowers in their
hair. In the final section, the narrator's story about Old Woman concludes in the same way, with the military putting the protagonist on
a train to Florida. When Thought Woman arrives, she meets the same
fate as the other mythical characters: the soldiers "throw her in Fort
Marion" (349).

In effect, King's novel promotes Benjamin's "allegorical way of seeing" by using fragments of the brutal historical episode to fashion an
allegory that speaks of the disastrous impact of the settler-invader
society on the Plains Indians. This objective, intellectual approach is
echoed by Dr Frank's formal academic lecture. Yet each humourous
repetition allows King to tell the story of the traumatic event – essentially to witness the apocalypse and convey its horror – without
transgressing Native beliefs about the impropriety of speaking
directly or accusingly about negative experiences. In addition to voic-
ing trauma, King's parodic imitations of the historical event are also
a form of resistance that reverse the hierarchy: readers are invited to
laugh at the settler-invader society; "Joking is an act of power and
Native people laughing at white society thus transgresses the usual
power dynamics. Furthermore, in a reversal of the standard direction
of the appraising gaze, Native people turn the eye of judgement back
on the whiteman" (Fagan 30).

Despite its subversive features, King's "trauma humour" nevertheless continually connects the characters back to an episode of
abuse. Ultimately, the repeated emphasis on the historical event con-

veys the overwhelming impression that North American Native people, scapegoated as members of the non-elect, remain trapped in a
sociopolitical situation akin to a rigged game of *Monopoly*. No matter
what card the Native characters draw from the Chance pile, it always
says the same thing: "Go to Jail." That being said, King could have
chosen any number of historical encounters between non-Native and
Native people to illustrate this point. Is there, then, something unique
about the Fort Marion incident that led King to select it?[4]

Given the novel's emphasis on the prisoner's artwork, King may
have chosen this incident because it draws specific attention to
Native acts of self-representation and to the status of the book, in particular. Unlike many other historical events, the Fort Marion episode
reflexively addresses what it means for Native people to disseminate
artistic representations of tribal life in the overarching context of
widespread domination by the settler-invader society. By adopting
the fate of the "Florida Boys" as a primary intertext, King self-consciously positions himself as a contemporary warrior-artist, whose
work, like that of the Fort Marion prisoners, speaks both of the need
for resistance and for the preservation of Native rituals and tradition.
For the inmates of Fort Marion and for King, the book serves as
repository of Native ritual and tradition. To borrow a central
metaphor from the novel – a metaphor that this chapter will go on to
explore – both the ledger books and *Green Grass, Running Water* serve
as maps that challenge European modes of apocalyptic plotting. In
keeping with Canadian writers' tendency to promote prophetic
eschatology as an alternative to apocalyptic eschatology, King's communal map looks to the past and can be used by Native and non-
Native people alike to counteract apocalypse's violent, individualistic, and future-oriented approach.

The role played by the map in Native culture should not be underestimated. Long before contact, Indian peoples of the Great Plains
were accomplished mapmakers.[5] They also possessed a strong sense
of history and were accustomed to plotting their history pictorially:
"Images inscribed on rock walls served for hundreds of years as a
large-scale, public way of marking historical events and visionary
experiences. Narrative scenes on buffalo hide robes and tipis provided records of a man's experiences and visions. His exploits in war
or success in the hunt would be painted on his garments and his shel-
ter to validate and memorialize those heroic deeds. This was personal

history made public, for all to see" (Berlo, *Drawing and Being Drawn In* 12). Modes of representation changed, however, when non-Native explorers and traders began travelling across the Great Plains introducing different methods and materials for inscribing history. Owing to their encounters with non-Natives, Plains Indians began drawing their maps and inscribing historical information into books. The Indians' newfound regard for books was twofold, resulting from the influence of white culture and also from "an indigenous Aboriginal belief in the power of history and of images, now combined with a new belief in the power of the written word" (16).

Through its allusions to the Fort Marion episode and Plains Ledger Art, King's novel emphasizes that, for Native writers, the tradition of drawing on paper and in books is fundamentally "an art of intercultural communication" (Berlo, *Drawing and Being Drawn In* 13). The self-conscious allusions to the Fort Marion Ledger Art also remind readers that books by Native authors (and *Green Grass, Running Water* is no exception) constitute a complex polyphonic discourse located at the interface between two radically distinct cultures. However, garnering a profit of upward of five thousand dollars, the Fort Marion ledger books painfully demonstrate that the "interface" between cultures was not based on equality. The patronage of whites, who placed orders for painted fans and requested duplicates of ledger books they fancied, exposed what some critics refer to as "the unspoken truth of the Anglo-Indian relationship," namely, that Indians "existed for the convenience and entertainment of white society" (Wade and Rand 48).

The text's references to the Fort Marion Ledger Art not only shed light on the exploitative and performative expectations that characterized Native/white relations, but also underscore the powerful role played by books in the preservation of Native culture. The creation of "small but eloquent" autobiographical images helped to keep a tribal spirit alive inside men "whose hair had been cut and who were forced to wear military-issue garments" (Berlo, *Drawing and Being Drawn In* 14). When a warrior who has been transformed into a schoolboy and forced to wear a blue serge uniform draws pictures of the old way of life, he is "keeping that way of life alive" because "to draw the past is to remember it and to convey it to others" (14). Thus, at a pivotal, apocalyptic moment in Native history, when Plains cultures were under siege, when people were being hounded onto reservations, and when the foundation of tribal existence was being challenged – violence unleashed in support of the creation of the purified nation-state – books served as repositories for Native wisdom and tradition. In *Headhunter* and *The English Patient*, the discourse of art was seen as crucial in resisting the apocalyptic paradigm. Similarly, for the Plains Indians, books served both as a means of witnessing the traumatic impact of the settler-invaders and, to borrow Benjamin's words, as an "index" or map that can direct humanity away from apocalypse. In accordance with the other works in this study, the aim of King's discursive map is to redeem history's anonymous losers, whose "cries for help, silent revolt, or their loud protests were not listened to by their contemporaries" (Honneth 128).

The words "revolt" and "protest" are especially apt in this case because ledger books and the Fort Marion books, in particular, did not simply record personal and public history, they were also inextricably connected to Native resistance. The simple act of writing in a ledger book must be considered, in and of itself, as a gesture of defiance and self-assertion: "During the most brutal and extensive period of U.S. government violence against Native Americans, between roughly 1860 and 1900, certain warriors of the Great Plains would take ledger books, turn them horizontally, and begin to draw. These narrow, lined vertical bound books, meant for recording details of commerce or tallying prisoners, were unmistakable artifacts of white settlers and the United States military ... [The Indians drew] over this space of foreign calculations, thereby transforming the nature of their own drawing and the ledger book itself, creating a middle place, an in-between place, in a place of writing" (Blume 40). Blume further likens the ledger book to a silent rifle, that, once possessed, "even without the necessary ammunition, could potentially give the warrior some of the power of his opponents, which had proven to be so devastating" (42).

Not surprisingly, given the circumstances of their production, the drawings of the Fort Marion prisoners register profound transformations in Native practices of self-representation. Whereas, in the past, Native peoples typically recorded individual heroic deeds, the warriors imprisoned in Fort Marion articulated an emerging sense of community and an appreciation of domestic life, both of which signalled a significant departure from earlier forms of representation: "The art of Fort Marion prisoners affirmed more general ideals of social solidarity through the exploration of tribal histories, elevation of the commonplace as a central artistic theme, and assertion of

Native American dignity in the face of cultural purification experiments. The drawings made at Fort Marion from 1875 to 1878 are nothing less than an incipient national literature" (Wade and Rand 45). Furnished with only this cursory understanding of the Fort Marion incident, readers can appreciate why King's text acknowledges its debt to this "incipient national literature" – a national literature that recalls prophetic eschatology.

Turning to *Green Grass, Running Water*, one can identify virtually all of the characteristics associated with the creation of Fort Marion Ledger Art. First, as many critics have argued, King's narrative self-consciously locates itself at the politically charged intersection between Native and non-Native culture.[6] In keeping with the warrior-artists who first appropriated ledger books, King has likewise created a palimpsest – a work that both recognizes and draws "over the space of foreign calculations." Second, the novel emphasizes the thematic elements associated with the radical changes introduced by the Fort Marion drawings, including the affirmation of solidarity, the elevation of the commonplace, and the assertion of Native dignity. Third, by populating the novel with characters who work in the service and/or entertainment industry, the narrative interrogates the "unspoken truth" that Native people exist "for the convenience and entertainment of white society." Finally, and most importantly, in accordance with the traditional role played by the book in Native culture, *Green Grass, Running Water* exposes the violence that constitutes "the *beginning* of the nation's narrative" (Bhabha 310) and serves as a tool for the preservation and transmission of tribal traditions and wisdom. This feature connects the novel to contemporary Canadian fiction's characteristic emphasis on prophetic eschatology, which emphasizes the value of community and history in contrast to apocalypse's focus on the elect's pursuit of the New Jerusalem.

In his autobiographical narrative *The Names*, Kiowa author N. Scott Momaday offers insight into the precise nature of this tool when he describes his ancestor, Phod-lohk, taking out his treasured book: "Now that he was old, Pohd-lohk liked to look backwards in time, and although he could neither read nor write, the book was his means. It was an instrument with which he could reckon his place in the world" (48). In keeping with Momaday's association between the book and an instrument used to reckon one's place, this study argues that King's novel serves as a map; with the aid of this map, both characters and readers can "reckon ... [their] place in the world." In keeping with prophetic eschatology, the emphasis is on this world rather than the next.

The relation between Native fiction and mapping is a long-standing one; "the figuration or mapping of space in time, the undoing of imposed boundaries and enclosures and the negotiation of rightful passage and claim" (Gray 15) remain foregrounded concerns in works by American Indian writers, including King's. Bonnie Berthold argues further that "recent Native American fiction can be read specifically in reaction to the modern European mode of mapping" (quoted in Gray 56–7). She contrasts this "specifically Native American mode of temporal mapping, which she calls 'story-mapping,'" (57) with the analytical techniques of Western mapping.

From the start, King's book signals its interrelated preoccupation with mapping and the Fort Marion episode. Images of trains, cars, roads, traffic lights, as well as the act of driving abound. Together, these images highlight the novel's ongoing interrogation of what Bakhtin cites as one of literature's most common "chronotopes," the spatial and temporal setting established by "the road." This setting evokes the age-old concern with mapping one's journey through life, although it assumes a straightforward, linear unfolding of plot. It is no coincidence that all three of the younger characters, namely, Lionel Red Dog, Alberta Frank, and Charlie Looking Bear lack direction in their lives and are in dire need of guidance and/or maps, for at one point or another all three embark on road trips that go awry. Yet the novel intimates that their journeys will never assume a meaningful direction, so long as they stick to the manmade road and continue to rely on non-Native, apocalyptic discursive maps. Furthermore, owing to the novel's account of the experiences of Amos Frank (Alberta's father) and Portland Looking Bear (Charlie's father), readers appreciate that the younger generation's inability to reckon its place in the world stems, in part, from the fact that generation after generation of Native peoples have been forced to take direction from non-Natives, who expect them to play stereotyped, overdetermined roles.[7]

In a wonderfully comic scene, the novel brings together both the cartographic and performative connotations associated with the word "direction." On the morning of Lionel's birthday, Lionel's boss, Bill Bursum, owner of the Home Entertainment Barn, screens one of Portland Looking Bear's early Hollywood films, *The Mysterious Warrior*, on a wall entirely covered with television sets that Bursum has arranged to form a map of Canada and the United States. When Eli, Charlie, and the four mythical Indians arrive at the store to wish Lionel a happy birthday, Bursum seizes the opportunity to explain that "the Map" was "more than advertising ... It was a concept, a concept that lay at the heart of business and Western civilization" (249). For Bursum, "the Map" serves as a means to gain power: "It was like having the universe there on the wall, being able to see everything, being in control" (109). Like most Western maps, it offers a vision of wholeness, permanence, and stability; everything is known, named, and claimed. King's depiction of "the Map" recalls the distinction drawn in *The English Patient* between future-oriented mapping whose goal is the "possession of objects," aligned with "the Nietzschean 'will to power'" (Wolin 93), and communal and historically oriented mapping, characterized by an "intentionless state of being" and "total immersion and absorption" (Benjamin, *The Origin of German Tragic Drama* 46).

Rather than allow "the Map" to maintain its power and broadcast the film and reinstall the cowboys' apocalyptic age-old slaughter of the Indians, the four magical escapees from Fort Marion decide to "fix" the ending of "the best Western of them all" (157). To revise the script, they begin to chant, and their ceremonial performance produces startling effects; the film changes from black and white to colour (perhaps because the relationship between whites and Indians is, after all, not a black and white issue) and the Indians begin to massacre the cowboys. Bursum, Lionel, Charlie, and Eli watch the Map in amazement, as bullets rip through John Wayne's chest (267). Overcome with pride for his father, who, for the first time, is clearly not taking direction from Hollywood, Charlie hollers, "Get 'em, Dad" (267). This episode is instructive because the escapees successfully alter "the Map" – a graphic mode of representation "whose systematic inscriptions upon an 'empty' landscape (figured here as blank television screens) support the territorial imperative of 'literate' cultures"; to effect this change, they introduce an oral chant, and through this story/songline they construct "a polyphonic acoustic space, a network of interconnected voices" (Huggan 144). Again, the use of humour and parodic repetition in this episode invites readers both to witness the trauma of the genocide of Native North Americans, which was celebrated in Hollywood films, and to participate in an act of resistance by subverting the familiar hierarchy and laughing at whites.

The Indians' simultaneous subversion of "the Map" and the Hollywood script again recalls the impact of the Fort Marion Ledger Art. By "fixing" the film, King's escapees from the Fort continue to adopt and adapt the technology of non-Native society to represent more accurately Native perspectives. Like the warrior-artists of the 1800s, who appropriated the ledger books of their captors, King's mythical escapees also create "a middle place, an in-between place, in a place of writing" (40). At bottom, this episode intimates that Native people must come to grips with "the Map" inscribed by the settler-invaders – a map that is reinscribed on a daily basis through the media.

While tampering with "the Map" and reversing the linear Hollywood script offer instantaneous comic relief, the novel treats Western modes of figuration far more subversively. King's text implicitly suggests that readers must not simply revise the content of apocalyptic racist and sexist scripts but challenge their fundamental conventions, specifically, the linear, monologic, narrative structure itself. In *Green Grass, Running Water*, oral storytelling, chanting, dancing, and the circle of performance epitomized by the Sun Dance, interrupt and contest the linear trajectory of the printed word.

Readers are no doubt familiar with the distinction between white "linear" time and Native "circular" time, a distinction whose significance in Native culture cannot be underestimated. While Native spiritual leaders repeatedly refer to the circle as the basis of the Indian Way of Life, the circle continues to play a central role in Native writing.[8] According to Harmond Lutz, Native authors have made "their greatest inroads into mainstream literature, without giving up the belief in the circle" ("The Circle" 88). Tomson Highway once drew a circle on a piece of paper to clarify the difference between Native and non-Native narrative models. He insisted on the difference between the never-ending circle and the European system, the straight line he calls "the Genesis to Revelations line: progress, progress, progress from point A to point B, until the apocalypse comes" (8). Similarly, when asked about the parallels between the structure of contemporary Native novels and the image of the circle, Native author Jeannette Armstrong also insisted on the importance of the circle. Speaking of her own fiction, she stated: "Native people have asked me, 'Is this accidental that there are four parts [in your novel] and it's like the four Directions, and there are the prologue and the epilogue being the direction above us and below us?' And I said, 'No, it wasn't, actually.'" (quoted in Lutz, *Contemporary Challenges* 20). Like the work of Highway and Armstrong, King's fiction also examines Western culture's reliance on a teleological narrative structure – epitomized and conveyed primarily by the Bible – and engages in modes of figuration other than those the linear narrative sequences seem to be driving toward. In this way, *Green Grass, Running Water*, like *Headhunter*, disputes Kermode's assertion that novels must have beginnings and ends "even if the world has not" because this is the only way to "convert the otherwise meaningless chaos of existence into meaningful patterns" (*The Sense of an Ending* 138, 135).

Through its playful subversion of linear trajectories, ranging from road trips to traditional Western modes of storytelling, King's novel revises the narrative map and questions a few highly cherished assumptions of Western culture, specifically, the belief that there are no alternatives to Western culture's end-driven stories, with their "Genesis to Revelations line." To interrogate the linear narrative – one of the West's essentially tragic "terminal creeds" (Gray 18) – and install the essentially comic worldview of Indian tribes, the novel tackles the problem at its root. From the start, the novel invokes the biblical story of Genesis, "point A" of Christianity's narrative of progress.

On page 1, echoing Genesis 1:1–2, the text proclaims that in the beginning was nothing – nothing, that is, but water and Coyote. Next, we are told that Coyote has a "silly" Dream, which he names a Dog Dream. This Dream, which is contrary by nature, gets "everything backward" and insists on being called GOD (2). Following the narrative's playful logic, readers become aware that the Judeo-Christian God is merely a troublesome figment of the Native trickster's imagination.

The text continues to undermine canonical beginnings when the four escapees from Fort Marion, who are given power to narrate the story, explore different ways of introducing their tales. Initially, First Woman, who goes by the name of the Lone Ranger, tests a variety of opening phrases, including "Once upon a time ... " (7), "A long time ago in a faraway land ... " (8), and a parody of Native storytelling, "Many moons comechucka" (9). But her companions reject each narrative foray, insisting that she begin again until she gets it right. At one point, in an attempt to appease her friends, she cites the opening of *Genesis*, only to be informed that it, too, is "the wrong story" (10). As it turns out, the only beginning deemed acceptable consists of phrases drawn from the opening of a Native divining ceremony. The words, written in Cherokee syllabics, invite the people to "listen up" (Hoy). This ceremony, in which the movement of pine needles floating on water are used to read the future, "playfully subverts the fixity of history in its official (meaning written) form by focusing on the possibilities yet to come" (Andrews 18).[9] Just as the escapees from Fort Marion "fix" the ending of the Hollywood movie, in this instance, they likewise draw over the space of foreign calculation and revise the non-Native beginning of the book. Rather than install a linear, print-based, end-driven trajectory, the four Indians offer a beginning rooted in oral performance, just as later they rely on chanting to subvert the filmic narrative.

Again, humour is used in this instance because, traditionally, laughter has helped Native people to cope with traumatic events. As Mohawk actor Gary Farmer states: "Because Native communities have gone through probably the worst situations in North America that any peoples have gone through they had to have the ability to laugh. If they didn't they wouldn't be existing today. So humour has been a means of survival, the only means" (quoted in Ryan, *The Trickster Shift* 72). In accordance with the desire to witness and resist apocalyptic violence, the text relies on parody in conjunction with an emphasis on alternative oral traditions to undermine the legitimacy of the fixed map, which stands for the sum total of Western culture's hegemonic linear narratives.

To further derail the map's linear trajectory, secured by the story of Genesis, the first section offers both a retelling and a realistic displacement of the story of the Garden of Eden. In the text's version, readers encounter Dr J. Hovaugh (Jehovah),[10] whose garden serves as a pleasant distraction from the mental institution, which he oversees. In a brilliant comic gesture, the text conflates the Garden of Eden with Fort Marion; it is within this asylum that King's four magical Indians are finally incarcerated. The text appropriately designates Dr J. Hovaugh's place of work as an "insane asylum," presumably because it is insane to believe that constructs such as the Garden of Eden and, by extension, Judeo-Christianity (not to mention reservations and places like Fort Marion) afford any kind of asylum to Native peoples. King's narrative also exposes the deathly aspects of Western culture's asylum; in Hovaugh's garden, the trees are all moribund (see 60, 79). Moreover, it appears that the Tree of Knowledge has been axed. Dr Hovaugh proudly sits behind a dead tree, a massive wooden desk, which, as he points out, represents a "rare example of colonial woodcraft" (12). The tree has been "stripped, repaired, stained blond, and moved into his office as a surprise"; nevertheless, it continues to remind him of "a tree cut down to the stump" (12). Owing to its references to the garden and the dead tree, the text subtly aligns the death of knowledge with colonization, a practice that petrifies living entities and stains them white or "blond."

.By portraying Hovaugh as a man who, like Findley's Kurtz, views events in the world from the warped perspective of his own "terminal creed" – the Bible's apocalyptic narrative – the novel continues to highlight the limitations of linear narratives that underwrite the colonial tales of progress. Wedded to dreams of catastrophe and death, Hovaugh misguidedly associates the four old Indians' repeated escapes from his asylum with global disasters, and he can find only one solution to the paranoid scenario he has invented; he demands that his friend John Eliot sign the escapees' death certificates, even though they are alive and well. A sensible man, Eliot tries to convince Hovaugh that the paranoid plot he has concocted bears no resemblance to reality. After Hovaugh rattles off a series of dates on which the Indians escaped and insists that they establish a pattern, Eliot counters his argument, saying, "Maybe there wasn't [a pattern] .... Maybe nothing happened on those dates. Or maybe something good happened on those dates. You ever think of that?" (39). Eliot invites Hovaugh to consider more important issues, such as where the Indians go when they escape (40). Captive to his morbid train of thought, Hovaugh does not even hear his friend's remarks; instead, he sets off on a road trip to round up the Indians.

In King's novel, road trips have a tendency to go awry. In a series of comic, magic-realist episodes that confirm the validity of Charlie's initial association between cars and flowing rivers, several of the characters' cars are submerged in pools of water that mysteriously appear and sweep away the vehicles. At one point or another, the cars driven by Charlie, Alberta, and Hovaugh all disappear. At the end of the novel, they reappear, floating in Parliament Lake, where they act as battering rams to destroy the dam.[11]

Again, these comic images are used with subversive intent to remind readers that Native tales of origin begin not with a void to be mapped and driven across but with water (Matchie and Larson 158). Therefore, the image of a car being washed away offers a tangible image of the clash between non-Native apocalyptic and Native anti-apocalyptic narrative structures. Located at the interface between two radically distinct cultures, *Green Grass, Running Water* deploys both linear narrative trajectories: the A to B route from Genesis to Revelation, represented by cars, roads, and driving; and non-linear narrative trajectories – identified with the circular worldview of the Native peoples and conveyed by the organic flow of water, the cloud cycle, and, most strikingly, by the Sun Dance. The latter ritual is crucial in King's novel because embedded in the Sun Dance is what Benjamin terms a "secret agreement between past generations and the present one" (*Illuminations* ii). In keeping with the intergenerational structure of this agreement, in King's novel, the Sun Dance serves as a repository in which "past ages have deposited their collective dreams and longings, their aspirations for a better life, aspirations which adverse historical conditions have heretofore frustrated ... [so that] it falls due to future generations to preserve such hopes for a better life, if not to redeem them outright" (Wolin 217). To orient themselves in a meaningful direction, however, the younger characters must relinquish the apocalyptic trajectory of Western culture, put themselves in the hands of those who can guide them, and embark on the organic path of the circle and performance favoured by Coyote – a path whose emphasis on community and history recalls the characteristic features of prophetic eschatology.

Prompted by his aunt Norma's repeated suggestion, Lionel's uncle, Eli, takes Lionel under his wing and drives him to the Sun Dance. As they drive, Eli talks to Lionel about the direction his own life has taken. Although he never states it explicitly, Eli knows that he should never have lived the greater part of his life as a white man, removed from people and traditions; he perceives his error now that he has returned home and is fighting on behalf of his people and their land. Lionel, who has no idea where they are going, listens to his uncle without comprehending Eli's message. Ultimately, the latter's awareness of the importance of the land and community is tangibly conveyed when Eli leaves the paved road and turns onto the lease road. Together they share the experience of exchanging the familiar linear route for the road less travelled: "It had been a long time since Lionel had travelled the lease road. Normally, he came in through Medicine River on the road that ran to Cardston. That road was all asphalt and mileage signs and billboards. This road was a wild thing, bounding across the prairies, snaking sideways, and each time they came to a rise, Lionel had the uneasy feeling that just over the crest of the hill the road would vanish, and they would tumble out into the tall grass and disappear" (301–2). Their journey to the Sun Dance entails a move away from the predictable non-Native trajectory to a non-domesticated, vital path that virtually fuses with the natural world.

In many respects, Alberta's journey mirrors Lionel's. She, too, is escorted to the Sun Dance by a woman who, like Eli, knows where home is and understands the importance of Native tradition. As they turn off the lease road, Alberta's guide, Latisha, observes that, for as long as she could remember, her aunt Norma's lodge was "always in the same place on the east side of the camp. And before that Norma's mother. And before that" (307). Both Lionel's and Alberta's guides have internalized a sense of Native history and, therefore, can reckon their place in the world and help others to do the same.

Throughout the novel, primarily owing to Eli's reminiscences of the ceremony, readers are given a foretaste of the power and centrality of the Sun Dance. At one point, while driving Lionel to the ritual site, Eli pulls onto the side of the road as they reach the crest of a hill, so that Lionel can survey the scene that lies before them: "Below in the distance, a great circle of tepees floated on the prairies, looking for all the world like sailing ships adrift on the ocean" (302). Images of ships and the ocean recall the text's overarching emphasis on water imagery. Taken together, the images in the passage suggest that, in contrast to Western culture and its great map (a fixed concept associated with Bursum's television screens and the Great Baleen Dam), ideally, the Native peoples live a nomadic existence invested with the meaning of ceremonial performances, which, although based on the principle of the circle, remain open to the contigencies of chance.

The vision of the "great circle of tepees," however, provides far more than a simple contrast between Native and non-Native philosophies. Throughout the novel, the circle and the Sun Dance, in particular, are offered as alternatives to the Western, apocalyptic map. The importance accorded to the Sun Dance only makes sense when readers understand that its goal lies in furnishing participants with a map of the universe in which their location is clearly demarcated.

The Sun Dance is an annual, communal festival, celebrated outside during the summer. It takes place in ritual space defined by a tree that is cut and replanted for the purposed of forming the centre of a circle. The tree selected is always the "rustling tree," also known as the cottonwood. In Black Elk's tale of the Sun Dance, the warrior Kablaya explains the purpose of the tree: "He will be our center, and will represent the way of the people" (47). All the ritual action of the dance takes place within and around the circle, which is typically forty to one hundred feet in diameter. Spectators watch the dancing from the periphery, generally under an awning made of evergreen boughs.

The Sun Dance circle is variously described as the sacred hoop and/or the mystery circle, and, as many Native spiritual leaders have argued, it serves as a tangible model of the universe. At the centre of the circle is an altar, also in the shape of a circle, in which a cross has been inscribed. The lines of the cross are oriented to the four cardinal points and represent the four winds; hence, at the centre of the Sun Dance is a map of the Sacred Circle. Within this map of the cosmos, the dancers move in a sunwise or clockwise direction in harmony with the motion of the Earth.[12]

In Black Elk's *The Gift of the Sacred Pipe*, the leader of the ritual, known as the intercessor, sums up the meaning of the dance at the end of the ceremony: "'By your actions today, you have strengthened the sacred hoop of our nation. You have made a sacred center which will always be with you, and you have created a closer relation with all things of the universe'" (148). The "sacred center" of which Black Elk speaks is, in fact, a map of sorts. Participants create a "sacred center" by inscribing the map of the universe onto their bodies: a black circle is drawn around the face, representing Wakan Tanka (the Lakota term for the godhead); next, a line is drawn on each cheek and the chin. Taken together, the four lines represent the four directions.[13] In this way, during the Sun Dance, the body itself becomes a map.

Armed with this cursory sketch of the ceremony, readers can appreciate how the references within King's text to the Sun Dance serve to champion Native modes of representation based on the circle over Western culture's linear apocalyptic trajectory. An awareness of the Sun Dance ceremony alters the reader's perception of the text. Thus, readers are in a position to understand "what Eli's dancing signifies, why Eli takes Lionel there to celebrate his birthday, and why Lionel's getting his face painted is not a trivial or childish birthday treat" (Fee and Flick 5). Moreover, rather than view the text's contrapuntal narrative structure as a postmodern innovation, it can be seen as an attempt to replicate the structure and rhythms of the Sun

Dance, whose circular structure and emphasis on the entire nation is decidedly anti-apocalyptic.

King's novel oscillates among at least nine different narrative perspectives, all overseen by the narrator and his companion, Coyote. In many ways, the narrator serves as the intercessor or announcer at the Sun Dance, who supervises "the constant activity in a general way" (Holler 174). Typically, the announcer provides a running commentary on the dance, makes necessary announcements, enforces order, and introduces various leaders; he is also responsible for enforcing "a standard of traditional behaviour," which, during a dance that Holler attended, "occasioned an intermittent stream of censure directed toward those present who lacked sufficient knowledge of traditional ways" (173). In King's novel, the narrator acts as an intercessor, by overseeing the different focalizers and by teaching Coyote about Native stories and modes of storytelling; at times, the narrator also chastises Coyote for his ignorance about Native history and tradition.

The carnivalesque rotation among focalizers in King's text also parallels the multifaceted structure of the Sun Dance. More important, its inclusive, communal structure undermines the apocalyptic notion of the elect; "since the ritual takes place 'in the round,' different points of view on the dance reveal different aspects of it," and the effect is "kaleidoscopic" (Holler 174). The circular or kaleidoscopic structure of King's text is both implicit in the constant shift in focalizers and reflexively underscored by the four Indians, who each ceremonially take a turn in narrating one of the four sections (see 87, 192, 273).

At various points in the novel, the mythical Indians refuse apocalypse's binary opposition between the elect and the non-elect by emphasizing that everyone, save perhaps Coyote, deserves to take a turn to narrate his or her version of the story. The use of the word "turn," in these instances, denotes both a change in the speaker or player of the narrative game as well as a physical shift or "turn" in the story's narrative direction. Indeed, both the content and the linear form of the apocalyptic paradigm are challenged by King's text: viewed cartographically, the sum of the turns taken by each of the elderly Indians composes a circle.

In the novel, the word "turn" is also associated with the act of turning something on and off (see 201, 273). For instance, while they are discussing whose turn it is, one of the Indians suggests that maybe

Coyote "can turn on the light" (192). Shortly after this episode, they admire a sunrise:

As the old Indians watched, the universe gently tilted and the edge of the world danced in light.
"Ah," said Hawkeye. "It is beautiful."
In the east the sky softened and the sun broke free and the day rolled over and took a breath.
"Okay," said the Lone Ranger. "Did Coyote turn on the light?"
"Yes," said Robinson Crusoe. "I believe he did." (195)

By playing on the various meanings associated with the word "turn," the text challenges the primacy of the apocalyptic paradigm. Moreover, it links the circular structure of its own narrative with the circular motion of the sun and, by extension, its human representation, the Sun Dance.[14]

What is perhaps most astounding about the novel's subversion of the apocalyptic paradigm is that it does not simply refer to the Sun Dance. Instead, like a participant in the dance itself, the text internalizes and embodies the cosmic rite with its sacred circle. *Green Grass, Running Water* serves as a map – a tool with which one can reckon one's place in the world. To come to grips with the nature of this anti-apocalyptic map, however, readers must pay attention to Native codes. For example, at the beginning of each section is a word in Cherokee. Rather than signify a linear progression, such as chapter 1, 2, etc., each word announces one of the four directions and the sacred colour associated with it. The narrative begins with east and red, then proceeds to south and white, west and black, and north and blue, in that order (Hoy). In *Wisdom and Power*, Native spiritual leader, Fools Crow offers a catalogue of the directional and colour system of the Cherokees and identifies these colours with the cardinal directions (60). At bottom, these references to the sacred directions and colours, in conjunction with the description of the four Helpers and the Sun Dance, suggest that King's novel does not simply describe the Native ceremony but is itself an evocation or map of the ritual.

In a bizarre, Trickster-inspired coincidence, the hardcover edition of *Green Grass, Running Water* physically inscribes a circle, ending as it does on page 360. It also now makes sense that on page 180 the text portrays Lionel asleep in his chair with the "tumbling light [of the television] pouring over him like water." Here the "tumbling light" of the television foreshadows the novel's conclusion – the tumbling water that destroys the Great Baleen Dam. Thus, midway through its own circular journey, the text looks across its horizontal axis and catches a glimpse of events that take place at the end, or beginning, of its narrative orbit.

In the end, the escapees from Fort Marion, together with the community, fix the world by defending the Sun Dance against an intruder, Latisha's abusive husband, George. He tries to take pictures of the ceremony and sell the images for profit; his behaviour uncannily echoes the treatment of the Plains Indians' Ledger Art. The reference to pictures recalls Kat's skill in photography and iconography in Atwood's "Hairball." In this work, as in King's novel, pictures and picture-taking are associated with apocalyptic greed and the creation of static commodities, as opposed to a vital and respectful engagement with a world in flux. In King's novel, when the picture-taking ordeal is over and the spiritually vacant, individualistic opportunist has been vanquished, Lionel turns to the four Indians and asks, "Is that it? ... This is how you help me fix my life?" The Lone Ranger replies, "You bet." Robinson Crusoe goes on to explain that, in "years to come ... you'll be able to tell your children and grandchildren about this" (322). Thus, in keeping with their real-life counterparts, King's escapees from Fort Marion continue to safeguard Native tradition, while engaging in acts of resistance that highlight the significance of representation, in this case, storytelling.

Although they magically return to Dr J. Houvagh's asylum, where they are once again confined "by some ass who is in authority," to borrow Lanier's words, the fate of the warrior-artists remains ambiguous. Despite the fact that they are imprisoned, in the light of the trip they have taken and the message they have conveyed to the younger generation, the novel implies that it is possible for Native people who are traumatized and lost to escape the restrictions imposed by Western culture and to find direction. According to the text, gaining a meaningful direction in life involves earthquaking the map,[15] the seemingly entrenched apocalyptic plot, and opening oneself to tribal ways of understanding, which as Gray observes, arise "in pre-novelistic, oral performance contexts more closely associated with land and community" (4). Perhaps, then, there is no definitive answer to Helen Mooney's question about what happened to the prisoners. If they are forgotten, then they will remain consigned to the category of history's anonymous losers, silenced by the apocalyptic violence unleashed in the creation of the nation-state. If, however, both their traumatic experience and their protests are remembered, then, as the novel demonstrates, their subversive energy remains available to contemporary Native artists such as King, who adopt the book and draw the circular map of Native ritual and tradition over the space of foreign calculations.

King's novel portrays the traumatic impact of the clash between the settler-invaders and North American Native people. However, because "in many Native cultures it is considered unethical to speak directly or accusingly about bad experiences" (Fagan 18), King adopts a humourous approach to this apocalyptic event, which allows him to tell stories of trauma and not tell them at the same time and thereby avoid transgressing Native ethics. In addition to bearing witness in this covert fashion, *Green Grass, Running Water* also highlights the ways in which Native traditions and rituals, epitomized by the Sun Dance, can both resist and function as an alternative to apocalyptic eschatology.

The next chapter examines Kogawa's *Obasan*, a novel that links the traumatic experience of Native North American peoples with that of the Japanese Canadian community during the Second World War. In contrast to *Green Grass, Running Water*, *Obasan* does not offer a radical alternative to apocalyptic thinking. Instead, in bearing witness to an apocalyptic event, *Obasan* emphasizes brokenness and fragmentation, recalling *The English Patient* and "Hairball," and suggests that the traumatic legacy of apocalypse may never entirely be resolved.

5

Broken Letters: *Obasan* as Traumatic Apocalyptic Testimony

All of the works in this study interrogate the secular view of apocalypse as a fanciful biblical story that addresses the problem of evil by fabricating images of the violent destruction of the earthly world and the creation of a new and perfect heavenly world. As these fictions illustrate, apocalypse – far from being a quaint literary artifact that merely describes the categories of good and evil – functions as a vital, discursive mechanism for the *inscription* of these categories. More important, rather than contain violence in the realm of art or imagination, these texts, owing to their emphasis on historical events, demonstrate how apocalypse repeatedly blurs the boundaries between life and art, instigating processes of signification that can legitimize forms of sociopolitical violence. The previous chapter focused on Tom King's *Green Grass, Running Water*, and this final chapter examines Joy Kogawa's novel *Obasan*. The decision to address these texts last was made largely to dispel any lingering illusions that Canada has resisted the siren song of apocalypse. For many Canadians, particularly those of Native and Japanese heritage, the dreams of apocalypse, to borrow Kermode's words, have already "usurped waking thought," and there is an urgent need as we enter the new millennium to consider the impact of the applying the logic of apocalypse to the earthly world.

Kogawa published *Obasan* in 1981 and based the novel on her experience of the internment and suffering of Japanese Canadians during the Second World War. By self-consciously alluding to Revelation in its representation of the expulsion of the Japanese Canadian community from Canada's West Coast and of the atomic bombing of Japan, *Obasan* signals its status as an apocalyptic text and affords a chilling view of the disaster from the perspective of the non-elect. Unlike King's text, humour is not used to deflect the horror of apocalyptic violence; nor is there any prohibition against bearing witness to the catastrophe. Read as the testimony not of the triumphant seer but of the traumatized survivor, the novel offers key insights into the connections among apocalypse, violence, amnesia, and the creation and maintenance of Canada as a nation-state.

In *Obasan*, the narrator, Naomi Nakane (who is the same age Kogawa was when the persecution began) writes of the loss of her home in Vancouver and the even more traumatic loss of her mother, who left Canada in 1941 to visit relatives in Japan and, mysteriously, never returned.[1] During the war, Naomi's father is sent to a work camp where he dies from tuberculosis; meanwhile, Naomi and her brother, Stephen, are cared for by their father's half-brother, Uncle Isamu, and his wife, Aunt Obasan. Throughout her life, Naomi is haunted by the same urgent question: why did her mother not return? At the end of the novel, a letter reveals that her mother was in Nagasaki when the bomb dropped.

One of the first books to name the victimization of Japanese Canadians, *Obasan* had a profound impact on both the Canadian literary and political scene. The novel has enjoyed tremendous popularity, receiving praise from reviewers and numerous prizes, including the *Books in Canada* First Novel Award (1981), the Canadian Authors Association Book of the Year Award (1982), and the Before Columbus Foundation American Book Award (1982). *Obasan* is now one of the most widely read Canadian novels and the subject of numerous scholarly articles in Canada, the United States, Europe, and Japan. It is taught in most Canadian literature courses as well as in the social sciences. The text, with its poignant association between Japanese Canadians and innocent yellow chicks, was adopted as a quasi-historical document that defined Japanese Canadian identity on the basis of loss and the demand for redress.[2] *Obasan* was "instrumental in influencing the Canadian government's 1988 settlement with Japanese-Canadians for their loss of liberty and property in Canada during wwII" (*Canadian Who's Who*). When the settlement was announced, parts of the novel were read aloud in Canada's House of Commons "as a fitting tribute to the novel's role in achieving this end" (Davidson 14–15).

Arnold Davidson boldly proclaims that *Obasan* "is one of the most important Canadian books to appear in recent decades" (13). But

why has the novel had such a profound impact? Davidson argues
that *Obasan* "tells us something about ourselves as a society that we
long preferred not to hear" (13).[3] In his study of apocalypse, however,
James Berger argues that society does not simply wish to "not hear"
information that it has avoided facing; in fact, society aims to neutralize such information: "forms of representation that both activate
and keep alive yet at the same time neutralize and assimilate a culture's central traumatic concerns will become objects of the most
intense feeling" (Berger 29). *Obasan*, I would argue, serves as an ideal
site for this contradictory and doubled negotiation. This chapter
offers a more detailed discussion of Berger's theories in order to
analyse *Obasan*'s status as an ambivalent, canonical text that both
attempts and resists working through the traumatic impact of the
destruction of the Japanese Canadian community during the Second
World War. After discussing the nature of trauma and revealing how
the narrative articulates the characteristic doubleness of traumatic
testimony, this chapter examines *Obasan*'s subversive engagement
with Revelation. An understanding of trauma, which wounds the
mind and throws communication into crisis, and its key features,
specifically, its association with memory loss and belatedness, help to
explain why Kogawa's novel juxtaposes the traumatic experience of
Japanese Canadians with other national catastrophes, most obviously
those of Native North American peoples. Ultimately, Kogawa's narrative, in keeping with Walter Benjamin's writings and Ondaatje's
The English Patient, advocates a strategy of melancholy rather than of
mourning and champions an aesthetics and politics of brokenness
and woundedness over that of wholeness and healing (strategies portrayed in *Green Grass, Running Water*). Whereas King's novel
acknowledges the traumatic impact of the settler-invader society's
treatment of Native North Americans by allowing fragments of the
brutal incarceration of the Plains Indians to recur throughout the text,
Green Grass, Running Water suggests that the trauma and suffering
can be resolved by embracing Native rituals and traditions, epitomized by the Sun Dance. By contrast, in *Obasan* the emphasis on brokenness and fragmentation suggests that the trauma cannot be
healed and thus recalls *The English Patient*'s and "Hairball"'s reliance
on the allegorical fragment as an emblem of the ongoing damage
caused by apocalyptic thinking.

As critics have observed, *Obasan*'s exposure of Canada's treatment
of so-called ethnic "enemy" minorities during the war challenged

Canada's self-image as a "peaceable kingdom" and "multicultural mosaic" (see Davidson 13). The cover of the Penguin edition, for instance, describes the work as a "moving novel of a time and a suffering we have tried to forget." By acting as a catalyst for the return of the forgotten or "repressed" content of Canadian experience, *Obasan* provides a locus for negotiating traumatic events. While most critics agree that *Obasan* constitutes an antidote to such forgetting and repression, they disagree about what it is that Canada has forgotten and what the novel's attitude is toward this repressed history. In keeping with the Penguin cover's emphasis on "*a* time and *a* suffering" (my emphasis) the majority of critics read *Obasan* as a narrative that restores a memory of a particular moment, an isolated incident within Canadian history. Read in this way, the novel neutralizes a traumatic experience, providing a healing resolution to an unfortunate racist episode in the nation's past and offering "a sign of possible recovery from racism, of leaving such issues behind" (Karpinski 2). "Academics who analyze the novel in detail, despite differences of approach, all tend to incorporate a resolutionary (not revolutionary) aesthetics in their overall critical framing of the novel"; the "agreement seems to be that Naomi resolves her silenced past, so establishes peace with the human rights violations that caused such havoc and grief to her, to her family, and to her community" (Miki 115). The process of canonization requires that "the critical or even potentially transformative – non-canonical or anticanonical – dimensions of texts and other artifacts be repressed or radically downplayed" (LaCapra 6). Accordingly, in the case of *Obasan*, other critics, including Miki himself, focus on these "repressed" elements and offer less resolutionary and consoling readings. Moreover, in response to the Penguin cover's description of the novel as a "moving novel of a time and suffering we have tried to forget," Scott Toguri McFarlane rightly asks: "Who is the 'we' in this statement? 'We' seems to refer to an imagined community made up of those possessing an homogenous 'Canadian memory' ... Furthermore, the comment suggests that the novel has filled in gaps in this imagined Canadian memory. Whoever the 'we' are, they are made more complete, or perhaps 'redeemed,' by the novel. Finally, the imagined Canadian community...does not include Japanese Canadians who have not forgotten about the internment" (407). Despite these academic skirmishes, the challenge in approaching *Obasan* is not to privilege one set of readings over another (the resolutionary versus the non-resolutionary), but to explore how the text itself functions (and how critics have responded to its function) as a traumatic symptom that exhibits what can be described as the characteristic doubleness of traumatic, apocalyptic testimony.

While I will be discussing various theories concerning trauma later in this chapter, at this point, it is useful to consider the fundamentally ambivalent nature of traumatic testimony. On the one hand, testimony about catastrophic events constitutes an attempt to recall and articulate the traumatic event and, thereby, work through it. On the other hand, this type of testimony also partly demonstrates "the inability or refusal to work though; it is a remembering of the trauma that seeks to eternize its traumatic impact" (Berger 79–80). Recognizing the ambivalence expressed by many apocalyptic texts, Dominick LaCapra contends that working through and acting out cannot always be distinguished and that "in cases of trauma, acting-out may be necessary and perhaps never fully overcome" (205). A discourse utterly without symptomatic traces, LaCapra tells us, is impossible. Such a response could only be a fetishistic narrative of fake redemption (220).[4] To read *Obasan* solely as a novel of recovery and closure would thus entail treating the text as a fetish and denying the symptomatic traces of apocalypse that testify to irrevocable losses sustained by the exiled and traumatized Japanese Canadian community.

To explore *Obasan*'s status as the traumatized testimony of the nonelect and locate the traces of apocalypse, it is necessary to reveal how the text engages in a dialogue with Revelation. *Obasan* signals an immediate engagement with apocalypse by using a passage from Revelation as its first epigraph:

> To him that overcometh
> will I give to eat
> of the hidden manna
> and will give him
> a white stone
> and in the stone
> a new name written ...

This excerpt from Rev. 2.17 concerns St John the Divine's relation of God's promise to the seven churches if they repent and remain faithful. In the preceding verse, however, John warns those who do not repent that God has sworn to come to them "soon and war against them with the sword of [his] ... mouth" (Rev. 2:16). Thus, the epigraph and its context direct our attention to the very different fates of the elect, who conquer and are given "power over nations" and "rule with a rod of iron," and the non-elect who, like "earthen pots," will "be broken in pieces" (Rev. 2:27).

Readers cannot forget these apocalyptic promises and threats because images from the epigraph – bread or "manna" and stone – are woven throughout the narrative. The novel opens, for instance, with the death of Naomi's uncle, Isamu. After hearing the news, Naomi returns to Granton, Alberta to comfort Obasan and prepare for the funeral. While staying at her aunt's house, awaiting the arrival of her brother, Stephen, and her mother's sister, Aunt Emily, Naomi contemplates the past. She is immediately confronted with the "stone bread" that Isamu used to bake – bread that for Naomi remains inedible (12–13). Later, Naomi finds and opens Aunt Emily's package of documents, containing her aunt's diary of events concerning the internment and newspaper clippings, remarking that it is "as heavy as a loaf of Uncle's stone bread" (32). Aunt Emily's package also includes, among other things, a grey folder that holds the letters written in Japanese explaining Naomi's mother's mysterious disappearance (the letters provide an eyewitness account of the mother's gruesome experience at Nagasaki) (32). Naomi describes this package of documents "piled as neatly as the thin white wafers in Sensei's [the Anglican priest's] wafer box" as "white paper bread for the mind's meal" (200). Although the text metaphorically suggests that Naomi receives this bread or manna, she distinguishes herself from the elect by emphasizing that "[w]e were the unwilling communicants receiving and consuming a less than holy nourishment, our eyes, cups filling with the bitter wine of a loveless communion" (200). These references to the Eucharist recall Atwood's gruesome parody of communion as experienced by the non-elect in "Hairball," in which an ovarian cyst serves as "less than holy nourishment" and likewise symbolizes a "loveless communion."

In categorizing *Obasan* as an apocalyptic work, then, I am responding both to the recurring allusions to Revelation that create the weft and weave of the text and to the insights of other critics who also trace the text's dialogue with Revelation.[5] Yet, while I share these critics' recognition of the novel's preoccupation with apocalypse, it is problematic that their readings try to impose absolute closure and unity – an expression, perhaps, of the critics' need for a New Jerusalem. Merivale, for instance, claims that "Naomi finally succeeds in joining the divergent voices of Emily and Obasan, history and poetry, document and lyric, into the unified elegiac voice of her mother found again in herself" (80). Similarly, Davidson asserts that Naomi "finally puts her past and her mother to rest" (73). In a chapter entitled "Resolution and Release," he states that "[w]e last see her [Naomi] concerned not with past suffering, but with the present" (Davidson 75). Coral Ann Howells goes so far as to adopt the language of apocalypse and psychoanalysis in her discussion of *Obasan*'s conclusion. The novel, she says, "*works through* strategies of silence and enigma toward *revelation*" (93; my emphasis).

Readings that situate *Obasan* solely within the progressive, consoling, psychoanalytic framework of "work[ing] through" and that emphasize Naomi's "final sense of resolution" (Harris 41) repress the ways in which the text remains divided, articulating both a desire and an inability or refusal to work through the traumatic experience. "In the centre of my body," Naomi writes at the beginning of her psychic journey, "is a rift. In my childhood dreams, the mountain yawns apart as the chasm spreads. My mother is on one side of the rift. I am on the other. We cannot reach each other. My legs are being sawn in half" (69–70). The trauma associated with Naomi's separation from her mother and, later, with the account of her horrific ordeal in Nagasaki permanently wounds both the mind of the child and the body of the text. Toward the conclusion, after the letters explaining the mother's fate have been read aloud, Naomi writes: "I hear the screams and feel the mountain breaking. Your [the mother's] long black hair falls and falls into the chasm. My legs are sawn in half. The skin on your face bubbles like lava and melts from your bones" (266). The return of the earlier images of woundedness and division, coupled with the use of the present tense and the repetition of the word "falls," signals the text's inability or refusal to work though the traumatic impact of a series of irreparable losses. Ironically, impositions of closure reinstall the apocalyptic vision of wholeness and order that the traumatized narrative forces readers to interrogate; such readings also drain the work of ethical and political force – a force that rests on the narrative's power to insist on its woundedness.

The emphasis on wounds in *Obasan* is particularly relevant to this discussion because the word *trauma* is Greek for *wound*. Although, as we will see later in this chapter, theorists have much to say about the complex features of trauma: in its most general definition, trauma describes "an overwhelming experience of sudden or catastrophic events in which the response to the event occurs in the often delayed, uncontrolled, repetitive appearance of hallucinations and other intrusive phenomena" (Caruth, *Unclaimed Experience* 11). While "trauma" originally referred to an injury inflicted on a body, in its later usage, particularly in medical and psychiatric literature, the term came to be understood as a wound inflicted "upon the mind" (3). Atwood's short story "Hairball" captures this duality by portraying, on the one hand, the trauma associated with the presence of Kat's cyst and, on the other, the equally traumatic impact the cyst has on Kat's psyche. After communing with Hairball, Kat shakes her head in wonder: "What are you doing, sitting on the floor and talking to a hairball? You are sick, she tells herself" (47). Thus, owing to the ways in which trauma defies and demands our witness, it has been characterized as a "double wound" (Caruth, *Unclaimed Experience* 3). Traumatic experiences defy witnessing because they instigate a crisis of communication. In trauma, one moves forward "into a situation that one has little capacity to imagine and that's why it shatters whatever one had that was prospective or experiential in the past" (Lifton 137). Communication is thrown into crisis because, for the survivor, there are "never enough words or the right words, there is never enough time or the right time, and never enough listening or the right listening to articulate the story that cannot be fully captured in *thought, memory,* and *speech*" (Laub 63).

The language Naomi uses to describe the painful loss of her mother bears an uncanny resemblance to contemporary accounts of trauma: "In my dreams, a small child sits with a wound on her knee. The wound on her knee is on the back of her skull, large and moist. A *double wound*. The child is forever unable to speak. The child forever fears to tell. I apply a thick bandage but nothing can soak up the seepage. I beg that the woundedness may be healed and that the limbs may learn to dance" (267; my emphasis). The wound on the knee refers to "the sexual wound, to an incident with [Naomi's neighbour] Old Man Gower" (Gottlieb 45). Gower used the nonexistent scratch on her knee as a pretext to take her into his house and molest her.[6] The wound at the back of the skull refers to the damage to the psyche, the "wound that comes from the internalization of guilt of violation" (Gottlieb 45–6). The double wound also refers to Naomi's "inability to articulate this traumatic memory or to find a stable system of communication with which to assimilate her traumatic past into consciousness" (Visvis 14). The child is, as Naomi insists, "forever unable to speak." Moreover, the suppurating head wound alludes to the particular devastation wrought by the atomic bomb. The letter read aloud at the end of the novel, for instance, describes Naomi's grandmother stumbling upon a woman so badly wounded that she was utterly disfigured: "Her nose and one cheek were almost gone. Great wounds and pustules covered her entire face and body. She was completely bald. She sat in a cloud of flies and maggots wriggled among her wounds ... the woman gave her a vacant gaze, then let out a cry. It was my mother" (263).

It is difficult to think of a more horrifying and traumatic experience. To a large extent, responses to the novel including those by Merivale, Davidson, and Howells cited above, that emphasize resolution and healing have been informed by the needs and desires of the dominant members of society to soften and, in some cases, negate the traumatic impact of the internment and the Allied bombing of Japan; "The cultural politics around Kogawa's book, and especially the novel's quick assimilation into the mainstream of literary criticism and pedagogy, involve mechanisms of co-optation that can tame and contain even the most 'disagreeable' message, revealing that the invention of national history, including the one structured around the nation's guilt, is ultimately a conserving and conservative enterprise" (Karpinski 3).

Karpinski argues further that the need "for closure, healing, coming to terms with the past, is motivated by the refusal or impossibility to conceive of the nation's history as founded on racist premises" (4). But there are other, less pernicious explanations for the overwhelming insistence on wholeness and healing. "Only the most traumatized, or iconoclastic, person can let traumatic wounds remain unhealed: "[t]hinkers as disparate as Kermode and Zizek agree that the unspeakable chasm, the void, the trauma, the apocalypse will be crossed by means of narrative. People *will* create closure for the wound ... [It] *must* ... be filled out or covered over with language" (Berger 83). The broader problem raised by the debate about the translation and untranslatability of trauma is whether it is possible to read *Obasan* without fabricating some sort of closure – can we have Revelation without the New Jerusalem? Can one ever hope to resist the process of canonization and come to terms with what apocalypse means for the damned? Laying the foundation for such an anticanonical reading involves a return to Revelation to see if, by reading it against the grain, the seer's vision can serve as a guide.

John of Patmos's account of apocalypse offers only a glimpse of the traumatic impact of the destruction of the city of Babylon on its inhabitants (Rev. 18:15–19); "all shipmasters and seafaring men, sailors and all whose trade is on the sea, stood far off and cried out as they saw the smoke of her burning 'What city was like the great city?' And they threw dust on their heads, as they wept and mourning, 'Alas, alas, for the great city where all who had ships at sea grew rich by her wealth'" (Rev. 18:17–20). Read in conjunction with Revelation, it becomes more significant that *Obasan* opens with the death of Naomi's "shipmaster" and "seafaring" uncle Isamu. Together with Naomi's father and grandfather, Isamu built boats in British Columbia. After learning of Isamu's death, Naomi recalls that the last time her uncle saw a boat was in 1941, when the RCMP officer confiscated the handmade yacht designed by Naomi's father (22). Shortly after, Isamu was taken away. Naomi speculates that her uncle's entire life was spent mourning the loss of the sea: "He was waiting for that 'some day' when he could go back to the boats. But he never did" (22). By eliciting pathos for Naomi's uncle, from the start, the text undermines the logic of apocalypse with its strict opposition between the elect and the non-elect.

As God's servant, John feels no sympathy for those labelled wicked. He describes the fate of Babylon's evil inhabitants and their lamentations primarily to juxtapose their experience with the angel's triumphant account of the rewarding of the elect and the creation of the new Jerusalem: "Then I saw a new heaven and a new earth; for the first heaven and the first earth had passed away, and the sea was no more" (Rev. 21:1). Before this event occurs, however, John informs his audience that Satan and his ilk will be thrown into "the bottomless pit" and, later, into "the lake of fire that burns with sulpher" (Rev. 19:20–20:1), and that the city of Babylon "shall be burned with fire":

And the kings of the earth ... will weep and wail over her when they see the smoke of her burning; they will stand far off, in fear of her torment, and say, "Alas! Alas! Thou great city, thou mighty city, Babylon! In one hour has thy judgement come." (Rev. 18:8–9)

By concluding with the fiery destruction of Nagasaki, *Obasan* offers an anguished reply to Revelation, with a testimonial from those who were thrown into the pit, burned in the lake of fire, and whose

city, in keeping with the terrible prophecy, was destroyed in an
instant.

The text strengthens the link between the fate of the Japanese
Canadians and that of the Antichrist by referring to the expulsion
from the "paradise" of Vancouver (98) and by describing the internment as a journey of descent, a "pure hell" kept "hush hush from the
public" (99). In her account of the evacuation, Naomi writes: "We are
leaving the B.C. coast – rain, cloud, mist – an air overladen with
weeping. Behind us lies a salty sea within which swim our drowning
specks of memory – our small waterlogged eulogies. We are *going
down to the middle of the earth* with pick-axe eyes, tunnelling by train
to the Interior, carried along by the momentum of the expulsion into
the waiting wilderness" (119; my emphasis). The narrative continues
to reinforce the connection between the fate of the Japanese Canadians and that of the damned when Naomi explains that her family's
cabin in the interior of BC "feels underground" (130). The text also
alludes to Satan's descent in the episodes in which Naomi identifies
with the kitten thrown into the outhouse and left to die (172) and the
tiny red insect thrown onto the water, "trapped in a whirling well"
(154). In contrast to Revelation, which stresses destruction and renovation, *Obasan* forces readers to come to grips with unmitigated
destruction – in this case, the repercussions of the dispersal and
destruction of the Japanese Canadian community.

After the Second World War ended, a total of twelve thousand
Japanese Americans were permitted to return to their homes on the
West Coast, but the Japanese Canadians in the interior camps were
told to move themselves east of the Rockies or sign papers renounc-
ing their Canadian citizenship and agree to be "repatriated"
(deported) to Japan (see Oiwa 12). Aunt Emily informs Naomi that
the American Japanese "'were interned as we were in Canada, and
sent off to concentration camps, but their property wasn't liquidated
as ours was ... We weren't allowed to return to the West Coast like
that. We've never recovered from the dispersal policy'" (*Obasan* 35).
Naomi herself testifies to the impact of this second utterly devastating uprooting: "Trains do not carry us home. Ships do not return
again. All my prayers disappear into space" (208). Torn from her
mother and father, Naomi and Stephen relocate with Uncle Isamu
and Aunt Obasan from Slocan, BC, to Granton, Alberta. For Naomi,
Granton is a hellish inferno, a place of death that she can hardly bear
to remember (214). She describes the field where they picked beets as

"an oven" – one of many references to the biblical "fiery furnace" in the apocalyptic book of Daniel (Dan. 3:13) – and explains that her family "are tiny as insects crawling along the grill" (215). In this "place of angry air" where "skull-shaped weeds" careen off into the brown air and "skeletons" of farm machinery lie abandoned beside their one-room hut, Naomi is transformed into the living dead, "a scarecrow or a skeleton in the wind" (210–11). In contrast to the Tree of Life found in the New Jerusalem, whose "leaves were for the heal-ing of the nations (Rev. 22:2), the only tree near Naomi's family's hut "is dead" and, on spring evenings, she squats "on the tree's dead roots" (224).[7] All of these examples (the fate of the "seafaring" men, their loss of the sea, the destruction of the beloved city, the descent into middle earth, and the dead tree) show how *Obasan* affords read-ers a view of apocalypse from the perspective of the non-elect. These examples, however, do not imply a one-to-one correspondence between the novel and the biblical seer's apocalyptic vision. Instead, the narrative highlights the power shift involved in the appropriation of apocalyptic discourse, such that apocalypse becomes the tool of those in possession of worldly, political, and military power, not the tool of the marginalized and oppressed.[8] As well, the narrative illus-trates more generally the conjunction in Canada in the 1940s between distinctive features of the modern nation (a reliance on bureaucracy, a teleology of progress, and an increase in technological resources) and what are often considered the repressed aspects of modernism – "the 'timeless' discourse of irrationality" (Bhabha 292) – in this case, the eruption of apocalyptic thinking and scapegoating mechanisms, which label people as "the enemy."

Invocations of apocalypse serve as a means of eradicating what-ever the apocalyptic writer deems evil or alien because apocalypse carves out an unmistakable distinction between true and false, good and evil. Aunt Emily highlights how this type of apocalyptic think-ing consistently informed attitudes and behaviours toward Japanese Canadians: "Over here they say 'Once a Jap always a Jap,' and that means us. We're the enemy" (89). Later, she admits that "[n]one of us ... escaped the naming. We were defined and identified by the way we were seen" (126). Naomi likewise emphasizes the traumatic impact of naming when she describes an episode in which a young girl teases her brother, Stephen. The girl, offering a simplified version of John of Patmos's threat, informs Stephen that all "the Jap kids at school are going to be sent away and they're bad and you're a Jap"

(76). Naomi asks her father if it is true, but he tells her, "'We're Canadian.'" "'It is a riddle,'" Stephen explains to Naomi. "'We are both the enemy and not the enemy'" (76).

The "riddle" and the novel as a whole underscore the inability of apocalyptic thinking to encode complexities and how this inability supports racist attitudes. Kogawa herself has commented in interviews that pure dichotomies (as well as the infamous metaphor of the mosaic of Canadian culture) cannot render the "hyphen" between Japanese-Canadian (Kogawa, "Interview" 99). In Canada during the Second World War, apocalyptic discourse, with its characteristic erasure of the hyphen, served specific sociopolitical interests. Aunt Emily confirms this when she records in her diary that a "letter in the papers says that in order to preserve the 'British way of life', they should send us all away. We're a 'lower order of people'" (*Obasan* 94).

Returning to a question posed at the beginning of this chapter, namely, what has Canada forgotten, it would appear that *Obasan* illustrates that what *some* Canadians have forgotten is not a discrete historical moment, but the fact that in creating and maintaining the nation-state, the proverbial New Jerusalem, Canadians from the British Empire invoked apocalyptic discourse to claim native status while brutally denying that same status to immigrants, in this instance, from Japan. But *Obasan* moves beyond the boundary of this particular historical moment to link the experience of Japanese Canadians during the Second World War with those of Native North Americans at the time of first contact. In doing so, the text bears witness to the more fundamental alliance among apocalypse, violence (specifically, the cannibalistic violence associated with the creation of the New Jerusalem) and amnesia. In this respect, it is useful to recall again Homi Bhabha's essay "DissemiNation," where he describes the peculiar combination of national violence and memory loss – what he terms the "strange forgetting of the history of the nation's past: the violence involved in establishing the nation's writ." Although Bhabha does not delve into the reasons for this bizarre memory loss, it bears a striking resemblance to latency, one of trauma's most unusual features.

Trauma's complexity was most thoroughly documented by Freud in two central works, *Beyond the Pleasure Principle* and *Moses and Monotheism*, written during the turmoil surrounding the First and Second World Wars, respectively. The groundwork for these two studies, however, was laid in *Studies on Hysteria*, which focuses on the relationships between trauma, repression, and symptom formation. Here, Freud describes how an overwhelming experience that the conscious mind cannot assimilate is forgotten, yet returns in the guise of somatic symptoms: the body speaks what the mind refuses to know. Freud developed his initial hypotheses about trauma in *Beyond the Pleasure Principle*, a work based on his treatment of shell-shocked veterans from the First World War – what was known in that era as "war neuroses" (see Caruth, *Unclaimed Experience* 59). The experience and symptoms exhibited by these battlefield survivors contradicted Freud's axiom that all dreams represent a desire for wish fulfillment: "Dreams occurring in traumatic neuroses have the characteristic of repeatedly bringing the patient back into the situation of his accident, a situation from which he wakes up in another fright. This astonishes people far too little ... Anyone who accepts it as something self-evident that their dreams should put them back at night into the situation that caused them to fall ill has misunderstood the nature of dreams" (*Beyond the Pleasure Principle* 13). Freud concluded that there must be a psychic force that undergirds the pleasure principle; he termed this force "repetition-compulsion." According to Freud, individuals who have undergone a trauma, which is often forgotten and repressed, are forced to repeat the repressed material of the past as "a contemporary experience" instead of "remembering it as something belonging to the past" (18). In referring to the dreams of his shock patients, Freud argues that the dreams that take them "back with such regularity to the situation in which the trauma occurred ... are endeavouring to master the stimulus retrospectively, by developing the anxiety whose omission was the cause of the traumatic neurosis" (32).

In *Moses and Monotheism*, his final work on trauma, Freud turned his attention to one of the most puzzling features of trauma – the return of the event after a period of delay: "It may happen that someone gets away, apparently unharmed, from the spot where he has suffered a shocking accident, for instance a train collision. In the course of the following weeks, however, he develops a series of grave psychical and motor symptoms, which can be ascribed only to his shock or whatever else happened at the time of the accident. He has developed a 'traumatic neurosis.' This appears quite incomprehensible and is therefore a novel fact. The time that elapsed between the accident and the first appearance of the symptoms is called the 'incubation period,' a transparent allusion to the pathology of infectious disease ... It is the feature one might term *latency*" (Freud, *Moses and Monotheism* 84). The concept of latency explains why the memory of the traumatic event is typically inaccessible to the conscious mind and is only available when triggered by a similar event in the present. Or, put another way, trauma produces symptoms "in its wake, after the event, and we reconstruct trauma by interpreting its symptoms, reading back in time" (Berger 21).

For the purposes of this study, an awareness of the delayed response characteristic of trauma explains the amnesia that obscures the violence involved in "establishing the nation's writ" (Bhabha 310). Trauma's belatedness also elucidates, in part, why thinking about the internment and the bombing of Japan remained latent in Canada, roughly during the interval between the end of the war and the publication of works such as Ken Adachi's *The Enemy That Never Was* (1976), Ann Gomer Sunahara's *The Politics of Racism: The Uprooting of Japanese Canadians During the Second World War* (1981), and, finally, Kogawa's *Obasan* (1981). The peculiar aspect of latency and the fact that recollections of traumatic experiences are triggered only in conjunction with events in the present also means that trauma forges an "indissoluble, political bond to other histories" (Caruth, *Unclaimed Experience* 18); "each national catastrophe invokes and transforms memories of other catastrophes, so that history becomes a complex entanglement of crimes inflicted and suffered, with each catastrophe understood – that is, misunderstood – in the context of repressed memories of previous ones" (Berger 23). In Kogawa's novel, the factor of latency explains why the narrative introduces temporal paradoxes that create links with other histories, shattering the comforting illusion that racism, to recall the words on the Penguin cover, can be contained to a specific "time and suffering." By aligning seemingly distinct peoples and disparate moments in the nation's past, the novel alerts readers to the shared trauma of Canada's racialized non-elect.

On the opening page, Naomi records the date, 9 August 1972, the anniversary of the Allied bombing of Japan, and explains that she and her uncle journey to the coulee "every year around this time" (1). She goes on to suggest that "Uncle could be Chief Sitting Bull squatting here. He has the same prairie-baked skin, the deep brown furrows like dry river beds creasing his cheeks. All he needs is a feather headdress, and he would be perfect for a picture postcard – 'Indian Chief from Canadian Prairie' – souvenir of Alberta, made in Japan"

(2).[9] The use of the word "souvenir" (from the French verb *to remember*) is apt, signalling as it does the operation of memory and prompting readers to remember Canada's betrayal of the aboriginal peoples in the light of the betrayal of Japanese Canadians during the Second World War. But Naomi illustrates that it is not merely her uncle who resembles a Native man. "Some of the Native children I've had in my classes over the years," Naomi says, "could almost pass for Japanese, and vice versa" (2). Ultimately, what binds the two groups, as the previous chapter on *Green Grass, Running Water* suggests, is their mutually traumatic experience of apocalypse and their inability to communicate what has happened.

Traumatic experiences shock their victims into silence because, as noted above, there are simply no words to describe what has occurred: "The trauma is the confrontation with an event that, in its unexpectedness or horror, cannot be placed within the schemes of prior knowledge ... and thus continually returns, in its exactness, at a later time" (Caruth, *Trauma* 153). For this reason, victims of trauma often remain numb and silent (see Caruth, *Unclaimed Experience* 11). Early on, Naomi remarks on the Native girl in the class she teaches, who "sits at the back and never says anything" (*Obasan* 9). In a comment that refers to herself as much as to her Native students, Naomi acknowledges that "it's the children who say nothing who are in trouble more than the ones who complain" (36).

Naomi is not alone in discerning the connection between the traumatized silence of the Japanese Canadians and Native North Americans. After the family is exiled to Slocan, BC, a sympathetic loner, Rough Lock Bill, befriends Naomi and asks her name. When she does not answer, he replies, "'Don't talk much do ya ... Like that fella up past the mine. Never said a word. Almost like a mute, he was ... Don't you never talk?'" (158). As it turns out, the "fella up past the mine" was the last member of the tribe of Native peoples that once lived in Slocan. Rough Lock explains that when his grandfather arrived, "there was a whole tribe here," and pointing a stick at his own cabin, he says, "'Right there was the chief's teepee. But last I saw – one old guy up past the mine – be dead now probably'" (158).

Silence is doubly linked to trauma in this episode because the fanciful story that Rough Lock proceeds to tell Naomi about how Slocan received its name continues to emphasize the chilling connection between the genocide of the Native peoples and the destruction of the Japanese Canadian community. Rough Lock prefaces his story by saying, "'Red skin, yellow skin, white skin, any skin ... Don't make sense, do it, all this fuss about skin?" After opening with the consoling incantation, "long time ago," Rough Lock introduces the story's protagonist, "an Indian brave" who escorts the remnant of his tribe, "so weak they have to be carried," across the mountains. The brave tells his people, 'If you go slow, you can go'" (158). "'We call it Slocan now,'" Rough Lock tells Naomi. "'Real name is Slow-can-go'" (158).

For the purposes of this study, Rough Lock's introduction to the tale is crucial because it graphically illustrates the familiar constellation among apocalyptic violence, the founding of the nation-state, and amnesia. "'Long time ago these people were dying,'" Rough Lock begins. "'All these people here. Don't know what it was. Smallpox maybe. Tribe wars. Starvation. Maybe it was a hex, who knows? But there's always a few left when something like that happens'" (158). His inability to remember the exact cause of the catastrophe coupled with his precise references to the disastrous impact of the settler-invaders' arrival, namely, "smallpox" and "starvation," recall Bhabha's description of the "strange forgetting of the history of the nation's past: the violence involved in establishing the nation's writ." Rough Lock cannot remember perhaps because it would entail facing the traumatic recognition that he and his ancestors are implicated in and profited from the genocide.[10] Rough Lock's inability to remember also indicates more generally that the ability to think of Canada as a nation depends on a similar "obligation to forget" the destruction of the Native peoples and the appropriation of their land; "being obliged to forget becomes the basis for remembering the nation, peopling it anew" (Bhabha 311).[11]

Not everyone, however, has the luxury of forgetting. Referring to the genocide of the Native tribe, Rough Lock tells Naomi: "'There's always a few left when something like that happens'" (158). Like the "Indian brave" in Rough Lock's story, Naomi herself is a survivor of a traumatic experience, and, owing to the nature of trauma, she *cannot* forget. In the novel *Crackpot*, by Canadian writer Adele Wiseman, a Holocaust survivor aptly named Lazar alludes to the impossibility of forgetting. Referring to his experience of the Holocaust, Lazar asks his girlfriend: "How can you remember what can never become the past?" (422). Owing to the factor of latency, trauma destabilizes the sequence of past and present, and the process of remembering and forgetting. *Headhunter* also underscores the destabilization of memory in its portrait of "the brood," the traumatized victims of the Club of Men, children who cannot remember their experiences of torture and sexual assault but ultimately act it out in the grisly murder of their therapist. In *The English Patient* the burned man's amnesia likewise reflects the impact of trauma.

As critics observe, since the traumatic event is neither experienced nor integrated when it occurs, technically speaking, it has not been "forgotten." Nor is it "remembered" in the present because the event is only fully evident "in connection with another place and in another time" (Caruth, *Trauma* 8). The puzzling belatedness characteristic of trauma means that it is never simply the "story of the individual in relation to the events of his own past"; instead, it is the story "of the way in which one's own trauma is tied up with the trauma of another" (Caruth, *Unclaimed Experience* 8).[12] The use of the word "tied" is apt because, in addition to the links noted above, in Kogawa's novel a blood-red thread literally runs throughout the text, binding the fate of Native peoples to that of Japanese Canadians.

The text immediately begins to establish the links in this lengthy and convoluted chain that starts with the traumatic experience of Japanese Canadians and ends with that of the Native peoples. When the novel opens, Naomi dreams of her dead uncle: in his mouth is a "red red rose with an endless stem." As Naomi explains, he is performing a "flower dance – a ritual of the dead" (30). Through a series of poetic associations, the narrative identifies the "endless stem" of the red rose in Uncle's mouth with the last tangible bond between Naomi and her mother – a paper streamer. When the boat departs for Japan, carrying Naomi's grandmother and her mother to their deaths, Naomi is too small to see above the crowd: "All I know is that Mother and Grandma are at the other end of a long paper streamer I clutch in my fist" (70). The endless stem of the rose and the streamer are, in turn, connected to the long "red string" that binds the folder containing the letters that describe the mother's ordeal at Nagasaki (48, 241). Toward the end of the novel, Naomi has a dream that reinforces the connections among these disparate images. In her dream, her mother, rather than her uncle, performs the ritual of the dead. As Naomi tells us, "the dance ceremony of the dead was a slow courtly telling, the heart declaring a long thread knotted to Obasan's twine, knotted to Aunt Emily's package" (250). According to Gottlieb, references to the ball of twine that Obasan collected from bits and pieces saved over the years indicate that "both the central secret and the key to its unravelling in the appropriate moment ... have been in

Obasan's hands all along" (48). But this crimson thread ultimately leads beyond the silent Obasan to the fate of the Native peoples. After learning of her mother's gruesome death, Naomi dreams that her mother is a "maypole" around whom she dances. "I dance," Naomi says, "with a long paper streamer in my hand. But the words of the May Day song are words of distress. The unknown is a hook that pierces the bone. Thongs hang down in the hot prairie air. Silence attends the long sun dance" (266). Here the Japanese funerary ritual of the flower dance gives way to the Native Sun Dance, emphasizing that both Native peoples and Japanese Canadians have been pierced by the unspeakable trauma of apocalypse.[13]

In response to this account of the novel, some readers might argue that the Second World War and the atomic bombing were inevitable (did we really want Hitler to win?), that the Canadian government responded admirably to the crisis of the bombing of Pearl Harbour and behaved as it did toward Canadians of Japanese descent out of necessity, and, finally and most importantly, that the past is past. Naomi herself echoes this view after learning about her mother's death: "Some people return home. Some do not. War, they all say, is war and some people survive" (266). This view, however, rests on the belief that what happened *had* to happen, that it was a predictable – even predestined outcome.

In *Lament for a Nation* (1965), the historian George Grant forcibly challenges this perspective, which, as he points out, either implicitly or explicitly identifies "necessity" with "goodness." Not surprisingly, the argument of necessity is often used to justify the behaviour of the settler-invader society toward North American Native peoples. The destruction of their way of life was, according to this logic, inevitable. Robertson Davies perhaps best illustrates this attitude when he states: "[The Native peoples] ... belonged to the stone age. You cannot mix modern people with stone age people and expect the stone age people to get the best of it, because they won't. Also they were not as numerous as the newcomers, whose technology was rather good. Nowadays, the Indians suffer painfully and their trouble is a horrible one, but I think it is *the inevitable impact of modern civilization* upon some people who have not advanced beyond the stone age and who are still alive ... There is always collective guilt when a highly civilized group takes a country from primitive groups. *It is just one of the facts of history*" (364–5; my emphasis). As Grant argues, those "who worship 'evolution' or the facts of 'history' consider that what must come in the future will be 'higher,' 'more developed,' 'better,' 'freer' than what has been in the past" (88–9). Grant also points out that the doctrine of progress or providence was given its best philosophical expression by Hegel, who wrote: "World history is the world's judgement" (Hegel quoted in Grant 88–9). But there is, Grant insists, a serious flaw in this reasoning: "[I]f history is the final court of appeal, force is the final argument. Is it possible to look at history and deny that within its dimensions force is the supreme ruler? To take a progressive view of providence is to come close to worshipping force. Does this not make us cavalier about evil? The screams of the tortured child can be justified by the achievements of history. How pleasant for the achievers, but how meaningless for the child" (Grant 89).[14] In accordance with Grant's view, Kogawa's narrative adopts a non-progressive view of history that refuses to dismiss the perspective of the tortured child – the child "forever unable to speak" (*Obasan* 267). Unlike the infamous unveiling experienced by John, the visions afforded to Kogawa's characters – most obviously, Naomi – and her readers, are not progressive and proleptic but analeptic (Visvis 3). Like Benjamin's melancholy "angel of history" the narrative turns to the past and surveys the ruins. This stance does not signal defeatism, however; in keeping with Benjamin's insights and Ondaatje's narrative strategy, Kogawa's narrative underscores the strategic necessity of witnessing the past and of identifying with brokenness, rather than wholeness, to counteract teleological and messianic or redemptive historical narratives, and, in doing so, establishes an aesthetics and politics of melancholia.

Within the novel, Naomi repeatedly stresses that her family has been shattered beyond repair. Both her mother and father die as a result of the government's decision to expel the Japanese Canadians from the West Coast, and her only sibling, Stephen, repeatedly compared to Humpty Dumpty (124), flees "to the ends of the earth" (15). As in *The English Patient* and "Hairball," in *Obasan* there is no possibility of gathering together the fragments or of undoing this damage; worse, Naomi recognizes that her entire bloodline will likely disappear. Stephen is childless and both Naomi and her aunt, scarred in different ways by the catastrophe, remain unmarried, suffering from what Naomi disparagingly refers to as a "crone-prone syndrome" (8). As she says, "Some families grow on and on through the centuries, hardy and visible and procreative. Others disappear from the earth without a whimper" (21).

Nor is the irreparable impact of the crisis restricted to Naomi's family. Within the novel, the family functions as a synecdoche for the wounded and terrified Japanese Canadian community. Using the governing metaphor of chickens to describe the plight of her community, Naomi states: "The paper battles rage through the mails onto the desks of busy politicians, while back in the chicken yard one hawk after another circles overhead till the chickens are unable to come out of hiding and their neck feathers moult from the permanent crick. The seasons pass and the leghorns no longer lay eggs. The nests are fouled and crawl with lice" (208).[15] Finally, when forced by her Aunt Emily to face the "facts" associated with the Canadian government's decision to prevent the Japanese Canadians from returning to the West Coast after the war, Naomi reluctantly complies: "The fact is that families already fractured and separated were permanently destroyed" (201).

Unlike Aunt Emily, who retains faith that gaps in history can be filled, Naomi insists that for her there is no healing: the "old sores" remain (219). Although she can cry "for the people who no longer sing ... [and] for Obasan who has turned to stone," she knows that crying will not restore what has been lost: "Uncle does not rise up and return to his boats. Dead bones do not take on flesh" (219). Even the Anglican priest, who arrives at Obasan's home after Uncle's death and translates the letter for Naomi and Stephen that reveals their mother's fate, attests to the brokenness of his community. "'That there is brokenness,'" Sensei says quietly. "'That the world is broken-ness'" (264). The use of incomplete phrases reinforces the reader's awareness that both the community and its ability to speak coherently about its experience have been shattered. Although the priest tries to offer hope, suggesting that "within brokenness is the unbreakable name" and enjoining the family to pray and forgive, Naomi says grimly, "I am not thinking of forgiveness" (264).

In interviews, Kogawa has commented on the experience of "brokenness." She began one interview by stating that her experience of the Japanese Canadians is "of a vastly and profoundly disparate and broken people" ("Is There a Just Cause?" 24). Surprisingly, rather than advocate healing and wholeness as a solution to the crisis, she maintained that people need to come to terms with brokenness: "Rather than abandoning the way of brokenness, I believe we need to remember the paradoxical power in mutual vulnerability. Where there is doubt, the authority of certainty is put aside, but the capacity to hear is heightened. We broken ones then, are not people who shout and stride, confident that our cause is just. But we listen, and we limp. In our limping we may discover that we walk with others who also limp and that even our enemies know pain. That sudden 'eureka' when we recognize a fellow human being where once we'd seen only the delusions of our monstrous imaginings is a miraculous moment" (20). Put somewhat differently, the power of the non-elect – those who have been traumatically wounded – lies in their ability to testify to their "mutual vulnerability." Furthermore, by exposing their brokenness, they dispel the "delusions of our monstrous imaginings," including our apocalyptic dreams of wholeness, purity, and perfection that repeatedly threaten life and community, rather than sustain them. There is, however, another way of conceiving of the novel's insistence on brokenness that gives us further insight into Kogawa's text (as well as into Benjamin's writing and its influence on Ondaatje's work). It entails viewing the opposition between brokenness and wholeness or healing in terms of the difference between mourning and melancholia. In essence, both *The English Patient* and *Obasan* demonstrate that melancholia is preferable to mourning in response to apocalypse.

In "Mourning and Melancholia," Freud argues that the work of mourning allows us to come to terms with the loss of a loved one by withdrawing one's attachment to the object and incorporating it within the ego. By accomplishing this labour, "the ego succeeds in freeing its libido from the lost object," and, in time, another object can be substituted for the one that is lost. In contrast to supposedly healthy grief, the inability to free the libido from the lost object and move on, yet another central aspect of melancholia, appears to Freud as the mark of "a morbid pathological disposition" (252).

As Hélène Cixous's critique of Freud's model reminds us, however, Freud does not consider factors such as gender nor, it should be added, race. Cixous writes: "Man cannot live without resigning himself to loss. He has to mourn ... Mourning, resigning oneself to loss, means not losing. When you've lost something and the loss is a dangerous one, you refuse to admit that something of yourself might be lost in the lost object. So you 'mourn,' you make haste to recover the investment made in the lost object" ("Castration or Decapitation" 355). Mourning, the incorporation of the lost object, allows men to recover the lost object in the language of the symbolic. By contrast, Cixous argues that women "do not mourn": "[T]hat is where their pain lies! When you've mourned, it's all over after a year, there's no more suffering. Woman, though, does not mourn, does not resign herself to loss. She basically takes up the challenge of loss in order to go on living: she lives it, gives it life, is capable of unsparing loss" ("Castration or Decapitation" 355).[16] In accordance with Cixous's observations, Kogawa's novel portrays Naomi taking up "the challenge of loss" rather than acquiescing to mourning, which may involve an inappropriate and impossible denial of loss and a conscious or unconscious complicity with hegemonic assimilationist strategies.

In the case of Naomi and, more generally, Canadians of Japanese ancestry who experienced devastating losses, loss cannot be relegated to memory because it cannot be contained by the symbolic. How can one begin to mourn, if one cannot name what has been lost? What could take the place of an absent home, an absent community, a history disrupted by expulsion and exile, and the lives that were never lived? Furthermore, Naomi also senses that she has lost something of herself; like the figure of Beloved in Toni Morrison's novel of the same name, the ghost of the mother haunting Naomi represents the other who "invades and constitutes the self" (Heffernan 565).

In the context of Kogawa's novel, the inability to mourn, to replace what has been lost – far from what Freud terms "a pathological symptom" – attests to the racialized losses sustained by the Japanese Canadian community. Furthermore, the portrayal of melancholia, with its characteristic feature of self-blame, must also be understood in the broader historical and political context that promoted, and continues to promote, internalized racism. As a small child, Naomi cannot fathom why her mother disappears. Grasping for some explanation, she imagines that because she withheld a secret from her mother (the experience of sexual abuse by her neighbour, Old Man Gower), she drove her mother away: "If I tell my mother about Mr. Gower, the alarm will send a tremor through our bodies and I will be torn from her. But the secret has already separated us" (69). This tendency toward self-reproach, which as Freud notes, is entirely absent in the case of mourning, remains one of the defining characteristic of melancholia.

In an effort to account for melancholia's defining trait of self-abasement, Freud posits that all of the self-reproaches actually apply to someone else: "If one listens patiently to a melancholic's many and various self-accusations, one cannot in the end avoid the impression that often the most violent of them are hardly at all applicable to the patient himself, but with insignificant modifications they do fit someone else, someone whom the patient loves or has loved or should love ... So we find the key to the clinical picture: we perceive that the self-reproaches are reproaches against a loved object which have been shifted away from it on to the patient's own ego" ("Mourning and Melancholia" 256–7). Freud argues further that the melancholic's "complaints" about himself should really be thought of as "plaints" in the old [legal] sense of the word (257). He goes on to explain that melancholics "always seem as though they felt slighted and had been treated with great injustice," an attitude that prevails because "the reactions expressed in their behaviour still proceed from a mental constellation of revolt, which has then, by a certain process, passed over into the crushed state of melancholia" (257).

In the light of the Canadian government's decision to revoke citizenship and confiscate the property of Canadians of Japanese ancestry, Kogawa's protagonist's complaints can legitimately be interpreted as plaints against the state – plaints arising not simply from the loss of an object but, in this case, from the theft of an object: "We are the despised rendered voiceless, stripped of car, radio, camera and every means of communication, a trainload of eyes covered with mud and spittle" (119). As Maria Sarita See has aptly noted, with reference to the case of colonial melancholia in contemporary Filipino/American texts, this is a "layered theft: not merely losing an object, or losing the right to own that object, but losing the right to own that loss" (2). But why, to borrow Freud's words, is the melancholic's "mental constellation of revolt" transformed into "the crushed state of the melancholia"? Why is the melancholic's plaint consistently deflected from the outside world and directed at the self?

Naomi's mother was gravely injured during the Allied bombing of Japan. A child at the time, Naomi did not cause her death; yet she feels responsible for the loss: "the secret has already separated us. The secret is this: I go to seek Old Man Gower in his hideaway. I clamber unbidden onto his lap" (69). Observing that the melancholic "reproaches himself, vilifies himself and expects to be cast out and punished" ("Mourning and Melancholia" 254), Freud views this behaviour as part of the psychic complex in which the ego introjects the lost object, then debases and rages against itself (267). However, the racial and political context complicates the portrayals of melancholia in Kogawa's novel. Here the "extra-ordinary diminution of self-regard" (254) cannot be prized apart from racism and internalized racism. Systems of domination actively coerce sub-ordinated racialized subjects to internalize negative perceptions of themselves, to be self-hating (hooks 28). In particular, Japanese Canadians found themselves at the mercy of a colonialist discourse that codes the non-white body as "a sign of the monstrous 'Asiatic,' then later as a deviancy to be assimilated, and more recently, as a variance that is scripted as the 'multicultural'" (Miki 208). Naomi recognizes that she is "self-denigrating" when she calls herself "crone-prone" (*Obasan* 8) and tells us that she has "the social graces of a common house-fly" (7). Taken together, her isolated reproaches and self-recriminations serve as a reminder of how the community as a whole was coerced into acting as a scapegoat, "forced to incorporate and hence disguise the relentless power of an underlying violence ... toward otherness in all its forms" (Miki 31).[17] By turning against herself and internalizing the hatred of her oppressors, Naomi likewise veils the actual source of her oppression. But the source is never entirely obscured because melancholy, like trauma, relentlessly demands a witness. In the light of their similarities, it is not surprisingly that Freud repeatedly likens melancholy to "an open wound" ("Mourning and Melancholia" 262, 268).

After tracing Kogawa's commitment to an anti-apocalyptic aes-thetics and politics of brokenness – a commitment that reflects the impact of trauma and melancholy – it is now possible to return to the question about the novel's ending and decide whether, as the major-ity of critics assert, it offers unity and closure. In the last chapter, Naomi returns to the coulee, a month after her uncle's death. The ending recalls the opening with an important difference: after sifting through her aunt's diary and the historical documents in the package and after hearing the contents of the letters concerning her mother's death, Naomi now has answers to the questions that haunted her. She knows, for example, why she and her uncle began visiting the coulee on 9 August every year after the war and why her mother never returned. The ending, according to Coral Ann Howells, is about for-giveness: "Naomi has rehabilitated herself as a speaking subject and the story ends on a fragile promise for the future" (194). But this vision of wholeness is called into question for several reasons. Even Howells is subsequently forced to admit that Naomi remains "silent and alone in a secret place on the Alberta coulee" (94). Gottlieb, who skilfully analyses *Obasan*'s concentric structure – "container hidden within container within container" (34) – loses sight of this structure when addressing the conclusion and mistakenly argues that the first and last chapters "are symmetrical like book ends" (37). Simply put, critics and readers alike seem to have forgotten (or have been obliged to forget) the doubleness of the ending. Yet, "Naomi's gesture and its fade-out does not close the novel, as many readers assume" (Miki 115–16). There are, in fact, two endings. The first "comes dangerously close to over-resolution, to the implicit assumption that the events of the text have conspired to leave the protagonist standing firm at the end, finally master of those same events she can now narrate" (Davidson 77). If the first ending represents an attempt to remember and tell the traumatic event, thereby working through it, the second ending reminds us that such a cleansed text is not possible. The "over-resolution" and falseness of the first ending together with the presence of a second ending signal an inability or refusal to work through.[18] In keeping with Kermode's view that novels must have beginnings and ends "even if the world has not" (*The Sense of an Ending* 138), *Obasan*'s conclusion has been understood as a means of promoting unity and closure. However, in contrast to Kermode's desire for elegant linear forms, *Obasan*'s doubled ending appears rather to stage the tensions between wholeness and brokenness and ultimately to reveal the limits of apocalyptic thinking.

The second ending consists of a brief postscript entitled: "Excerpt from the Memorandum sent by the Co-Operative Committee on Japanese Canadians to the House and the Senate of Canada, April 1946" (272). This document, signed by three white men, protests against the government's plan to deport Japanese Canadians. In the light of this supplementary ending, Miki contends that *Obasan* lacks closure. "A silence," he writes, "still haunts in the absence of a Japanese Canadian name on this political document submitted to the government" (116). The implication of the document for Miki is that "nothing has happened to change the social and political background to Naomi's experiences" (116). Are we not witnessing, Miki asks, "the same dominant social system (these three men are, after all, from the same white society that inflicted the suffering on the Japanese Canadians) talking back to itself, resolving its own contradictions through the disguise of petition and pleas?" (116).

While Miki's reading of the postscript shows scrupulous attention to what has been described here as the anti-canonical dimensions of the narrative, it must be argued further that it is in the nature of Kogawa's apocalyptic testimony to disrupt this type of solipsistic exchange. The challenge to language as a wholly transparent medium of exchange is perhaps best illustrated by the letter that describes the mother's fate. Rather than simply offer a revelation that allows the signifying system to carry on intact, the letter forces readers to contend with precisely those elements that cannot and have not been represented by the symbolic order.

The narrative itself alludes to the issue of revelation when Naomi describes the Japanese writing on the thin blue rice paper as "a bead curtain of asterisks" (256). But is this curtain or "veil" ever torn aside to reveal the truth? The text's challenge to the symbolic order, seen in the portrayal of the letters and their transmission, may be analyzed in the light of the theoretical insights of poststructuralist critics, including Derrida and Lacan. When the family is gathered to mourn Uncle's death, the priest arrives and reads the letters. After learning that their contents have been kept secret from the children, he informs Obasan and Aunt Emily that it is time for Naomi and Stephen to know what happened to their mother.

The text emphasizes that the children do not have unmediated access to their mother's presence: for one, the letters were written not by the mother but by their grandmother, Grandma Kato, and are addressed to her husband. "It is clear," Naomi says, "as he [the priest] reads that the letters were never intended for Stephen and me" (255). As well, the letters travel a circuitous path. Written by the grandmother, they are sent initially to her husband and, when he dies, they end up with Aunt Emily. She, in turn, makes two attempts to bring them to Naomi but eventually leaves them with Obasan. After reading the letters, however, Obasan decides not to share their contents with Naomi. Finally, eighteen years later, after passing through many hands, the letters are read aloud by the priest. Paradoxically, although they were neither written by the mother nor read by her, they are said to represent her voice. "'Naomi,' he [the priest] says softly, 'Stephen, your mother is speaking. Listen carefully to her voice'" (256). Naomi's subsequent comment confirms that he reads Grandmother Kato's letters without translating them. As she says, "Many of the Japanese words sound strange and the language is formal" (256). In the succeeding chapter, Naomi provides readers with an elaborate translation. In effect, efforts at locating the mother's voice – efforts at an apocalyptic unveiling that never takes place –

recall similar episodes in the works already discussed. In *Headhunter*, for instance, the photographer who tries to take a picture of Emma Berry's perfect face end up recording only the artistry of her husband, the famous cosmetic surgeon, Maynard Berry. Similarly, when invited by Kurtz to write an essay in answer to the question "Who do you think you are?" Fabiana does not give Kurtz the truth about herself; instead, she gives him a fiction composed by her "writing friend" (342).

Generally speaking, these episodes, as well as the circuitous path of the letters in *Obasan*, demonstrate the impossibility of achieving divine revelation by recalling poststructuralist theories about the signifying system. In "Structure, Sign, and Play," for example, Derrida describes how language creates the illusion of "a point of presence, a fixed origin" (247). In contrast to the classical view of language, which conceived of the linguistic system as an "inexhaustible field" because it was so vast, Derrida argues that the system is infinite because of a gap: "there is something missing from it: a center which arrests and founds the freeplay of substitutions" (260). The movement of "freeplay," Derrida contends, is permitted "by the lack, the absence of a center or origin" (260). He goes on to explain that the "presence of an element is always a signifying and substitutive reference inscribed in a system of differences and the movement of a chain" (263). That is, the interplay between presence and absence that produces meaning is posited as one of difference and deferral created through the potentially infinite process of referring to other, absent signifiers (Moi 106). Derrida's conception of the symbolic order radically challenges notions of truth and agency: "Derrida's analysis of the production of meaning thus implies a fundamental critique of the whole of Western philosophical tradition, based as it is on a 'metaphysics of presence,' which discerns meaning as fully present in the Word (or Logos). Western metaphysics comes to favour speech over writing precisely because speech presupposes the *presence* of the speaking subject, who thus can be cast as the unitary *origin* of his or her discourse" (Moi 106–7). Derrida's theories about the language and his keys concepts of "differance"[19] and "trace" highlight the significance of Grandma Kato's letters and their wanderings, which come to an end only when they arrive in the hands of the priest. As Derrida argues, the sign can never return to the origin, in this case, the mother. The convoluted passage of the letters and their transmission demonstrate further that her supposed presence is nothing more

than an effect of the signifying system with its characteristic "movement of a chain." Thus, there can be no apocalypse.

The dissemination of the letters also recalls Lacan's account of the
workings of the symbolic order, which is anchored, according to
Lacan, by the primary, transcendental signifier, the phallus.[20]
Kogawa's narrative, repeatedly classified as an "elegy for a lost community,"[21] disrupts the symbolic because the narrative refuses the
closure associated with the discourse of the Father. Although the
priest attempts to effect closure through the recitation of the Lord's
Prayer, Naomi will not listen. We are told that the "sound of Sensei's
voice grows as indistinct as the hum of distant traffic" (264). For her,
the dominant, patriarchal discourse loses its privileged status as the
bearer of the Logos and becomes merely noise.[22]

Examining *Obasan* with the writings of Derrida and Lacan does not
minimize the narrative's depiction of the horror arising from specific
historical and racialized events; nor does it suggest that these events
can be subsumed under the normal operations of the signifying system.[23] A post-Holocaust Jew, Derrida's singular contribution to critical theory, deconstruction, contains traces of the crisis of the Second
World War. Derrida admits that "the best paradigm for the trace...is
not, as some have believed ... , the trail of the hunt, the fraying, the
furrow in the sand, the wake in the sea, the love of the step for its
imprint, but the cinder (what remains without remaining from the
holocaust, from the all-burning, from the incineration, the incense)"
(*Cinders* 43). When Naomi turns away from the priest's voice and
attends her mother's "voicelessness" she is following the same inex-
orable path of the trace: "How shall I attend that speech, Mother, how
shall I trace that wave?" she asks. At first, she uses the familiar Der-
ridean trope of "the furrow in the sand," comparing the mother to
"the tide rushing moonward pulling back from the shore" (*Obasan*
265). But she finally arrives, as Derrida does, at the "all-burning"
atomic blast: "The skin on your face bubbles like lava and melts from
your bones. Mother, I see your face. Do not turn aside" (266). Readers are thus alerted both to the workings and to the limits of language
after the traumatic experience of the Holocaust and the bombing of
Japan by the letters (which are, in fact, not the "mother's voice"), by
Naomi's refusal to forgive and to recite the Lord's Prayer, and, finally,
by Naomi's impossible claim of seeing her mother's ravaged face.

The survivor's testimony also illustrates the limits of language
because the survivor speaks – as Naomi's earlier description of her-

self as a "skeleton" suggests – as the living dead, but this is not the same as being dead. Even when the survivor attempts to speak for the dead or to see "the face" of the dead, she ultimately bears witness to an absence, a wound that is translated and made intelligible only through language.[24] In his study of American apocalypses, Douglas Robinson reminds us that apocalypse falls under the broad category of eschatology; whereas this term is often understood to mean "the study of last things," the etymological meaning of the eschaton is actually "the furthermost boundary," "the ultimate edge" in time or space (xii). Read in this context, *Obasan*, like *Headhunter*, invites readers not to pull aside a curtain that obscures their vision but to consider the location and nature of the threshold itself. Rather than shore up the symbolic order, Kogawa's text invites readers to scrutinize the cultural and political investment in maintaining the outermost limit between what is deemed familiar and whatever supposedly lies beyond.

Moreover, when we turn our attention to the threshold, it becomes immediately apparent that it is gendered: the mother cannot be represented except through a ventriloquism act by the priest. In this way, the text gestures to the fact that throughout the history of Western thought, the unrepresentable, the space of alterity or difference beyond the conscious subject, has relentlessly been associated with the feminine. In her study of patriarchy, the historian Gerda Lerner traces this view to Aristotelian philosophy, which assumes that women are "beings of an entirely different order than men" (10). In a groundbreaking 1974 essay, the anthropologist Sherry Ortner argued persuasively that in virtually every known society women are viewed as being closer to nature than to culture. Within the realm of literary theory, Hélène Cixous contends that Western philosophy and literary thought have always been caught up in a series of hierarchical binary oppositions – nature/culture, active/passive, reason/emotion—based on the fundamental opposition between male and female (*La Jeune Née* 115–16). Finally, in her doctoral thesis *La Révolution du langage poétique* (1974), Julia Kristeva acknowledges and reinscribes this dichotomy when she contrasts the Lacanian male-identified mode of the symbolic order with what she terms the feminine semiotic. This site of negativity, perceived only as disruptions, absences, and silences in the symbolic language, according to Kristeva, provides the source for challenges to the subject of the symbolic order and the meanings it generates. In light of this gendered structure of the symbolic, critics, including Derrida, have recognized that one can read apocalypse as resisting such alterity or difference by expressing "a desire for closure in the final 'truth' represented by a single, male deity" (Woodland 51). In Kogawa's text, Naomi refuses closure in favour of difference. But this is a difference with a difference: *Obasan* also highlights how "the furthermost edge" is determined by conceptions of race. Since Naomi's Canadian mother was raised and died in Japan, the letter describing her death is written in Japanese. Thus, in addition to the disruption signalled by the refusal of the Lord's Prayer, the act of translation also undermines attempts to install closure.

In "The Task of the Translator," Walter Benjamin argues that while "the content and language form a certain unity in the original, like a fruit and its skin, the language of the translation envelops its content like a royal robe with ample folds" (*Illuminations* 75). Benjamin goes on to explain that the language of translation "signifies a more exalted language than its own and thus remains unsuited to its content, overpowering and alien" (75). His comments help to illuminate the cultural politics surrounding Naomi's translation of the letters – a translation from (unrepresented) Japanese text into Standard English. In terms of the novel as a whole, Benjamin's suggestion that translation envelops its content "like a royal robe" perfectly captures how, within the racialized national context, the Japanese-Canadian minority group's traumatic experience is enveloped in the dominant group's overarching discourse, which is both "overpowering and alien."

Despite the potential pitfalls, engaging in acts of translation remains an absolutely necessary and strategic task. As a child, Naomi imagines that once upon a time all the different birds sang in unison and their song was comprehensible: "they sang together, a great bird choir, each bird adding its part to the melody, till some catastrophe happened and the songs disappeared into chirps and tweets" (153). Her dream of prelapsarian harmony recalls Derrida's comment concerning the two potential responses to poststructuralist views of the signifying system:

One seeks to decipher, dreams of deciphering, a truth or an origin which is free from freeplay and from the order of the sign, and lives like an exile the necessity of interpretation [and translation]. The other, which is no longer turned toward the origin, affirms free play and tries to pass beyond man and humanism, the name man being the name of that being who, throughout history of metaphysics or of ontotheology – in other words, through the history of all of his history – has dreamed of full presence, the reassuring foundation, the origin and the end of the game ... There are more than enough indications today to suggest we might perceive that these two interpretations of interpretation – which are absolutely irreconcilable even if we live them simultaneously and reconcile them in an obscure economy – together share the field which we call, in such a problematic fashion, the human sciences. ("Structure, Sign, and Play" 264–5)

In fact, Naomi's traumatic, doubled narrative articulates both a longing for presence combined with an acute awareness that we need to move beyond "the origin and end of the game." The necessity of moving beyond the game is graphically evident when one considers that, in the 1940s, the symbolic functioned akin to the board game called *The Yellow Peril* that Naomi's brother, Stephen, receives as a Christmas present. In this game, the Japanese are characterized as "weak and small" (165); "people are reduced to a set of binary signifiers" (Visvis 7). Translation exposes and, to a certain extent, disrupts the arbitrary and barbaric rules of the game.

In his discussion of the cultural politics of translation, Homi Bhabha insists that "cultural difference" (his term for the awareness of cultural hybridity that calls into question the myth of national cohesion) emerges from "the borderline moment of translation" (314). According to Bhabha, the transfer of meaning "can never be total" between discourses (314). This means that in the act of translation the "'given' content becomes alien and estranged; that, in turn, leaves the language of translation *Aufgabe*, always confronted by its double, the untranslatable – alien and foreign" (315). With respect to *Obasan*, by paying careful attention to the gaps among the ample folds of translation's "royal robe," readers catch a glimpse of the very thing that makes the conception of Canada as an "imagined community" possible and what the dominant discourse was, according to Derrida, "designed to leave in the domain of the unthinkable" ("Structure, Sign, and Play" 254). Rather than attend to the Logos, Kogawa's narrative envisions "the Other/Woman as an (im)possible national subject," and, in doing so, brings Canadians "*to the limits* of understanding themselves as a nation; in fact through this gesture, the book stages a crisis of nationalist discourses as such, as an offshoot of the patriarchal state's attempt to ensure the 'purity' of its progeny" (Karpinski 6; my emphasis). Naomi's translation of her mother's ordeal is central in staging this crisis. Moreover, English must be used in order to address non-Japanese Canadians whose traumatic history, while it may have been forgotten, is nevertheless tied to the catastrophic events at Nagasaki and, even earlier, to the betrayal of Native peoples. If Naomi offers us a vision from the perspective of the non-elect, at bottom, her testimony demonstrates that we are implicated in each other's traumas; "It may be that when the seals are broken and absolute evil is identified and isolated, the Blessed will look across the abyss and see themselves" (Berger 8).

To conclude, Kogawa, like Findley and Ondaatje, views the Second World War as a defining historical moment that calls for a profound reconsideration of the apocalyptic paradigm and a recognition of the suffering and trauma experienced by the non-elect. And, in keeping with Ondaatje's and Atwood's preoccupation with the fragment, Kogawa also recognizes the power of brokenness. In *Obasan*, images of fragmentation attest to the lethal repercussions of Manichean apocalyptic thinking, "the delusions of our monstrous imaginings" (Kogawa, "Is There a Just Cause?" 20). Moreover, viewed in terms of the difference between mourning and melancholia, images of fragmentation in *Obasan* signal the impossibility of mourning owing to the traumatic, racialized losses sustained by the Japanese Canadian community. Finally, by emphasizing that the letter describing Naomi's mother's death is written in Japanese, and by translating this letter into English in all its gruesome detail, *Obasan*, like the other works in this study, prompts readers to recognize that apocalyptic violence is designed to eradicate the Other/Woman. Thus, for those who naively assume that Canada has never succumbed to the lure of apocalypse, *Obasan*'s traumatic testimony, which outlines the fate of Japanese Canadians and links their fate to that of Native North Americans, demonstrates that the fires of apocalypse have burned here, at home.

Adrift after the Apocalypse

Fashioning an ending for a book about fictions that advocate skepticism about endings is, admittedly, a tricky business. However, in
light of this study's findings that it is dangerous to ignore the myth
of the end, it seems prudent to offer some concluding remarks. This
study began with the desire to explore the treatment of the apocalyptic paradigm from the ex-centric perspective of contemporary
Canadian writers. In effect, their works confirm Ronald Granofsky's
observation that 1945 was "the year a certain innocence ended for the
human race, a Second Fall" (2). Using the grammar of apocalypse
outlined in the introduction, chapters 1 and 2 traced the characteristic features of apocalypse adopted and, in many instances, adapted in
Findley's and Ondaatje's novels. While they rely on basic features of
apocalypse, including intertextuality, allegory, revelation, an overarching temporal perspective, and the opposition between the elect and
the non-elect, *Headhunter* and *The English Patient* nevertheless challenge the apocalyptic paradigm in important ways.

Headhunter destabilizes the apocalyptic paradigm, on one level, by
revealing the permeable boundary between the categories of good
and evil, the elect and the non-elect. By demonstrating Marlow's
belief in "that most dangerous of concepts, the concept of men and
women who were superior" (380), *Headhunter* shows how fundamentally benevolent and educated individuals can be seduced by the
logic of apocalypse. In this way, *Headhunter* demonstrates that,
despite its Manichean divisions, the apocalyptic boundary between
the elect and the non-elect remains subjective and indeterminate.

Headhunter also forcibly resists apocalypse by omitting its key
vision of the New Jerusalem. This omission underscores the novel's

fundamental rejection of apocalypse's fascist promise of perfection and its faith in a future predicated on the violent destruction of the earthly world. Both *Headhunter* and *The English Patient* are haunted by the absence of the biblical New Jerusalem. In these novels, the absence of this key biblical trope helps to promote prophetic eschatology, a less radical alternative to apocalypse, which, in contrast to apocalypse's future-oriented vision of divine intervention, stresses responsible action in an earthly, communal context.

Although they share a desire to subvert the apocalyptic paradigm, *Headhunter* and *The English Patient* nevertheless emphasize different strategies for challenging the biblical narrative. Whereas *Headhunter* destabilizes the apocalyptic paradigm by exposing the permeable boundary between the elect and the non-elect, *The English Patient* reconsiders allegory, another basic apocalyptic element. However, in contrast to Revelation, which uses allegorical fragments to promote its vision of progress, wholeness, and order, *The English Patient* relies on fragments for the opposite effect. In Ondaatje's novel, allegorical fragments contribute to a portrait of human history as a process of decline. And, whereas Revelation intimates that progress, wholeness, and order are predicated on a violent rejection of the past and an embrace of the future, *The English Patient*, in accordance with Walter Benjamin's allegorical way of seeing, valorizes a potentially redemptive engagement with the past and history's anonymous losers.

In contrast to the initial chapters on *Headhunter* and *The English Patient* and the final chapters on *Green Grass, Running Water* and *Obasan*, which explore novels that promote prophetic eschatology in a bid to resist apocalypse, chapter 3 serves as the study's apocalyptic centre. Unlike the other fictions, Atwood's short story "Hairball" depicts what happens when apocalyptic thinking goes unchallenged. Furthermore, whereas *Headhunter* and *The English Patient* implicitly and explicitly allude to the historical events surrounding the Second World War, Atwood's story draws on Native Wendigo tales to indicate that apocalyptic violence dates back to Canada's formation as a nation-state. At bottom, by highlighting the parallels between the grisly plot of Revelation, specifically the murder of the Whore of Babylon and the conquest of Native North Americans, "Hairball" suggests that the settler-invader society relied on apocalyptic thinking to subjugate Native peoples, women, and the wilderness.

Whereas links between the apocalyptic paradigm and the brutal treatment of women and Canada's Native peoples remain implicit in

"Hairball," these links are explicit in King's *Green Grass, Running Water*. Like Atwood's "Hairball," King's text also aims to cure non-Native North Americans' amnesia concerning apocalyptic violence. To this end, his novel offers readers a history lesson about the US government's ruthless campaign to force the remaining Plains Indian tribes onto reservations. In its efforts to resist apocalypse, King's text recalls the tactics adopted in Findley's and Ondaatje's novels. In effect, like *Headhunter* and *The English Patient*, King's novel advocates a return to something akin to prophetic eschatology to counter the linear, future-oriented, genocidal, apocalyptic plot. And in keeping with *The English Patient*'s emphasis on maps and mapmaking, *Green Grass, Running Water* likewise demonstrates how the book, adopted and adapted by Native writers, can serve as a communal map that provides an alternative to apocalypse's individualistic, future-oriented map. But King takes the emphasis on prophetic eschatology to a new level by rejecting the Western map of apocalypse in favour of a circular, Native mode of figuration based on the Sun Dance.

By emphasizing Canada's treatment of Native North Americans and Japanese Canadians in the wake of the Second World War, the final chapters on *Green Grass, Running Water* and *Obasan* vividly portray apocalypse from the perspective of Canada's traumatized non-elect. In effect, both King's and Kogawa's texts shed light on the importance of bearing witness, another crucial facet of the apocalyptic paradigm. Although *Green Grass, Running Water* adopts a comic approach to apocalypse, whereas *Obasan*'s is elegiac, both novels highlight the importance and difficulty of bearing witness to apocalyptic violence. In the case of *Green Grass, Running Water*, bearing witness is complicated by the fact that the process contravenes traditional ethics of Northern Native peoples. For this reason, King relies on "trauma humour" to examine the impact of apocalyptic thinking on Native North Americans. This strategy allows him simultaneously to evade and uphold Native ethics. However, in addition to ethical problems, the impact of trauma also greatly complicates the act of bearing witness to apocalyptic violence.

In chapter 5, discussions of trauma and its symptoms by Freud, Caruth, Berger, and LaCapra help to explain why *Obasan* both attempts and resists working though the corrosive impact of traumatic events unleashed on Japanese Canadians during the Second World War. Moreover, puzzling and idiosyncratic features associated with trauma, such as memory loss and belatedness or latency, also

clarify why *Obasan* and other fictions considered in this study repeatedly portray traumatic events in light of prior traumatic events. Thus,
although it concerns the internment of Japanese Canadians, *Obasan*,
like "Hairball" and *Green Grass, Running Water*, prompts readers to
consider how the myth of apocalypse shaped earlier moments in
Canadian history, specifically the encounters between the settler-
invaders and Native North Americans. In *Obasan*, a blood-red thread
literally binds the apocalyptic fate of the Native peoples to that of
Japanese Canadians.

Ultimately, with the exception of Atwood's "Hairball," rather than
fully complying with the apocalyptic paradigm, each of the works in
this study attempts to follow the traces of apocalypse to the limits of
the biblical narrative. By invoking basic features of the paradigm,
such as the division between the elect and the non-elect, allegorical
fragments, and the act of bearing witness, the fictions under consideration show how these features can be used to deconstruct the biblical narrative. Furthermore, owing to the links between apocalyptic
thinking and the founding of nation-states, in the process of exploring the furthermost edge of apocalypse, these fictions unveil the limits of the discourse of Canadian nationalism – a discourse that constructs an imagined community only by relegating certain peoples to
the margins – what Derrida terms "the domain of the unthinkable."
Indeed, as Derrida and other critics have observed, the apocalyptic
narrative, which represents its desire for closure in the form of a final
truth embodied by a single, male God, is designed to resist alterity.

At its most basic level, Revelation wrestles with the problem of
home, informing readers in no uncertain terms that their old home
will be destroyed and offering a vision of a heavenly and perfect
home. Now that Canadians have entered the new millennium, it is
tempting to speculate on the fate of apocalypse. In *The Politics of
Home: Postcolonial Relocations and Twentieth-Century Fiction* (1996),
Rosemary Marongoly George maintains that "homes are not about
inclusions and wide open arms as much as they are about places
carved out of closed doors, closed borders and screening appara-
tuses" (18). Later, she insists that home is "neither where they have to
take you in nor where they want to take you in, but rather the place
where one is in because an Other(s) is kept out" (26–7). Faced with
the deadly binary logic of apocalypse, made glaringly apparent after
the Second World War, the Holocaust, and the bombing of Japan, fictions by Canadian writers are challenging the apocalyptic impulse to

claim a home predicated on a violent exclusion of the Other. Yann
Martel's novel *Life of Pi* (2002) is a perfect example: it takes place on
the ocean, adrift between religions, countries, and traditions, and features a boy who, rather than face the prospect of drifting alone in his
lifeboat, invites another passenger aboard, a three-year-old adult
Bengal tiger. Indeed, rather than accept the myth of apocalypse, its
distinction between the elect and the non-elect, and its promise of the
New Jerusalem, which, translated into secular terms, often entails
embracing exclusionary and violent forms of nationalism, many ex-
centric contemporary Canadian authors champion, instead, what
might best be described as placelessness and drifting.

In *Territorial Disputes*, Graham Huggan observes that contemporary Canadian writers "seem less interested than their immediate or
more distant predecessors in evoking a sense of place than in expressing a kind of placelessness through which the notion of a fixed location, and the corresponding possibility of a fixed identity, are resisted
... [in these texts] the self ... becomes a transitory, contingent, and
fluid phenomenon" (56). In *The English Patient*, the nameless hero
recalls happier days before the Second World War and makes an
impassioned plea for rejecting nationalism in favour of placelessness.
Indeed, the passage cited earlier champions a politics of drifting:
"There were rivers of desert tribes, the most beautiful humans I've
met in my life. We were German, English, Hungarian, African – all of
us insignificant to them. Gradually we became nationless. I came to
hate nations ... The desert could not be claimed or owned – it was a
piece of cloth carried by winds, never held down by stones, and
given a hundred shifting names long before Canterbury existed, long
before battles and treaties quilted Europe and the East ... We disappeared into landscape. Fire and sand. We left the harbours of oasis.
The places water came to and touched ... Ain, Bir, Wadi, Foggara,
Khottara, Shaduf. I didn't want my name against such beautiful
names. Erase the family name! Erase nations! I was taught such
things by the desert" (138–9). Findley, like Ondaatje, was equally
obsessed by apocalypse and the dark side of nationalism. For Findley, the Holocaust – specifically, the systematic plan to rid the world
of so-called undesirables – gruesomely demonstrated that aspects of
nationalism are perversely exclusionary and are bound up with
ensuring that the supposedly "right" people are accorded power and
privilege, while the supposedly "wrong" sort are expelled or, better
yet, never allowed in.

To illustrate the dangerous exclusionary elements of nationalism Findley wrote *Not Wanted on the Voyage*. At the end of his retelling of this apocalyptic biblical story, Noah's wife sits aboard the drifting Ark. In a final gesture that has puzzled and angered readers, she looks up at the empty sky. Perversely rejecting the promise of an end to the voyage and a return to order epitomized by the new nation, she submits to the motion of drifting and she prays – "not to the absent God ... but to the absent clouds" – for more rain (352). Like Ondaatje's nameless hero, who also wants to erase the nation, Noah's wife prays for rain because she does not want Noah to find land and create a new nation that will, as Rosemary Marongoly George asserts (26–7), inevitably include certain people and viciously exclude others.

At the end of Atwood's story "Hairball," Kat likewise chooses namelessness, placelessness, and drifting over stasis and identity: "She puts on her coat and goes out, foolishly. She intends to walk just to the corner, but when she reaches the corner she goes on ... She feels light and peaceful and filled with charity, and temporarily without a name" (48). Drifting is also featured in King's novel, most obviously in the episode in which Eli drives Lionel to the Sun Dance. Before they arrive at the ritual site, as they reach the crest of a hill, Eli pulls onto the side of the road so they can survey the scene that lies before them: "Below in the distance, a great circle of tepees floated on the prairies, looking for all the world like sailing ships adrift on the ocean" (302). In contrast to Western culture and its apocalyptic map – a fixed linear structure that excludes both the non-elect and the contingencies of chance – the images in this passage highlight a fluid alternative. Finally, in *Obasan*, Naomi describes the Japanese-Canadian community as "rooted nowhere" (248). She is last seen slipping out of the house and driving her car to the coulee. Standing on the bank of the river, she recalls her uncle's words about the prairie landscape: "'Umi no yo,' he always said. 'It's like the sea'" (271).

Following these writers' lead, a host of contemporary ex-centric Canadian writers have begun to champion drifting, forging transnational, often diasporic alliances over apocalyptic nation-building. Recently, for instance, the award-winning novelist and poet Dionne Brand argued explicitly against viewing oneself in nationalist terms. As a black woman from the Carribean, Brand is deeply aware of exclusionary practices, including slavery and racism, which prompted her to question the meaning of home: "Too much has been made of origins ... Here at home, in Canada, we are all implicated in this sense of origins. It is manufactured origin nevertheless, playing to our need for home, however tyrannical. This country, in the main a country of immigrants, is always redefining origins, jockeying and smarming for degrees of belonging" (*A Map to the Door of No Return* 68–9). Brand goes on to insist: "Belonging does not interest me. I had once thought that it did. Until I examined the underpinnings. One is misled when one looks at the sails and majesty of tall ships instead of their cargo" (85). In keeping with the writers considered in this study, rather than cling to notions of home and nation, Brand's fiction emphasizes an alternative possibility, namely, tracing the wandering paths and solitary spaces of history's beautiful losers, the non-elect barred from paradise. In her novel *At the Full and Change of the Moon*, the female descendant of an infamous slave contemplates the word "drift" and confesses that "she liked the word, suggesting streams of her appearing and dissipating in air" (215). In keeping with prophetic eschatology, the alternative to apocalypse favoured by the fictions in this study, Brand's texts conceives of drifting as linking individuals to their past and to the experiences of history's anonymous victims.

Viewed within a broader context, Canadian writers' reconsideration of the apocalyptic paradigm can be seen to coincide with what Stuart Hall terms "the most profound cultural revolution." According to Hall, this revolution has come about as a consequence of the margins coming into representation: "The emergence of new subjects, new genders, new ethnicities, new regions, new communities, hitherto excluded from the major forms of cultural representation, unable to locate themselves except as de-centered or subaltern, have acquired through struggle, sometimes in very marginalized ways, the means to speak for themselves for the first time. And the discourses of power in our society, the discourses of the dominant regimes, have been certainly threatened by this de-centered cultural empowerment of the marginal and the local" (34). However, as the texts in this study demonstrate, those on the margins are not immune to the exclusionary logic of the apocalyptic paradigm: "When the movements of the margins are so profoundly threatened by the global forces of postmodernity, they can themselves retreat into their own exclusivist and defensive enclaves. And at that point, local ethnicities become as dangerous as national ones. We have seen that happen: the refusal of modernity which takes the form of a return, a rediscovery of identity which constitutes a form of fundamentalism"

(Hall, "The Local and the Global" 36). Moreover, in light of the impact of this revolution, one could argue, as James Clifford does, that even the binary opposition between margin and centre has given way: the "old localizing strategies – by bounded *community*, by organic *culture*, by region, by *center* and *periphery*" – no longer account for the contemporary transnational routes taken by populations, and capital.[1] Indeed, with all the attention contemporary Canadian writing is currently receiving, it is difficult to conceive of Canada as on the margins.

Taken together, then, a host of factors – including the apocalyptic violence unleashed during the Second World War; the empowerment of the marginal and local; the increasing impact of globalism and transnationalism, which is rendering the old localizing strategies of margin and centre obsolete; the unsavoury aspects of fundamentalism; and the rising tide of apocalyptic rhetoric in the United States – have prompted contemporary Canadian writers to fashion alternatives to the exclusionary and apocalyptic conceptions of home and the nation-state. Moreover, in their works, images of erasure and drifting often highlight the inadequacy of the nation-state, particularly its response to demands for social justice and its long-standing practices of exclusion. Notwithstanding the claims to nationhood that contribute to projects of decolonization, these anti-apocalyptic fictions portray prophetic eschatology, drifting, and reflecting on history's beautiful losers as equally legitimate resistant practices. At bottom, they offer a cautionary warning to recognize the exclusionary foundations and ongoing limitations of nationalism informed by the apocalyptic paradigm.

Notes

1 This famous quote can be found in many sources, including on the web at history.cbc.ca/history/
?MIval=EpContent.html&chapter_id=5&episode_id=1.

2 I am grateful to Ian MacLaren for alerting me to the pervasive use of apocalyptic tropes in exploration literature.

3 See studies by John R. May, Zbigniew Lewicki, Lois Parkinson Zamora, and Maxine Lavon Montgomery.

4 There are only a scattering of articles on apocalyptic motifs in specific texts. See, for instance, W.J. Keith's "Apocalyptic Imaginations: Notes on Atwood's *The Handmaid's Tale* and Findley's *Not Wanted on the Voyage*" and Norman Ravvin's "The Apocalyptic Predicament: Timothy Findley's Predetermined Novel."

5 Eli Mandel named MacLennan "the father of the Canadian novel" (Mandel 112).

6 This study concerns itself with works of the recognized Canadian canon as popular and culturally significant examples of the apocalyptic paradigm's place within Canadian society and literature.

7 In Judaism, the shift from prophetic to apocalyptic eschatology was a gradual process. The worldly features of prophetic eschatology began to give way to apocalyptic eschatology owing to a series of disasters, including the fall of the northern kingdom in the 730s and 720s BCE, the fall of the southern kingdom of Judah, the abolition of Israel's political identity as a nation in 587 BCE, and, finally, the destruction of Solomon's temple in 586 BCE. In the wake of these catastrophic losses, the people of Israel lost faith in the prophets and in the hope that redemption would

occur within history; "apocalyptic eschatology is the mode assumed by the prophetic tradition once it had been transferred to a new and radically altered setting in the post-exilic community" (Hanson 10; see Reddish 20).

8 "The Bible and the apocalyptic writers know of no progress in history leading to the redemption … It is rather transcendence breaking in upon history, an intrusion in which history itself perishes, transformed in its ruin because it is struck by a beam of light shining into it from an outside source. The apocalyptists have always cherished a pessimistic view of the world. Their optimism, their hope, is not directed to what history will bring forth, but to that which will arise in its ruin, free at last and undisguised" (Scholem 10). As noted earlier, Salmond argues that eschatology portrays history as a moral process, "with a goal toward which it is moving" (734). Scholem's description of apocalypse, however, with its stress on divine intervention – "transcendence breaking in upon history" (10) – suggests that the biblical God's plans and goals may be beyond human comprehension.

9 The small island of Patmos was one of the Sporades Islands in the Aegean Sea, located about thirty-seven miles south and west of Miletus on the western coast of Asia Minor (roughly, present-day Turkey); see Thompson, 11.

10 Although interpreters continue to be stymied by many of the images, it is generally agreed that they correspond to historical figures and events surrounding the persecution of the early Christians and that the persecuting force is "clearly Rome, as represented both by the Emperor and by Emperor-worship" (Matthews 798). Interpretation is complicated because most of the images are intertextual and drawn from earlier apocalypses and prophecies.

11 For a detailed discussion of the biblical allusions in Revelation, see Thompson, 50–1.

12 Indeed, Revelation repeatedly highlights its status as a map and places John in the role of mapmaker on several occasions. The angel explicitly and repeatedly commands John to map the stage where the final battle will take place: "I was given a measuring rod like a staff, and I was told: 'Rise and measure the temple of God and the altar and those who worship there but do not measure the court outside the temple; leave that out, for it is given over to the nations, and they will trample over the holy city for forty-two months" (11:1–2). At the end of Revelation, the angel shows John "the holy city Jerusalem coming down out of heaven from God," and, once again, John proceeds to map the city. John

also observes that the angel who talked to him had "a measuring rod of gold to measure the city and its gates and walls," and he dutifully reports the angel's findings: "The city lies foursquare, its length the same as its breadth; and he [the angel] measured the city with his rod, twelve thousand stadia ... He also measured its wall, a hundred and forty-four cubits by a man's measure, that is, an angel's" (21–2). Although no literal map is produced, John creates a cognitive map.

13 It would be, however, an error to assume that the connection between past and present is based solely on nostalgia. In contrast to nostalgia, prophetic eschatology demonstrates the vital continuation of the past within the present.

14 The concept of the Saints of God or "the elect" has its roots in the Old Testament belief that the Jews are the Chosen People, a belief common to prophetic and apocalyptic eschatology. In the Book of Daniel, one can recognize "the paradigm of what was to become and to remain the central phantasy of revolutionary eschatology" (Cohn, *The Pursuit of the Millenium* 4). Daniel's prophecy refers specifically to the elect, "the Saints of God":

> The world is dominated by an evil, tyrannous power of boundless destructiveness – a power moreover which is imagined not simply human but as demonic. The tyranny of that power will become more and more outrageous, the sufferings of its victims more and more intolerable – until suddenly the hour will strike when the Saints of God are able to rise up and overthrow it. (4)

The elect inevitably direct their righteous anger against an enemy personified by the Antichrist. In Revelation, the figure of the Antichrist reappears as a pseudo-messiah who is once again "allowed to make war on the saints and to conquer them" (13:7). Like Satan, the Antichrist is typically portrayed as a gigantic embodiment of "anarchic, destructive power" (Cohn, *The Pursuit of the Millenium* 20). Readers of the Book of Daniel have identified the king in the prophet's dreams, who "shall exalt himself, and magnify himself above every god" (11:36), with the historical ruler Antiochus IV and labelled him the Antichrist. He "shall wear out the saints of the Most High, and shall think to change the times and the law; and they shall be given into his hand for a time" (7:25). According to Daniel, the false god's dominion "shall be taken away, to be consumed and destroyed to the end" (7:26).

15 In Revelation, John gleefully describes the punishment of the wicked by the angel of God: "the angel swung his sickle on the earth and gathered the vintage of the earth, and threw it into the great wine press of the

wrath of God; and the wine press was trodden outside the city, and blood flowed from the wine press, as high as a horse's bridle, for one thousand six hundred stadia" (14:17).

16 In his study of post-apocalyptic writing, James Berger analyses the relationship between trauma and apocalypse:

> Trauma is the psychoanalytic form of apocalypse, its temporal inversion. Trauma produces symptoms in its wake, after the event, and we reconstruct trauma by interpreting its symptoms, reading back in time. Apocalypse, on the other hand, is preceded by signs and portents whose interpretation defines the event in the future. The apocalyptic sign is the mirror image of the traumatic symptom. In both cases, the event itself is so overwhelming as to be fundamentally unreadable; it can only be understood through the portents and symptoms that precede and follow it. Both apocalypse and trauma present the most difficult questions of what happened "before," and what is the situation "after." The apocalyptic-historical-traumatic event becomes a crux or pivot that forces a retelling and revaluing of all events that lead up to it and all that follow. (20–1)

CHAPTER ONE

1 In a subplot inspired by Fitzgerald's classic, we are introduced to James Gatz, a mysterious and lonely man who throws lavish parties that never satisfy his longing for a lost love. When Gatz meets Emma Berry, the novel maps a fanciful intersection between *The Great Gatsby* and Flaubert's *Madame Bovary*. Like her literary predecessor, Emma Berry marries a doctor – a surgeon, in this case – but abandons her husband and daughter and compulsively engages in a series of doomed liaisons, which culminate in her affair with Gatz.

2 Nicholas Fagan's name first appears in the short story "Hello Cheeverland, Goodbye," in Findley's first collection, *Dinner Along the Amazon*; the "author" of *Essays and Conversations*, the fictional Fagan's comments on John Cheever are used as an epigraph. Fagan also reappears in *The Wars*. At the conclusion of the novel, we are given a quotation from the Irish essayist and critic: "the spaces between the perceiver and the thing perceived can ... be closed with a shout of recognition. One form of a shout is a shot. Nothing so completely verifies our perception of a thing as our killing of it" (191). The name Nicholas Fagan may also allude to the work of Charles Dickens – a combination of the title *Nicholas Nickleby* and the character "Fagin" from *Oliver Twist*.

3 Aspects of the novel are also drawn from Findley's early short stories, specifically, "What Mrs Felton Knew," "Cheeverland," and "Dinner Along the Amazon."

4 For more information on the temporal perspective of apocalypse, see Charles's "Apocalyptic Literature" and chapter 1 of Scholem's *The Messianic Idea in Judaism and Other Essays of Jewish Spirituality*.

5 *Headhunter* is heavy with italicized text; when quoting the novel, the emphasis is never mine.

6 The realization of the new world is also omitted in Findley's *Not Wanted on the Voyage* , a retelling of the story of Noah's Ark that concludes with an image of the ark seemingly doomed to an eternal voyage.

7 Frye uses this term to discuss the technique of adjusting "formulaic structures to roughly a credible context" (*The Secular Scripture* 36).

8 This metamorphosis seems all the more apt in the light of George Bernard Shaw's description of the Book of Revelation as "a curious record of the visions of a drug addict which was absurdly admitted to the canon under the title of Revelation" (quoted in Thompson 4).

9 In his portrayal of Fagan's passion for singing, Findley draws from his own corpus. In *Not Wanted on the Voyage*, Mrs Noyes is famous for playing her "favourite favourites" (175). When her beloved cat, Mottyl, sings her death song, the subject of her "litany of praise and sorrow" is the "last whole vision of the world before it was drowned" (333).

10 Their mutual status as gods is playfully compared in the episode in which Kurtz invites his friend Fabiana Holbach to attend the dinner in honour of Nicholas Fagan. At first Fabiana is overwhelmed and declines. When Kurtz asks for an explanation, she responds: "He's a god, Rupert" (266). Smiling, Kurtz replies: "Well, you've been sitting here with me this last while – and I'm a god. Or so you say. According to Slade" (266).

11 The metaphorical connection between children and the future is established early on when Amy Wylie's sister Olivia debates whether or not to abort her foetus. During her visit with her mother, Olivia longs to tell her "about the child – wanting to reassure her there was – or could be – a future" (26). At the end of the novel, Olivia decides to keep the baby, and the text juxtaposes the Club of Men's shout of death (596) with Olivia's affirmation of life and the future (602).

12 See Tom Hastings's exploration of this motif in *The Wars* in his article, "'Their Fathers Did It to Them': Findley's Appeal to the Great War Myth of a Generational Conflict in *The Wars*."

13 As Carol Roberts reports, the images were "more graphic and horrific

than any seen by the public up to that time" (*Timothy Findley: Stories from a Life* 38). Findley wrote about his reaction to the pictures in a speech, "My Final Hour": "the vision of Dachau in Ivan Moffat's photographs told me that I was just like everyone else. We are all a collective hiding place for monsters" (quoted in Roberts, *Timothy Findley: Stories from a Life* 39).

14 See Heather Sanderson's "(Im)Perfect Dreams: Allegories of Fascism in *The Butterfly Plague*" for an analysis of these issues in *The Butterfly Plague*.

15 Marlow's fallibility is evident on several occasions: he is completely mistaken about his wife's vicious character; his first impression of his secretary, Bella Orenstein, is likewise wildly inaccurate; and he transgresses the doctor-patient boundary by falling in love with his patient Emma Berry.

16 The narrator of *Famous Last Words*, Hugh Selwyn Mauberly, conveys the same idea when he insists that Ezra Pound is not solely to blame for inciting fascism: "It will be somebody's job to pull him down and say he was the cause of madness; thus disposing of the madness in themselves, blaming it all on him. 'We should never had done these things,' they will say, 'were it not that men like Pound and Mussolini, Doctor Goebbels and Hitler drove us to them.' ... Missing the fact entirely that what they were responding to were the whispers of chaos, fire and anger in themselves" (77).

17 In the introduction to Kermode's *Poetry, Narrative, History*, Schweizer and Payne point out the epistemological compromises in Kermode's system; in *The Sense of an Ending*, Kermode's referential assumptions concerning the "real" and "reality" constitute "unacknowledged miniature fictions" (Schweizer and Payne 21).

18 Ironically, whereas Findley climbs into his own fiction, destabilizing the narrative paradigm, he portrays another character, the black woman named Orley, disappearing from his text. Fed up with the way white authors portray blacks: "Black – with a white hand hovering over the page. All the pages of her life written by a white hand," Orley decides "[f]rom now on, I will write myself" (592). Clearly, Findley realizes that, as an author, his is simply one more "white hand hovering over the page." By allowing Orley to escape his fiction, he signals that it is time to throw into question and perhaps even relinquish the unquestioned right to represent marginalized groups. True to her word, Orley never appears in Findley's text again. This episode deftly counters Kermode's assertion that, in the novel, there can be no "just representation" of

human freedom because, if characters were entirely free, they "might simply walk out of the story" (*The Sense of an Ending* 138). See Lorraine York's article "'A White Hand Hovering over the Page': Timothy Findley and the Racialized/Ethnicized Other" for a detailed discussion of Findley's representation of race.

CHAPTER TWO

1 As Burger suggests, the "meaning may well be the message that meaning has ceased to exist" (70).

2 Such parallels also exist between the two novels' attempts to combat imperialism and colonialism. On one level, the patient's strategy of immersion can be likened to Findley's gesture of stepping down into his own text – a gesture that Ondaatje replicates when, toward the end of text, the narrator enters the fiction and discusses Hana, confessing that "[s]he is a woman I don't know well enough to hold in my wing, if writers have wings, to harbour for the rest of my life" (301).

3 The soldier's engagement with the discourses of art and religion can be compared to Benjamin's critical method of Dialectic at a Standstill, a process that involves subjecting familiar phenomena to forms of estrangement or shock effect. This critical method "temporarily freezes them as it slides them under the microscope of the critic, lifts them momentarily from their natural environment in order to make them relevant for the present" (Wolin 125). Throughout *The English Patient*, rifle telescopes and binoculars are used to perform the same task as the critic's microscope: to estrange familiar phenomena, specifically, works of art.

4 As far as Benjamin was concerned, in contemporary society, this type of "genuine experience (*Erfahrung*), continuous with past and future and containing elements of both the past and the future in itself," was in the process of being eroded (see Spencer 60–1).

5 In *The English Patient*, emphasis is placed on the construction and destruction of bridges. When he sees the portrait of the Queen of Sheba, Kip describes her as "a woman who would someday know the sacredness of bridges" (70). After he is tortured, Caravaggio makes his way to the Santa Trinità Bridge; as he lay there "the mined bridge exploded and he was flung upwards and then down as part of the end of the world" (60). Kip's experience at the end of the novel reinforces the apocalyptic tone of this earlier episode. While travelling across a bridge on his motorcycle, Kip's bike skids and he is flung down into the water.

As he enters the river, he, too, ponders the end of the world and recalls Isaiah's apocalyptic prophecy: "'He will toss thee like a ball into a large country'" (295).

6 The Dominican monk Girolamo Savonarola was one of history's most famous apocalyptic prophets. He believed that the troubles of northern Italy in the 1490s prefigured John's revelation of a final apocalyptic battle in the year 1500. Savonarola welcomed the invading forces of Charles VIII of France when they entered Florence on 10 December 1494, and he viewed Charles as a messiah. After the French army retreated and Florence established a republic, Savonarola switched sides and, after declaring "God's law in Florence and preaching zealously against luxury and excess," incited Florentines to burn their worldly goods in a huge "bonfire of vanities" (Kingwell, 42).

7 Melancholy remains the predominant feature of allegory because, although the allegorist creates emblems and, by extension, meaning, they soon become exhausted: "the profound fascination of the sick man with the isolated and insignificant is succeeded by that disappointed abandonment of the exhausted emblem" (Benjamin, *The Origin of German Tragic Drama* 185). Thus, there is no escape, even for the allegorist, from historical decline.

8 In Carravagio's eyes, "the rich" are the powerful, evil figures who have betrayed the powerless. In a conversation with Hana, Carravagio states: "'Kip will probably get blown up one of these days. Why? For whose sake? He's twenty-six years old. The British army teaches him the skills and the Americans teach him further skills and the team of sappers are given lectures are decorated and sent off into the rich hills. You are being used, boyo, as the Welsh say'" (121).

9 In several episodes, characters identify with and internalize discursive maps, which they later rely on to plot their own identities and lives in the present. For example, we are told that the patient's lover, Katherine Clifton, reads Herodotus's story of Gyges and Candaules from the pages of the patient's commonplace book. As a result of coming into contact with that quasimythical story from the past, a "path suddenly revealed itself in real life" (233).

A similar path opens when the sapper enters the Sistine Chapel and gazes at the face of Isaiah. As Kip explains, at this point in their lives, the soldiers' characters are threatened by the war: "[c]haracter that subtle art, disappeared among them during those days and nights, existed only in a book or on a painted wall" (70). Owing to this danger, which is nothing less than a threat to the individual's moral being, Kip turns to and internalizes the combination of gesture and knowledge – the character – embedded in this artifact. Readers recognize that Kip has absorbed the character of Isaiah because the sapper strikes Hana as "stern and visionary." Furthermore, during their game of hide-and-seek, Kip leans "against the corner of the vestibule like a spear" (221). Both of these descriptions are drawn from Kip's earlier account of the painting of Isaiah, whose face Kip likens to "a spear, wise, unforgiving" (77).

10 The text confirms this, by reminding readers that the patient is familiar with both geographic and narrative maps (94).

11 The relationship between catastrophe and the angel's countenance helps to explain the strange link in Benjamin's description of the Klee painting between paradise and the storm.

CHAPTER THREE

1 *The Robber Bride* explicitly links the diabolical antagonist, Zenia, with the biblical figure of the harlot or, more precisely, Jezebel. As the novel draws to a close, Zenia plunges to her death. When the women she has victimized discover the body, they realize that they have re-enacted the familiar apocalyptic plot: "Time has folded in upon itself, the prophecy has come true. But there are no dogs. Then it comes to her. *We are the dogs, licking her blood. In the courtyard, the Jezebel blood.* She thinks she's going to be sick" (518).

2 In his introduction to *Windigo: An Anthology of Fact and Fantastic Fiction*, John Robert Columbo provides the same, although more detailed, non-Native account.

3 The information concerning the Wendigo is drawn from my more detailed study "A Taste of the Wild."

4 Basil Johnston has repeatedly observed that non-Native people very often reduce the metaphorical aspects of words and seize on their literal interpretations (see "One Generation from Extinction" and "Is That All There Is?").

5 Telephone interview 11 May 1995.

6 Early references to the Wendigo relate to an evil god who posed a threat to humans and had to be propitiated. In these accounts, "characteristics which were later associated with the Windigo being *are absent*, including his gigantic stature, his anthropophagous or cannibal propensities, and his symbolic connection with the north, winter, and starvation" (Fogelson 77; my emphasis). The shift from evil deity to flesh-eating

monster prompted many anthropologists to argue that the creation of a
cannibalistic giant represents a post-contact phenomenon.

7　Marano confirms that the Native category "carried no semantic conno-
tation of cannibalism, but took on this ancillary meaning for 150 years
or more during crisis conditions of a particular kind" (124).

8　Europeans who made contact with Native communities introduced
deadly diseases, including smallpox, VD, and tuberculosis. As a result of
the spread of these diseases, kinship groups faced huge losses; hunters
died, and without them starvation was inevitable. Unwittingly, the
explorers and fur traders who reported the savagery of the Native peoples – a savagery epitomized by anthropophagy – were themselves
responsible for creating starvation conditions.

9　See Bishop's two studies "Northern Algonkian Cannibalism and the
Windigo Psychosis" (245) and *The Northern Ojibwa and the Fur Trade* (12).

10　The Wendigo theme and canonical Western apocalyptic cannibal fictions pervade Atwood's entire collection. For example, in "The Age of
Lead," references to the story of the Franklin Expedition reinforce the
dangers associated with imperialist consumption. Similarly, in the story
"Weight," and in the title story, "Wilderness Tips," the image of the
Titanic symbolizes the disaster that attends the West's voracious pursuit
of pleasure, material gain, and mastery over nature. As the story of the
Franklin Expedition is central to Atwood's fiction but may not be
widely known, I will outline the details.

In May 1845, Sir John Franklin and 135 men sailed from England in
search of the Northwest Passage. Europeans had been attempting to
find a way across North America for three hundred years. The voyage's
primary motive was economic, but "economic motives included, of
course, imperialist pride, power, and domination" (Grace 148). However, something went terribly wrong with Franklin's voyage of discovery. Predator ended up becoming prey when the men were swallowed
by the Arctic, virtually without a trace.

The expedition was last sighted in Baffin Bay in July 1845. After that,
the ships simply vanished. Almost ten years later, the surveyor John
Rae learned from some Inuit hunters that the ships had been crushed in
the ice and the expedition's men had starved to death while trying to
make their way south. The story of the Franklin Expedition is also a
cannibal fiction. As Atwood cheerfully explains, the men indulged "in a
little cannibalism along the way. (Mention has been made, for instance,
of a bootful of human flesh)" (*Strange Things* 13). Relishing every
opportunity to reveal the hypocrisy of Western culture, Atwood recalls

that the Inuit who relayed this information were "indignantly denounced as barbaric liars, because a Briton could not possibly have behaved so hungrily; though later research has proved them true" (13).

Eventually, bodies and remnants of the expedition were discovered, and, from samples of hair and fingernails, the scientists concluded that the men had been suffering from high levels of lead poisoning. Ironically, the seemingly godlike technological advancements on which their confidence was based betrayed them. The up-to-date tin cans they took with them, packed full of meat and soup, were soldered together with lead. The food and the landscape they expected to consume ended up consuming them.

In accordance with the Northern Algonkian use of the word "Wendigo" to denote an "individual who had lost his or her wits," Atwood's story "The Age of Lead" intimates that Franklin's men turned into Wendigos. Readers learn, for instance, that the sailors "set out on an idiotic trek across the stony, icy ground, pulling a life boat laden down with toothbrushes, soap, handkerchiefs, and slippers, useless pieces of junk" (168). Before they succumbed to the ice and snow, they lost the use of their human reason. The story goes on to draw a parallel between lead poisoning in the Arctic more than a hundred years ago and apocalyptic conditions in the contemporary urban wasteland. Just as Franklin's sailors perished at an early age owing to their desire for economic gain and imperialist pride, in the 1980s, disaster strikes again. The protagonist, Jane, recognizes that corporate greed is destroying the environment, and more and more people are succumbing to bizarre ailments; people began dying "too early": "It was as if they had been weakened by some mysterious agent, a thing like a colourless gas, scentless and invisible, so that any germ that happened along could invade their bodies, take them over" (166). She recognizes further that this sickness results from humanity's attempt to control the environment (yet another Frankensteinian experiment that ends up destroying the experimenter): "[m]aple groves dying of acid rain, hormones in the beef, mercury in the fish, pesticides in the vegetables, poison sprayed on the fruit, God knows what in the drinking water" (166). Mirroring the fate of Franklin's men, contemporary individuals also turn Wendigo; as Jane notes, something "invade[s] their bodies, take[s] them over" (166).

The story's final episode likewise alludes to the northern spirit of the cannibal monster. Jane visits the hospital to visit her close friend, Vincent, who has been infected by a mutated virus that is "creeping up his

spine";"[i]t was white in his room, wintry. He lay packed in ice" (167).
She considers the parallels between Vincent's experience and that of
Franklin's men. Like the poor sailors who were buried in the per-
mafrost, Vincent is also about to lose his mind and his life; Jane knows
that "when the virus reached his brain it would kill him" (167). At one
point, Jane asks Vincent to tell her what is destroying him; he replies,
"'Who knows? ... It must have been something I ate'" (168). His
deathbed humour continues to underscore the connection between his
fate and that of Franklin's men – a connection that foregrounds the terror of going Wendigo and the uncanny relationship in Western culture
between excessive consumption and self-destruction.

The final story, "Hack Wednesday," similarly highlights the related
motifs of apocalyptic disaster and consumption. The moment she
wakes up, the protagonist, Marcia, hears the radio announcer's voice
filled with heightened energy because he is describing "a disaster of
some kind" (219). Every catastrophe, from the Panama invasion to the
greenhouse effect, makes an appearance. In an episode that reinforces
the connections between disaster, imperialism, and consumption, Marcia's husband, Eric, battles against the destructive forces of neo-imperi-
alism by restricting his family's consumption. Marcia explains that he
won't eat Cheerios "because they're American." She recounts that "ever
since the Free Trade deal with the States went through he has refused to
purchase anything from south of the border" (222). However noble, his
efforts prove futile and despair is pervasive. On her way to work, Marcia sees two Native Indian men and imagines that they've "had it with
this city, they've had it with suicide as an option, they've had it with
the twentieth century" (225). Ultimately, "The Age of Lead," "Hack
Wednesday," and their intertexts reveal that the Wendigo constitutes a
prominent feature of contemporary Canadian society.

11 In keeping with Wendigo tales, *Frankenstein* also links the catastrophe to
the conquest of indigenous peoples. Initially, the monster, akin to
Rousseau's noble savage, is innately good and he condemns unjust
European practices. In a memorable episode, the monster weeps when
he learns about the colonization of the American hemisphere and the
Europeans' brutal treatment of its original inhabitants (147). In effect,
Western society's lust for power is seemingly embodied in Victor. Not
surprisingly, his fate also mirrors that of the Wendigo's victims: he ends
up losing his mind and personality and destroying his family members
and those he loves most.

12 For example, in the opening story, "True Trash," repeated parallels are

drawn between women and butchered meat. Similarly, in the story "Weight," the narrator's best friend, Molly, is dismembered by her psychotic husband. As outlined in "True Trash," society teaches boys to objectify women (the campers' use of binoculars is a familiar Atwoodian motif) and align them with meat. For example, we are told that, in the eyes of the boys, the waitresses basking in the sun resemble a "herd of skinned seals" (1). Later, Darce calls Ronette "summer sausage," and Donny describes women's legs as "hams in cloth" (25). The commodification of women, which turns them into food/meat, remains a longstanding concern in Atwood's writing. This issue is central to *The Edible Woman*. It surfaces again in *Bodily Harm*, when the narrator describes herself as her lover's "raw material" (212), and returns with a vengeance in *Cat's Eye*, when, as Barbara DeConcini notes, the narrator notices in her art history course "how naked women are presented in the same painterly manner as plates of meat" (DeConcini 116).

In the title story, "Wilderness Tips," a predatory man named George, a refugee from Hungary, marries into an wealthy, established Canadian family. From the start, the text portrays George as a Wendigo figure, motivated by hunger and aggression. During his youth, George faced starvation conditions: he "spent the forties rooting through garbage heaps and begging, and doing other things unsuitable for a child" (191). These experiences transformed him into a cold-hearted predator. In "Wilderness Tips" – echoing the allusions to misogyny, objectification, and dismemberment in "True Trash" and "Weight" – readers learn that, as a kid, George and a couple of his buddies took a poster of a film star "apart with the rusty blade from a kitchen knife" (192). As an adult, he recalls his "intense resentment of the bright, ignorant smile, the well-fed body" (192).

Early on, George describes his innocent and youthful future wife, Portia, as his "host." The girl's sister, Pamela, attempts to correct him, explaining that he should have said "hostess" because a "'host' is male, like 'mine host' in an inn, or else it's the wafer you eat at Communion. Or the caterpillar that all the parasites lay their eggs on" (211). Her comments, with their references to the Eucharist and to caterpillars devoured by parasites, bring together the sacred and profane facets of cannibalism associated with apocalypse.

In the end, George, a force of greed and destruction, responsible for "[a]cres of treelessness, of new townhouses with little pointed roofs – like tents, like an invasion" (206), adds Pamela to his list of conquests (he has maintained an affair with his other sister-in-law, Prue, for years). In true Wendigo fashion, George preys on his own family members.

Like the narrator in "Weight," Portia, who discovers that George has slept with Pamela – the sister she most trusted – equates the current disaster with the sinking of the Titanic. Listening to the tolling of the dinner bell, she fantasizes that she is on the sinking ship: "She sees herself running naked through the ballroom – an absurd, disturbing figure, with dripping hair and flailing arms, screaming at them, 'don't you see? It's coming apart, everything's coming apart, you're sinking. You're finished, you're over, you're dead!'" (216). In Atwood's collection, the allusions to Wendigo tales coupled with the references to the Titanic and to Revelation – references that are repeatedly associated with the act of eating – emphasize that, in Western society, women occupy the lower rungs of the food chain. They also support Pippin's belief that misogyny at the end of the twentieth century may be "more technologically advanced, but the roots and results of woman-hatred are the same" (53).

13 "The creature has no name. No one may know it and live to tell about it, so the Windigo must remain nameless" (Columbo 2).

14 References to the Eucharist can also be understood to express a desire to return to the premodern relationship between the real and the image. In "The Hazard of Modern Poetry," Erich Heller traces the origin of the modern predicament, the separation of the real from the symbolic, back to sixteenth-century Marburg, to the theological dispute between Luther and Zwingli about the nature of the Eucharist. For Luther, the bread and the wine were "the thing itself," the blood and the body of Christ; for Zwingli, they were "mere symbols." According to the postmodern theorist Jean Baudrillard, we have now reached a stage of simulation where "it is no longer a question of imitation, nor of reduplication, nor even of parody. It is rather a question of substituting signs of the real for the real itself" (4). Viewed in this context, Kat's transformation from a producer of images who glories in playing with "frozen light" and "frozen time" to a person who offers her cyst as food and insists that it "has the texture of reality, it is not an image" (47) represents a return to "the thing itself" and a healing of the rift between the real and the symbolic. Of course, a critic like Baudrillard would read this image of communion both as an indicator of Kat's nostalgia for the real and as further proof of the irrevocable loss of the real. "When the real is no longer what it used to be, nostalgia assumes its full meaning. There is a proliferation of myths of origin and *signs of reality*. There is an

escalation of the true, of the lived experience ... And there is a panic-stricken production of the real and the referential, above and parallel to the panic of material production" (Baudrillard 12–13).

15 For a discussion of the limitations of this strategy of erasure, see my essay "War and the Game of Representation in Michael Ondaatje's *The English Patient*."

16 Atwood's fictions repeatedly allude to apocalypse's degradation and destruction of the human community and the rituals that sustain it, specifically, the Eucharist. For example, in *Surfacing*, the narrator chastises people for their profane attitude toward violence and consumption, the latter a practice that she believes should be viewed as sacred: "The animals die that we may live, they are substitute people, hunters in the fall killing the deer, that is Christ also. And we eat them, out of cans or otherwise; we are eaters of death, dead Christ-flesh resurrecting inside us, granting us life. Canned Spam, canned Jesus, even the plants must be Christ. But we refuse to worship; the body worships with blood and muscle but the thing in the knob of our head will not, wills not to, the head is greedy, it consumes but does not give thanks" (150).

CHAPTER FOUR

1 Brotherson's understanding of the relationship between mapping and writing recalls the Russian semiotician Yuri Lotman's assertion that maps are merely one form of "modelling system" – a system that also includes literary texts. (For a discussion of Lotman's views, see Huggan 5.)

2 After the end of the Civil War in 1865, Americans began to pursue the project of westward expansion, and the army turned to Indian-fighting. Although the benevolence of those who advocated moving Indians onto reservations may well escape contemporary readers, it is important to understand that, within the historical context of the Indian Wars, the attempt to relocate the Indians and to civilize them was, in fact, the era's liberal humanitarian response to the army's ongoing slaughter of the Indians (Holler 111).

3 Interestingly enough, Pratt's system of penal education and subsequent creation of industrial boarding schools were used as the prototypes for Canadian Indian education. When Nicholas Flood Davin was charged by Prime Minister Macdonald to develop a school system in Canada, he took the simplest solution: he went to the United States to inspect their schools; he arrived at a time when Pratt's system was "enjoying its heyday" (Samek 138).

4 The Indian prisoners at Fort Marion were incarcerated for three years, whereas the entire Chiricahua and Warm Springs Apache people – men, women, and children – were held as prisoners of war for twenty-six years by the United States (see Meredith 101).

5 See Ewers, chapter 10: "The Making and Uses of Maps by Plains Indians Warriors," 180–90.

6 A number of critics highlight the text's hybrid status, including Fee and Flick, Andrews, Donaldson, Gray, and Matchie and Larson.

7 Latisha's first husband, George was pleased that she was, "as he said, a real Indian" (112). Similarly, Eli Stands Alone's girlfriend, Karen, also liked the fact that he was Indian and referred to him as her "mystic warrior" (138).

8 As spiritual leader of the American Indian Movement, Philip Deere stated: "[Y]ou hear the Indian people talking about the sacred book, – or the circle. That circle is important to us because we do not believe in the square measurements. But the ancient belief was in the circle. The moon is in a circle, the sun is round, and our ancestors knew the earth was round. Everything that is natural is in a round form" (quoted in Lutz, "The Circle" 85).

9 Alan Kilpatrick (46–7, 55) offers a more extensive description of this Cherokee ritual.

10 Dr J. Houvagh first appears in Thomas King's story "A Seat in the Garden" from *One Good Story That One* (83–94).

11 As Fee and Flick note, there is an important intertextual reference at work in this episode. Five hundred years after Columbus, three cars, a red Pinto (*Green Grass Running Water* 23), a blue Nissan (175), and a white Karmann-Ghia (235) (see Fee and Flick 133) – the Nina, the Pinta, and the Santa Maria – crash into the already stress-fractured Grand Baleen Dam and break it during an earthquake.

12 The purpose of the dance is multifaceted and has also changed over the years. Initially, it enshrined the fundamental aspects of Plains Indian life: "war and the buffalo hunt" (Holler 180). The principle reason for dancing to the sun was to "secure victory over enemies," although was also viewed as a way of offering thanks for recovery from "some sickness or trouble" (42, 69). However, the Sun Dance also served other important functions: for instance, it was the an effective mechanism for the redistribution of wealth, providing a means for "the poorer people in the society to obtain the goods needed to survive the extreme Dakota winter" (180). In addition, studies also confirm that the dance served an

important teaching function, "inculcating and preserving the values and mythology of the society" (180).

13   Holler 146–7; see also Black Elk (62). For an account of the symbolic meaning of the colour black, refer to Black Elk (146).

14   The episode cited above not only highlights the importance of the sun, but further derails the Judeo-Christian narrative by suggesting that Coyote, rather than God, is responsible for turning on the light and initiating the circular pattern of night and day, as well as the seasons.

15   The role played by the earthquake in King's text recalls Aritha van Herk's rejection of the desire to "fix" the prairie by imposing what Rudy Wiebe described as "great black steel lines of fiction." In response to Wiebe, van Herk asserts that the west has to be "earth-quaked a little, those black steel lines and the looming giant toppled. Not destroyed, on no, but infiltrated" ("Women Writers and the Prairie" 24). To an extent, her feminist project mirrors that of King's. In this case, however, the earthquake and the flood specifically signal the crying out of the Earth. As Fools Crow explains: "Grandmother Earth is crying out about it [environmental destruction]. She is shaking the land [earthquakes] more and more to tell us how she feels, and to get our attention. *Waken-Tanka* has told me that the Thunder Being will be sending great floods to show us the great cleansing that needs to go on within people" (quoted in Mails 67).

CHAPTER FIVE

1   In her essay on *Obasan*, Erika Gottlieb suggests that Naomi herself is the true seer: "it is through the silent Naomi's personal recollections that we ultimately get the impression of having heard the word of the prophet, the seer" (41). To a certain extent, Naomi's position is similar to that of John of Patmos, a man thought to be politically and socially marginalized and oppressed. However, Naomi's refusal to speak marks her refusal to adopt this position in apocalyptic discourse. I'm grateful to Malcolm Woodland for pointing out the implications of Naomi's commitment to silence.

2   Roy Miki writes that the redress movement was coeval with "the identity formation, 'Japanese Canadian' ('JC') " (11).

3   In addition, Davidson feels that *Obasan* is artistically and culturally significant (13).

4   In his analysis of trauma, Freud observes that there are two typical

responses. One response entails an intellectual acceptance, the equiva-
lent of asserting, "Yes, it happened, but it is over and I'm fine." Freud
terms this type of response "denial" or "negation." Although there is a
kind of intellectual acceptance of what is repressed, "in all essentials the
repression persists" ("Negation" 236). Freud also observes that
fetishization constitutes a potential response to trauma, in which the act
of denial "is played out in relation to a physical object: the object represents the event that did, and did not, take place" (Berger 27). See
Freud's "Fetishism," "Negation," and "The Splitting of the Ego in the
Process of Defence."

5 Visvis, for instance, characterizes *Obasan* as an "apocalyptic text that
draws on motifs from the biblical apocalypse and focuses on the theme
of revelation to situate an elided chapter in Canadian history as a sup-
pressed truth that requires unveiling" (20). Davidson concentrates on
the text's engagement with apocalypse as well but explores the ways in
which the novel supposedly fulfills the seer's promise to the elect (37).
By contrast, Merivale acknowledges that the text's biblical allusions
speak of the "punishments of the Apocalypse" (68). She argues that
Kogawa's novel portrays the collective experience of Japanese Canadians in terms of a "secular apocalypse, in the form of which, inevitably,
we all imagine it in our time, the dropping of the atomic bomb" (72).
Gottlieb's study opens with the assertion that the entire novel represents Naomi's attempt to answer the following question: "Can a human
being ever come to terms with the experience of evil on the psychological, the political, the universal level?" (34). Apocalypse establishes a
"unique temporal and teleological framework for understanding evil"
(O'Leary 6). Gottlieb implicitly and explicitly classifies *Obasan* as an
apocalyptic narrative. She goes on to observe that the disasters that
befall Naomi and her nightmares echo "the ultimate nightmare vision
of cosmic proportions – the total annihilation of the world as a result of
the overpowering forces of evil ... the vision of the Last Judgement, the
end of the world" (48).

6 This nonexistent mark recalls the overarching context of racialization,
specifically, the way that the "mark" (yellow skin and slanted eyes, for
instance) functioned, and continues to function, in the process of racialization as a sign that supposedly designates an essential nature. In her
study of the system of "marks," Guillaumin argues that the "invention
of the idea of nature cannot be separated from the domination and the
appropriation of human beings" (133). In using the term *racialization*, I
am referring to what Roy Miki describes as "the imposition of race con-

structs and hierarchies on marked and demarked 'groups' whose members come to signify divergence from the normative body inscribed by whiteness" (127).

7 Far from embracing the logic of apocalypse, *Obasan* forces readers to address the aspects of Revelation that led Harold Bloom to describe the book as "[l]urid and inhumane": "Resentment and not love is the teaching of the Revelation of St John the Divine. It is a book without wisdom, goodness, kindness, or affection of any kind. Perhaps it is appropriate that a celebration of the end of the world should be not only barbaric but scarcely literate. Where the substance is so inhumane, who would wish the rhetoric to be more persuasive, or the vision to be more vividly realized?" (4–5).

8 I'm grateful to Malcolm Woodland for drawing my attention to this shift in power. For more information about the adaptability of apocalyptic discourse, see Derrida's "Of an Apocalyptic Tone Recently Adopted in Philosophy."

9 Sitting Bull, chief of the entire Sioux nation, defeated Custer in 1876 and fled to Canada the following year. After serving two years in jail as a prisoner of war, touring with Buffalo Bill's Wild West Show, and travelling throughout the United States and Canada, Sitting Bull was eventually arrested in 1890 for supporting the Indian religion called the Ghost Dance. He was killed on his way to prison.

10 Marjorie Pickthall's short story "Third Generation" stages this type of return of the repressed, as Misao Dean's excellent essay on the subject illustrates.

11 Bhabha cites, as his example, Renan's account of the forgotten events that laid the foundations for the creation of France: "'yet every French citizen has to have forgotten [is obliged to have forgotten] Saint Bartholomew's Night's Massacre, or the massacres that took place in the Midi in the thirteenth century'" (Renan quoted in Bhabha 310).

12 The links among traumas are apparent within the text. For example, Naomi recalls bathing with her Grandmother as a child: "She urges me down deeper into the liquid furnace and I go into the midst of the flames, obedient as Abednego..." (52). Lying beside her grandmother in the bath, Naomi marvels at "the redness" of her body (52); note that her supposedly "yellow" body becomes "red," signalling connections between so-called red-and yellow-skinned people and alluding to the potential of burning. As critics point out, this passage foreshadows the grandmother's death during the internment and her cremation. Later, watching the grandmother's funeral pyre, Naomi once again recalls the

biblical story of Daniel, in which Daniel and his three companions:
Abednego, Shadrach, and Meshach were delivered from the burning
fiery furnace (Dan. 3:12–30). The fire is "a dancing bright-dark rage of
crackling in the night ... Who, I used to wonder could survive such
heat. The angel in the Old Testament story kept three men safe in the
middle of a place like that" (*Obasan* 141). Merivale argues further that
the atomic bomb – "that fieriest of all furnaces" – is carefully antici-
pated by these allusions "to the biblical fiery furnace with its angel pro-
tecting the believers" (72).

13 For a discussion of the funerary ritual, see Gottlieb.

14 In Canada, arguments about the inevitable facts of history continue to
be launched. In Canada's national newspaper, *The Globe and Mail*, for
example, a letter to the editor entitled "Natives Can't Undo History,"
published 17 July 2000, stated:

> We foreign-born Canadians do not understand what the fuss is about
> ... The natives were here before the Europeans. That is a fact. But they
> lost their power, and hence their land, because they were no match
> for the French or British, as far as warfare goes. Their arms were still
> of stone-age technology, their civilization was not as sophisticated as
> the Europeans'. In other words, the natives were defeated. That is
> also a fact.
>
> Today the overwhelming majority of Canadians are not native.
> Regardless of what Matthew Coon Come, the new Assembly of First
> Nations chief, says, this is not their land any more. This is our land,
> too – at least 95 per cent of it, if we base our calculation on a per-
> capita basis. The natives live here at our behest. This may sound rude
> but it is true: We feed them, we educate them, we subsidize their way
> of life. It would be better if they wanted to assimilate, but if they
> don't that's fine, too.
>
> Land claims? What land claims? Do the Germans claim the lands
> they lost to Poland and Russia? Do the Greeks have any claim on
> Sicily? Do the Dutch have a claim on Manhattan? History has spoken:
> Breslau is in Poland, Sicily belongs to the Italians and Manhattan is
> the real capital of the United States. There is nothing else to it. *Peter
> Dratsidis, Toronto*

The following day, a number of replies to this letter were published.
The following, witty response nicely captures Grant's view:

> "Land claims? What land claims?" asks Peter Dratsidis, whose
> entire argument really boils down to three words: Might makes right.
> Natives "lost their power, and hence their land because they were no

match for the French or British, as far as warfare goes." They have no valid claims because "history has spoken."

It is my sincere hope that Mr. Dratsidis is never assaulted and robbed at gunpoint. By his own argument, he would have no cause for complaint, and the assailant would not only escape punishment, but would actually get to keep the wallet. A late arrival at the scene might side with the perpetrator and treat the victim with sneering condescension. After all, Mr. Dratsidis would be no match for his clearly superior armed attacker. That would be a fact and, as he concludes in his letter, "there is nothing else to it." *David Farrant, Toronto*

15 In interviews, Kogawa similarly attests to the traumatic influence of the persecution of her community: "Many Nisei, like myself, who suffered the drawn out trauma of racial prejudice during our formative and young adult years have a deep timidity turned into our psyches with the injunction that we must never again congregate, never again risk the visibility of community. Perhaps as a result, no Japan town exists anywhere in Canada today" ("Is There a Just Cause?" 21).

16 My thanks to Teresa Heffernan for directing me to Cixous's interpretation of mourning and melancholia.

17 In her diary, Aunt Emily writes: "We are the billygoats and nannygoats and kids – all the scapegoats to appease this blindness. Is this a Christian country?" (95).

18 In the sequel to *Obasan* – *Itsuka*, which traces the struggle for apology and redress – Kogawa repeats the first epigraph, suggesting that it has not yet been fulfilled. Naomi has broken her silence but "that break has not produced a new Naomi"; closure continues to remain elusive (Davidson 86–8).

19 Derrida's use of "differance" spelt with an "a," is significant: "the anomolous 'a' in Derrida's spelling of difference, which he uses as a kind of marker that sets up a disturbance in our settled understanding of translation of our concept of difference is very important, because that little 'a,' disturbing as it is, which you can hardly hear when spoken, sets the word in motion to new meanings yet without obscuring the trace of its other meanings in its past. His sense of "differance" ... remains suspended between the two French verbs 'to differ' and 'to defer,' both of which contribute to its textual force, neither of which can fully capture its meaning" (Hall, "Old and New" 49–50).

20 Malcolm Woodland observes in the case of the mourning process articulated in elegies such as *In Memoriam* that they achieve closure only when the "elegist aligns himself with the discourse of God the Father

and Christ the Son, that is with the prophetic and apocalyptic discourse, the patriarchal discourse of truth that promises compensation in a perfect, unchanging world" (61).

21 See Patricia Merivale's "Framed Voices: The Polyphonic Elegies of Hebert and Kogawa," Diana Brydon's "Obasan: Joy Kogawa's Lament for a Nation" (465), and Coral Ann Howell's "Storm Glass: The Preservation and Transformation of History in *The Diviners*, *Obasan*, and *My Lovely Enemy*" (475).

22 Erika Gottlieb asserts that the text does not fulfill the apocalyptic promise of the New Jerusalem because the Christian apocalyptic vision gives way to a Buddhist view. The coincidence "of Buddhist and Christian symbols in the quest present the effect of superimposition or double exposure" (50).

23 In "Structure, Sign, and Play in the Discourse of the Human Sciences," Derrida himself attests to the racially inflected aspects of his theories, emphasizing how they coincide with developments in the social sciences, particularly ethnology: "One can in fact assume that ethnology could have been born as a science only at the moment when a de-centering had come about: at the moment when European culture – and, in consequence, the history of metaphysics and of its concepts – had been *dislocated*, driven from its locus, and forced to stop considering itself as the culture of reference" (251). Derrida's theories are doubly inflected by race because, as James Berger argues (106–30), poststructuralist theories about the signifying system must be understood as belated and traumatic responses to the Holocaust.

24 See Berger's "Representing the Holocaust after the End of Testimony," 59–105.

CONCLUSION

1 Clifford's "Diasporas," 303; see also Kaplan's discussion of Clifford (134).

Bibliography

Abrams, M.H. "Apocalypse: Theme and Romantic Variations." *The Revelation of St. John the Divine*, Harold Bloom, ed. (1988): 7–33.

– *Glossary of Literary Terms*, sixth ed. New York: Harcourt Brace College Publishers, 1993.

– *Natural Supernaturalism – Tradition and Revolution in Romantic Literature*. New York: W.W. Norton, 1971.

Adachi, Ken. *The Enemy that Never Was: A History of the Japanese Canadians*. Toronto: McClelland and Stewart, 1991.

Adorno, Theodor W. *Ästhetische Theorie*. Gretel Adorno and R. Tiedemann, eds. Frankfurt: Suhrkamp, 1970.

Andrews, Jennifer. "Reading Thomas King's *Green Grass, Running Water*: Cross-Border Humor and Laughter." Unpublished essay, 1998.

Atwood, Margaret. *Bodily Harm*. Toronto: McClelland and Stewart-Bantam, 1981.

– "Cannibal Lecture." *Saturday Night* Nov. 1995: 81–90.

– *Cat's Eye*. Toronto: McClelland and Stewart-Bantam, 1988.

– *The Edible Woman*. Toronto: McClelland and Stewart, 1969.

– *Oryx and Crake*. Toronto: McClelland and Stewart, 2003.

– *The Robber Bride*. Toronto: McClelland and Stewart, 1993.

– *Strange Things: The Malevolent North in Canadian Literature*. Toronto: Oxford, 1995.

– *Survival: A Thematic Guide to Canadian Literature*. Toronto: Anansi, 1972.

– *Wilderness Tips*. Toronto: McClelland-Bantam, 1991.

Bailey, Anne Geddes. *Timothy Findley and the Aesthetics of Fascism*. Vancouver: Talonbooks, 1998.

Bakhtin, Mikhail. *The Dialogic Imagination: Four Essays*. Translated by Caryl

Emerson and Michael Holquist. Michael Holquist, ed. Austin: Universityof Texas Press, 1981.

Baudrillard, Jean. *Simulations*. Translated by Paul Foss, Paul Patton, and Philip Beitchman. New York: Columbia/Semiotext(e), 1983.

Benjamin, Walter. "Central Park." *New German Critique* 34 (1985): 33–57.

– *Illuminations: Essays and Reflections*. Hannah Arendt, ed. New York: Schoken, 1968.

– *The Origin of German Tragic Drama*. Translated by John Osborne. London: NLB, 1977.

– *Reflections, Essays, Aphorisms, Autobiographical Writings*. Peter Demetz, ed. New York and London: Harcourt Brace Jovanovich, 1978.

Beran, Carol, L. "Ex-centricity: Michale Ondaatje's *In the Skin of a Lion* and Hugh MacLennan's *Barometer Rising*." *Studies in Canadian Literature* (1993) 18.1: 71–84.

Berger, James. *After the End: Representations of Post-Apocalypse*. London and Minneapolis: University of Minnesota Press 1999.

Berlo, Janet Catherine. "Drawing and Being Drawn In: The Late Nineteenth-Century Plains Graphic Artist and the Intercultural Encounter." *Plains Indian Drawings 1865–1935*, J.C. Berlo, ed. (1996): 12–18.

– ed. *Plains Indian Drawings 1865–1935: Pages from a Visual History*. New York: Harry N. Abrams in Association with the American Foundation of Arts and the Drawing, 1996.

Bhabha, Homi. "Dissemi/Nation: Time Narrative and the Margins of the Modern Nation." *Nation and Narration*, Homi Bhabha, ed. London and New York: Routledge (1990): 291–322.

Bible. Rev. Standard Ed. New York: William Collins, 1971.

Bishop, Charles. "Northern Algonkian Cannibalism and the Windigo Psychosis." *Psychological Anthropology*, T.R. Williams, ed. The Hague: Mouton (1975): 237–48.

– *The Northern Ojibwa and Fur Trade: An Historical and Ecological Study*. Toronto: Holt, Rinehart and Winston, 1974.

Black Elk. *The Gift of the Sacred Pipe*. Joseph Epes Brown, ed. Norman: University of Oklahoma Press 1953 (rpt. 1982).

Bloom, Harold. Introduction. *The Revelation of St. John the Divine*, H. Bloom, ed. Modern Critical Interpretations. New York: Chelsea House (1988): 1–5.

Blume, Anna. "In a Place of Writing." *Plains Indian Drawings 1865–1935*, J.C. Berlo, ed. (1996): 40–4.

Brand, Dionne. *At the Full and Change of the Moon*. Toronto: Vintage, 2000.

– *A Map to the Door of No Return: Notes to Belonging*. Toronto: Doubleday, 2001.

Britt, Brian M. *Walter Benjamin and the Bible*. New York: Continuum, 1996.

Brody, Hugh. *Maps and Dreams: Indians and the British Columbia Frontier*. Vancouver and Toronto: Douglas & MacIntyre, 1981 (rpt. 1988).

Brotherson, George. *Book of the Fourth World*. Cambridge: University of Cambridge Press, 1992.

Brown, J. and R. Brighton. *The Orders of the Dreamed: George Nelson on Cree and Northern Ojibwa Religion and Legend*. Winnipeg: University of Manitoba Press, 1988.

Brydon, Diana. *"Obasan*: Joy Kogawa's 'Lament for a Nation.'" *Kunapipi* 16.1 (1994): 465–70.

Bull, Malcolm, ed. *Apocalypse Theory and the Ends of the World*. Oxford: Blackwell, 1995.

Burger, Peter. *Theory of the Avant-Garde*. Minneapolis: University of Minneapolis Press, 1984.

Canadian Who's Who 1998, vol. 33. Elizabeth Lumley, ed. Toronto: University of Toronto Press, 1998.

Carpenter, Mary Wilson. "Representing Apocalypse: Sexual Politics and the Violence of Revelation." *Postmodern Apocalypse: Theory and Cultural Practice at the End*, Richard Dellamora, ed. Philadelphia: University of Pittsburg Press (1995): 107–35.

Caruth, Cathy, ed. and introd. *Trauma: Explorations in Memory*. Baltimore and London: Johns Hopkins, 1995.

– *Unclaimed Experience: Trauma, Narrative and History*. Baltimore and London: Johns Hopkins University Press, 1996.

Charles, R.H. "Apocalyptic Literature." *A Dictionary of the Bible*, James Hastings, ed.

Cixous, Hélène. "Castration or Decapitation." *Out There: Marginalization and Contemporary Culture*, Russell Ferguson, Martha Gever, Trinh T. Minh-ha, and Cornel West, eds. New York: The New Museum of Contemporary Art and Massachusetts Institute of Technology Press (1990): 345–56.

– *La Jeune Née*. Paris: UGE, 1975.

Clifford, James. "Diasporas." *Cultural Anthropology* 9.3 (1994): 302–38.

Cohn, Norman. *Cosmos, Chaos, and the World to Come: The Ancient Roots of Apocalyptic Faith*. New Haven and London: Yale University Press, 1993.

– *The Pursuit of the Millennium*. London: Secker and Warburg, 1957.

Columbo, John Robert, introd. and ed. *Windigo: An Anthology of Fact and Fantastic Fiction*. Saskatoon: Western Producer Prairie Books, 1982.

Conrad, Joseph. "Stanley Falls, Early September 1890." *Heart of Darkness*. 3rd ed. Robert Kimbrough, ed. New York: Norton, 1988. 186–7.

Coupland, Douglas. *Girlfriend in a Coma*. Toronto: HarperCollins, 1998.

Davidson, Arnold. *Writing against the Silence: Joy Kogawa's Obasan*. Toronto: ECW, 1993.

Davies, Robertson. "Interview with Kaarina Kailo." *Other Solitudes: Canadian Multicultural Fictions*, Linda Hutcheon and Marion Richmond, eds. Toronto: Oxford, 1990.

Dean, Misao. "Forgetting to Remember." Congress of Social Science and Humanities Conference, University of Edmonton, Edmonton, Alta. 26 May 2000.

DeConcini, Barbara. "Narrative Hunger." *The Daemonic Imagination: Biblical Text and Secular Story*, Robert Detweiler and William G. Doty, eds. Atlanta: Scholars P, 1990.

Derrida, Jacques. *Cinders*. Translated by Ned Lukacher. Lincoln: University of Nebraska Press, 1991.

– "Of an Apocalyptic Tone Recently Adopted in Philosophy." Translated by John P. Leavey, Jr. *Semia* 23 (1982): 63–97.

– "Structure, Sign, and Play in the Discourse of the Human Sciences." *The Structuralist Controversy*, Richard Macksey and Eugenio Donato, eds. Baltimore and London: Johns Hopkins University Press (1970): 247–65.

Donaldson, Laura. "Noah Meets Coyote, or Singing in the Rain: Intertextuality in Thomas King's *Green Grass, Running Water*. *SAIL* 7.2 (Summer 1995): 27–43.

Dratsidis, Peter. "Natives Can't Undo History." [Letter to the Editor] *The Globe and Mail*. Monday, 17 July 2000, A18.

Erdinast-Vulcan, Daphna. *Joseph Conrad and the Modern Temper*. Oxford: Clarendon, 1991.

Ewers, John, C. *Plains Indian History and Cultural Essays on Continuity and Change*. Norman and London: University of Oklahoma Press, 1997.

Fagan, Kristina Rose. *Laughing to Survive: Humour in Contemporary Canadian Native Literature*. Diss., University of Toronto. 2001.

Fawcett, Brian. "Scouting the Future." *Books in Canada* 20.7 (1991): 29–32.

Fee, Margery and Jane Flick. "Coyote Pedagogy: Knowing Where the Borders Are in Thomas King's *Green Grass, Running Water*." *Canadian Literature* 161/162 (1999): 131–9.

Findley, Timothy. *The Butterfly Plague*. New York: Viking, 1969. Rev ed. Markham, ON: Penguin, 1986.

– *Famous Last Words*. Toronto: Clark, 1981.

– *Headhunter*. Toronto: HarperCollins, 1993.

– *The Last of the Crazy People*. New York: Meredith, 1967.

– *Not Wanted on the Voyage*. Markham, ON: Penguin, 1985.

– "Turning Down the Volume." 1992 Graham Spry Lecture on Culture and Society. University of Toronto. 10 December 1992.
– *The Wars*. Toronto: Clark, 1977.

Fogelson, Raymond D. "Psychological Theories of Windigo Psychosis and a Preliminary Application of a Models Approach." *Context and Meaning in Cultural Anthropology: Essays in Honour of A. Irving Hallowell*, Melford E. Spiro, ed. New York: Free Press (1965): 74–99.

Freud, Sigmund. *Beyond the Pleasure Principle. The Standard Edition of the Complete Psychological Works of Sigmund Freud*. Translated by James Strachey, 18: 7–14. London Hogarth Press, 1955.
– "Fetishism." S.E. 21: 149–57.
– Moses and Monotheism. S.E. 23: 3–137.
– "Mourning and Melancholia." *On Metapsychology: The Theory of Psychoanalysis*. Penguin Freud Library, vol. 11. Angela Richards, ed. Harmondsworth, England: Penguin (1991): 245–69.
– "Negation." S.E. 19: 235–40.
– "The Splitting of the Ego in Self-Defense." S.E. 23: 271–8.
– "The Uncanny." S.E. 17: 218–52.
– with Josef Breuer. *Studies on Hysteria*. S.E. 2.

Frye, Northrop. *The Anatomy of Criticism: Four Essays*. Princeton: Princeton University Press, 1957.
– *The Secular Scripture: A Study of the Structure of Romace*. Cambridge, Mass.: Harvard University Press, 1976.
– "Typology: Apocalypse." *The Revelation of St. John the Divine*, H. Bloom, ed. Modern Critical Interpretations. New York: Chelsea House (1988): 69–72.

Gates, Nathaniel, ed. *Cultural and Literary Critiques of the Concept of "Race."* New York and London: Garland, 1997.

George, Rosemary Marangoly. *The Politics of Home: Postcolonial Relocations and Twentieth-Century Fiction*. Cambridge: Cambridge University Press, 1996.

Goldman, Marlene. "A Taste of the Wild: A Critique of Representations of Natives as Cannibals in Late-Eighteenth-and Nineteenth-Century Canadian Exploration Literature." *Literary Studies East and West* 10 (1996): 43–64.
– "War and the Game of Representation in Michael Ondaatje's *The English Patient*." *Reconstructing the Fragments of Michael Ondaatje's Works*, Jean-Michel Lacroix, ed. Paris: Presses de la Sorbonne Nouvelle, 1999.

Goldsmith, Stephen. *Unbuilding Jerusalem: Apocalypse and Romantic Representation*. Ithaca: Cornell University Press, 1993.

Gomer Sunahara, Ann. *The Politics of Racism: The Uprooting of Japanese Canadians During the Second World War*. Toronto: James Lorimer, 1981.

Gordon, Avery. *Ghostly Matters*. Minneapolis: University of Minnesota Press, 1997.

– and Christopher Newfield. "White Philosophy." *Cultural and Literary Critiques of the Concept of "Race,"* N. Gates, ed. (1997): 149–69.

Gottlieb, Erika. "The Riddle of Concentric Worlds in *Obasan*." *Canadian Literature* 109 (1986): 34–53.

Grace, Sherrill. "'Franklin Lives': Atwood's Northern Ghosts." *Various Atwoods: Essays on the Later Poems, Short Fictions, and Novels*, Lorraine York, ed. Concord, ON: Anansi (19950: 147–66.

Granofsky, Ronald. *The Trauma Novel: Contemporary Symbolic Depictions of Collective Disaster*. New York: Peter Lang, 1995.

Grant, George. *Lament for a Nation*. Toronto: McClelland and Stewart, 1965.

Gray, James. *Between Voice and Text: Bicultural Negotiation in the Contemporary Native American Novel*. Diss., University of Wisconsin-Madison, 1995.

Guillaumin, Colette. "Race and Nature: The System of Marks: The Idea of a Natural Group and Social Relations." *Cultural and Literary Critiques of the Concept of "Race,"* N. Gates, ed. (1997): 117–35.

Gunn Allen, Paula. Interview with Laura Coltelli. *Winged Words: American Indian Writers Speak*, Laura Coltelli. Lincoln and London: University of Nebraska Press (1990): 10–19.

Hall, Stuart. "The Local and the Global: Globalization and Ethnicity." *Culture, Globalization and the World System: Contemporary Conditions for the Representation of Identity*, Anthony D. King, ed. Minneapolis: University of Minnesota Press (1997): 19–39.

– "New Ethnicities." *Cultural and Literary Critiques of the Concept of "Race,"* N. Gates, ed. (1997): 373–408.

– "Old and New Identities, Old and New Ethnicities." *Culture, Globalization and the World-System: Contemporary Conditions for the Representation of Identity*, Anthony D. King, ed. Minneapolis: University of Minnesota Press (1997): 40–68.

Hanson, Paul, D. *The Dawn of Apocalyptic*. Philadelphia: Fortress Press 1975.

Harlow, Barbara. *Resistance Literature*. New York and London: Methuen, 1987.

Harris, Mason. "Broken Generations in Obasan." *Canadian Literature* 127 (1990): 41–57.

Harrison, John R. *The Reactionaries*. London: Victor Gollancz, 1966.

Hastings, James. *A Dictionary of the Bible*. 5 vols. New York: Scribners, 1898 (rpt. 1909).

Hastings, Tom. "'Their Fathers Did It to Them': Findley's Appeal to the Great

War Myth of a Generational Conflict in *The Wars." Paying Attention*, Anne Geddes Bailey and Karen Grandy, eds. Toronto: ECW (1998): 85–103.

Heffernan, Teresa. *"Beloved* and the Problem of Mourning." *Studies in the Novel* 30.4 (Winter 1998): 558–73.

Heller, Erich. "The Hazard of Modern Poetry." *The Disinherited Mind*, 4th ed. London: Bowes and Bowes (1975): 261–300.

Highway, Tomson. "Nanabush in the City." [Interview with Nancy Wigston.] *Books in Canada*, March 1989: 7–9.

Holler, Clyde. *Black Elk's Religion: The Sun Dance and Lakota Catholicism*. Syracuse: Syracuse University Press, 1995.

Honneth, Axel. "A Communicative Disclosure of the Past: On the Relation between Anthropology and Philosophy of History in Walter Benjamin." *The Actuality of Walter Benjamin*, Laura Marcus and Lynda Nead, eds. London: Lawrence and Wishart (1993): 118–34.

hooks, bell. "Representations of Whiteness in the Black Imagination." *Cultural and Literary Critiques of the Concept of "Race,"* N. Gates, ed. (1997): 27–40.

Howells, Coral Ann. "Storm Glass: The Preservation and Transformation of History in *The Diviners, Obasan*, and *My Lovely Enemy." Kunapipi* 16.1 (1994): 471–8.

Hoy, Helen. "Translation of Cherokee." Email to the author. 28 July 1998.

Huggan, Graham. *Territorial Disputes: Maps and Mapping in Contemporary Canadian and Australian Fiction*. Toronto: University of Toronto Press 1994.

Hunter, Catherine. "'I Don't Know How to Begin': Findley's Work in the Sixties." *Paying Attention*, Anne Geddes Bailey and Karen Grandy, eds. Toronto: ECW (1998): 13–31.

Hutcheon, Linda. *The Canadian Postmodern: A Study of Contemporary English-Canadian Fiction*. Toronto: Oxford University Press, 1988.

– "The Politics of Representation." *Signature* 1 (1989): 23–44.

Irvine, Lorna. *Sub/Version*. Toronto: ECW, 1986.

Iyer, Pico. *The Global Soul*. New York: Vintage, 2000.

Johnston, Basil. "Is That All There Is? Tribal Literature." *An Anthology of Canadian Native Literature in English*, Daniel David Moses and Terry Goldie, eds. Toronto: Oxford University Press (1992): 105–12.

– *Ojibway Heritage*. Toronto: McClelland and Stewart, 1976.

– "One Generation from Extinction." " *An Anthology of Canadian Native Literature in English*, Daniel David Moses and Terry Goldie, eds. Toronto: Oxford University Press (1992): 99–104.

– Telephone interview, 11 May 1995.

Kaplan, Caren. *Questions of Travel*. Durham and London: Duke University Press, 1996.

Karpinski, Eva. "Public Memory, Private Grief: Reinventing the Nations' (Self)Image through Joy Kogawa's *Obasan*." ACCUTE Conference. University of Edmonton. 27 May 2000.

Keith, W.J. "Apocalyptic Imaginations: Notes on Atwood's *The Handmaid's Tale* and Findley's *Not Wanted on the Voyage*." *Essays on Canadian Writing* 35 (1987): 123–34.

Kermode, Frank. *The Sense of an Ending*. New York: Oxford University Press, 1967.

– "Waiting for the End": *Apocalypse Theory and the Ends of the World*, M. Bull, ed. (1995): 250–63.

Kilpatrick, Alan. *The Night Has a Naked Soul: Witchcraft and Sorcery Among the Western Cherokee*. Syracuse: Syracuse University Press, 1997.

King, Thomas. *Green Grass, Running Water*. Toronto: HarperCollins, 1993.

– *One Good Story, That One*. Toronto: HarperCollins, 1993.

Kingwell, Mark. *Dreams of Millennium: Report from a Culture on the Brink*. Toronto: Penguin, 1999.

Kogawa, Joy. "Interview by Magdalene Redekop." *Other Solitudes: Canadian Multicultural Fictions*, Linda Hutcheon and Marion Richmond, eds. Toronto: Oxford (1990): 87–101.

– "Is There a Just Cause?" *Canadian Forum* 63, no. 737, March, 1984, 20–4.

– *Obasan*. Toronto: Penguin, 1983.

Kristeva, Julia. *La Révolution du langage poétique*. Paris: Seuil, 1974.

LaCapra, Dominick. *Representing the Holocaust*. Ithaca and London: Cornell University Press, 1994.

Lanier, Sidney. *Centennial Edition of the Works of Sidney Lanier*. Vol. 9. C.R. Anderson and A.H. Starke, eds. Baltimore: Johns Hopkins, 1963.

Laub, Dori. "Truth and Testimony: The Process and the Struggle." *Trauma*, Cathy Caruth, ed. (1995): 61–75.

Lerner, Gerda. *The Creation of Patriarchy*. New York: Oxford, 1986.

Lewicki, Zbigniew. *The Bang and the Whimper: Apocalypse and Entropy in American Literature*. Westport, Conn.: Greenwood, 1984.

Lifton, Robert Jay. "An Interview with Robert Jay Lifton by Cathy Caruth." *Trauma*, Cathy Caruth, ed. (1995): 128–47.

Lutz, Hartmut. "The Circle as Philosophical and Structural Concept in Native American Fiction Today." *Native American Literatures*, Laura Coltelli, ed. Pisa: Servizio Editoriale Universitario (1989): 85–97.

– *Contemporary Challenges: Conversations with Canadian Native Authors*. Saskatoon: Fifth House, 1991.

Mails, Thomas. *Fools Crow: Wisdom and Power*. Tulsa: Council Oaks, 1991.

Mandel, Eli. *The Family Romance*. Winnipeg: Turnstone, 1986.

Marano, Lou. "On Windigo." *Current Anthropology* 24.1 (1983): 120–5.

Martel, Yann. *Life of Pi*. Toronto: Vintage, 2002.

Matchie, Thomas and Brett Larson. "Coyote Fixes the World: The Power of Myth in Thomas King's *Green Grass, Running Water*." *North Dakota Quarterly* 63.2 (Spring 1996): 153–68.

Matthews, S. "Revelation." *A Dictionary of the Bible*, James Hastings, ed.

May, John R. *Toward a New Earth: Apocalypse in the American Novel*. Notre Dame, Indiana: University of Notre Dame, 1972.

McFarlane, Scott. "Covering *Obasan* and the Narrative of Internment." *Privileging Positions: The Sites of Asian American Studies*, Gary Y. Okihiro et al., eds. Pullman: Washington State University Press (1995): 401–11.

Meredith, Howard. *Dancing on Common Ground*. Lawrence, Kansas: University Press of Kansas, 1995.

Merivale, Patricia. "Framed Voices: The Polyphonic Elegies of Herbert and Kogawa." *Canadian Literature* 116 (1988): 68–82.

Miki, Roy. *Broken Entries: Race, Subjectivity, Writing*. Toronto: Mercury, 1998.

Moi, Toril. *Sexual/Textual Politics: Feminist Literary Theory*. London and New York: Routledge, 1985.

Momaday, M. Scott. *The Names: A Memoir*. Tucson: University of Arizona Press 1976.

Montgomery, Maxine. *The Apocalypse in African-American Fiction*. Gainsville: University Press of Florida, 1996.

Moodie, Susanna. *Roughing It in the Bush or Life in Canada*. Carl Ballstadt, ed. Ottawa: Carleton University Press, 1990.

Morrison, Bruce and C. Roderick Wilson. *Native Peoples and the Canadian Experience*. Toronto: McClelland and Stewart, 1986.

Mukerji, Chandra. "Visual Language in Science and the Exercise of Power: The Case of Cartography in Early Modern Europe." *Studies in Visual Communications* 10.3 (1984): 30–44.

Oiwa, Keibo, introd. and ed. *Stone Voices: Wartime Writings of Japanese Candian Issei*. Montreal: Véhicule Press 1991.

O'Leary, Stephen. *Arguing the Apocalypse: A Theory of Millennial Rhetoric*. New York: Oxford, 1994.

Ondaatje, Michael. *Anil's Ghost*. Toronto: McClelland and Stewart, 2000.

– *The English Patient*. Toronto: McClelland and Stewart, 1992.

Ortner, Sherry. "Is Female to Male as Nature Is to Culture?" *Women, Culture, and Society*, Michelle Zimbalist Rosaldo and Louise Lamphere, eds. Stanford: Stanford University Press, (1974): 67–88.

Paley, Morton. *Apocalypse and Millennium in English Romantic Poetry*. Oxford: Clarendon Press, 1999.

Patrides, C.A. "'Something like Prophetick Strain': Apoclalyptic Configurations in Milton." *The Apocalypse in English Renaissance Thought and Literature: Patterns, Antecedents and Repercussions*, C.A. Patrides and Joseph Wittreich, eds. Manchester: Manchester University Press (1984): 207–39.

Peterson, Karen Daniels. *Plains Indian Art from Fort Marion*. Norman, Oklahoma: University of Oklahoma Press, 1971.

Pickthall, Marjorie. "The Third Generation." *Early Canadian short Stories*. Misao Dean, ed. Ottawa: Tecumseh Press (2000): 247–59.

Pippin, Tina. *Death and Desire: The Rhetoric of Gender in the Apocalypse of John*. Louisville, Kentucky: Westminister/John Knox, 1992.

Preston, Richard J. *Cree Narrative: Expressing the Personal Meanings of Events*. National Museum of Man, Mercury Series, Canadian Ethnology Service Paper 30, 1975.

Ravvin, Norman. "The Apocalyptic Predicament: Timothy Findley's Predetermined Novel." *Fins de Siècle/New Beginnings*, special edition of *The Dolphin* (31). Aarhus University Press (2000): 163–76.

Reddish, Mitchell, ed. *Apocalyptic Literature: A Reader*. Peabody: Hendrickson, 1995.

Ricoeur, Paul. *Time and Narrative*, vol. 2. Translated by Kathleen McLaughlin and David Pellauer. Chicago and London: University of Chicago Press 1985.

Roberts, Carol. *Timothy Findley: Stories from a Life*. Toronto: ECW, 1994.

Roberts, Julian. *Walter Benjamin*. London: MacMillan, 1982.

Robinson, Douglas. *American Apocalypses: The Image of the End of the World in American Literature*. Baltimore and London: Johns Hopkins University Press, 1985.

Root, Deborah. *Cannibal Culture*. Boulder, Colorado: Westview, 1996.

Rowland, Christopher. *The Open Heaven*. London: Blackwell, 1982.

Ryan, Allan. *The Trickster Shift: Humour and Irony in Contemporary Native Art*. Vancouver: University of BC Press; Seattle: University of Washington Press, 1999.

Said, Edward. *Culture and Imperialism*. New York: Vintage, 1994.

Salmond, S.D.F. "Eschatology." *A Dictionary of the Bible*, James Hastings, ed.

Samek, Hana. *The Blackfoot Confederacy 1880–1920: A Comparative Study of Canadian and U.S. Indian Policy*. Albuquerque: University of New Mexico Press, 1987.

Sanderson, Heather. "(Im)Perfect Dreams: Allegories of Fascism in *The But-*

terfly Plague." Paying Attention, Anne Geddes Bailey and Karen Grandy, eds. Toronto: ECW (1998): 104–24.

Scholem, Gershom. *The Messianic Idea in Judaism and Other Essays of Jewish Spirituality*. New York: Schocken, 1971.

Schweizer, Harold and Michael Payne, introd. *Poetry, Narrative, History*. Oxford: Basil Blackwell, 1990. 1–28.

See, Maria Sarita. "An Open Wound." Racial Melancholia in the Late Twentieth Century. MLA Convention. Hyatt Regency, Chicago. 27 December 1999.

Shelley, Mary. *Frankenstein*. D.L. Macdonald and Kathleen Scherf, eds. Peterborough: Broadview, 1994.

Söderlind, Sylvia. *Margin/Alias: Language and Colonization in Canadian and Québécois Fiction*. Toronto: University of Toronto, 1991.

Spencer, Lloyd. "Allegory in the World of the Commodity: The Importance of *Central Park. New German Critique* 34 (1985): 59–77.

Thompson, Leonard. *The Book of Revelation: Apocalypse and Empire*. New York: Oxford, 1990.

Traill, Catherine Parr. "From *The Backwoods of Canada*." *An Anthology of Canadian Literature in English*, vol. 1, R. Brown and D. Bennett, eds. Toronto: Oxford (1983): 63–9.

van Herk, Aritha. "Women Writers and the Prairie: Spies in an Indifferent Landsape." *Kunapipi* 6.2 (1984): 14–25.

Vernon, John. *The Garden and the Map: Schizophrenia in Twentieth-Century Literature and Culture*. Urbana: University of Illinois Press, 1973.

Visvis, Vikki. "Removing the Veils of History: Revelation in Joy Kogawa's *Obasan*." Unpublished essay, 2000.

Wade, Edwin and Jacki Thompson Rand. "The Subtle Art of Resistance: Encounter and Accommodation in the Art of Fort Marion." *Plains Indian Drawings 1865–1935*, J.C. Berlo, ed. (1996): 45–9.

Wiseman, Adele. *Crackpot*. Toronto: McClelland and Stewart, 1974.

Wolin, Richard. *Walter Benjamin: An Aesthetic of Redemption*, 2nd ed. Berkeley and London: University of California Press 1994.

Woodland, Malcolm. Unpublished essay, 2001.

York, Lorraine. "'A White Hand Hovering over the Page': Timothy Findley and the Racialized/Ethnicized Other." *Paying Attention*, Anne Geddes Bailey and Karen Grandy, eds. Toronto: ECW (1998): 201–20.

Zamora, Lois Parkinson. *Writing the Apocalypse: Historical Vision in Cotemporary U.S. and Latin American Fiction*. Cambridge: Cambridge University Press, 1989.

Index

allegory: defined, 76; as feature of apocalyptic narrative, 18–19, 56, 58; as fragment, in theory of Walter Benjamin, 20, 58–9, 60

"Angelus Novus" (Paul Klee), 57–8

Anna Karenina (Leo Tolstoy), 48, 103

anti-apocalyptic narrative, Canadian: "Hairball" as, 13, 83–4; placelessness and drifting, as themes in, 166–7; as resulting from newfound voice of marginalized, 167

Antichrist (in Revelation), 30, 41, 171n14

apocalypse: Biblical concept of, 3, 4–5, 12; catastrophic signs of, 33–4; as central to Western culture, 11–12; closure in, as required by masculine nature of, 27, 157, 164; as culmination of linear storyline, 21–2, 47, 117–18; definition of, as often broadly applied, 12; "elect" and "non-elect," as divided by, 4, 20, 21, 23–4; as esoteric in nature, 16, 18–19; etymology of term, 50; as exceeding bounds of literature, 47–8; fragment, as emblem of, 20–1; human body, as emblem of, 20–1; as map, 21–3; New Jerusalem, as reward of elect, 6, 19, 170–1n12; placelessness and drifting, as alternatives to, 165; as predicated on violent exclusion of unacceptable "Others," 164–5; redemption of humanity through, as alien to non-Christian teleology, 21–3, 117–20; traditional views of, as negated by Second World War, 7–9, 10, 11, 21; traumatic nature of, 26–7, 172n16;

unveiling of "truth" by, as problematic or impossible, 14, 49–51, 154–5; as way of understanding evil, 21. *See also* apocalyptic narrative; apocalyptic violence; elect; non-elect; Revelation

apocalyptic narrative: allegory, as feature of, 18–19, 56, 58; of Christian teleology, as linear, 21–3, 47, 117–18; deconstruction of, by Canadian approach to, 164; as exceeding bounds of literature, 47–8; as form of protest or resistance, 17, 39; fragmentation and ruin in, 20–1; intertextuality of, 18–19; literary tradition of, 5–6; of non-Christian teleologies, as cyclical, 21–3, 106, 117–18; as panoramic vision of, 19, 33; temporal perspective of, 20, 33. *See also* Revelation

apocalyptic narrative, Canadian: "beautiful losers," as central characters of, 4, 30, 33, 55, 92; as challenging traditional apocalyptic concepts, 6, 8–10, 11; colonization and imperialism in, 13, 17, 18, 25–6; continuity of past and present, as valued by, 22–3; as "crisis literature," 11, 17, 39; early examples of, 7–8; as elegiac, 9–10; "ex-centric" perspective of, 4, 5, 30, 43, 56–7; fragmentation of, 54, 56, 59–60, 81; human body, as emblematic in, 20–1; intertextuality of, 19; locus of, as familiar place, 31, 39, 46, 53, 92; map, as central icon in, 19–20, 22–3; placelessness and drifting in, 164–7; technological progress in, as destructive, 9, 11, 62–4,

85–6; as "Other," 25, 160; power of, as threat to male hierarchy, 25, 97–8; as responding to loss by refusing to mourn, 149–50; specific figures: Bride (in Revelation), 86, 97, Jezebel, 9, 25, 85, 177n1, Whore of Babylon, 9, 25, 85, 86, 97. *See also* "Hairball" (Margaret Atwood); Hana (*English Patient*); Kat ("Hairball"); Kemp, Lilah (*Headhunter*); Naomi (*Obasan*)

Words of My Roaring, The (Robert Kroetsch), 8

Yeats, William Butler, apocalyptic sentiments of, 44–5